DATE DUE

THE THEORY OF FISCAL ECONOMICS

Publications of the
Bureau of Business and Economic Research
University of California

THE THEORY OF FISCAL ECONOMICS

BY

EARL R. ROLPH

UNIVERSITY OF CALIFORNIA PRESS

BERKELEY, LOS ANGELES, LONDON

1971

UNIVERSITY OF CALIFORNIA PRESS
BERKELEY AND LOS ANGELES

UNIVERSITY OF CALIFORNIA PRESS, LTD.
LONDON, ENGLAND

COPYRIGHT, 1954, BY
THE REGENTS OF THE UNIVERSITY OF CALIFORNIA
CALIFORNIA LIBRARY REPRINT SERIES EDITION 1971

ISBN: 0-520-01926-1
LIBRARY OF CONGRESS CATALOG CARD NUMBER: 54-10435

PRINTED IN THE UNITED STATES OF AMERICA
BY THE UNIVERSITY OF CALIFORNIA PRINTING DEPARTMENT

TO MY
MOTHER AND FATHER

Preface

Fiscal economics is a difficult subject. A fiscal student should be an expert in every field of economics. Government finance, expenditures, taxes, subsidies, and debt operations have repercussions in every field of private economic affairs as well as in international economic relations. Few have this comprehensive command of economics; certainly I do not. Even moderate success in explaining fiscal operations requires the research of workers in the many divisions of economics. But if such investigations are to provide a systematic body of knowledge, some guiding principles are needed to assist in formulating significant questions and to provide criteria as to what constitutes relevant information. I hope that this study may contribute to fulfilling this important need.

The main ideas set forth in the study are elaborations and applications of what is usually called economic theory. Fiscal theory is economic theory as it applies to effects of government actions. Yet many incorrect fiscal ideas can be traced to the use of a tax to illustrate a theory, such as import duties in the theory of international trade, and excise taxes in the theory of price. Taxes cannot be successfully explained by treatment of them as a series of footnote thoughts on price theory. Such explanations lead to self-contradiction. Fiscal ideas need to be treated with more respect. In turn, they must not be found to deny any valid proposition in the corpus of economic theory.

This study leans heavily upon the work of A. C. Pigou, especially his book A Study in Public Finance. The many points at which I have found it necessary to express a difference from his views merely testify to the importance attached to them. It is, perhaps, fortunate that Marshall's dominating position in neoclassical economic thought did not extend to public finance. I must confess that I find Marshall's views on taxation rather uninstructive. This is no criticism; he did not choose to devote his attention to this area to the extent he did to many others. In addition to Pigou's writings, special acknowledgment should be made to the works of Sir Dennis H. Robertson and of Professor Abba P. Lerner. Robertson, almost

[ix]

*alone, has kept monetary theory from degenerating into stultifying
dogma and thereby has done fiscal theory a service because of the
close association of these two areas of thought. Lerner, whose views
may have suffered in influence from their association with catchy
labels, such as "Functional Finance," should be given much of the
credit (some may say discredit) for reëmphasizing the crucial importance of the Pigou-Edgeworth technique of attributing to each
public finance act, such as a tax, a transfer payment, or a government expenditure, the effects of that act. The popularity of the
opposing view, that of identifying a tax with the expenditures of
the tax proceeds, threatened for a time to end systematic theorizing
about public financial operations.*

*Fiscal theory in certain aspects is applied monetary theory, and
hence the monetary approach that is adopted takes on some importance. The main ideas on this score, herein adopted, which are set
forth in chapter 5, are a stock-flow type of theory. Stocks—the inherited past—together with human choice are viewed as the determinants of flows, namely, the actual present. In adopting this theory,
it is unfortunately necessary to part company with the monetary
theory that is dominant in contemporary thinking—the Keynesian
system. By adopting this position, I do not mean to belittle Keynes'
contributions. But neither he nor anyone else has said the last word
about fundamentals in any area of economic theory. Had he lived,
Keynes might have broken with the new orthodoxy as he had with
the old; his restless and iconoclastic mind ill suited him for the role
of schoolmaster.*

*Chapters 4, 6, 8, and 9 contain material which has previously
been published in journals. Chapter 4 is a revision of an article
entitled "The Concept of Transfers in National Income Estimates," appearing in the* Quarterly Journal of Economics, *Vol.
LXII (May, 1948), pp. 327–360. Chapter 6 is a revision of two
articles, "A Proposed Revision of Excise Tax Theory," appearing
in the* Journal of Political Economy, *Vol. LX (April, 1952), pp.
102–117, and "A Theory of Excise Subsidies," appearing in the*
American Economic Review, *Vol. XIII (September, 1952), pp.
515–527. Chapter 8 is a revision of the article "The Burden of Import Duties," appearing in the* American Economic Review, *Vol.
XXXVI (December, 1946), pp. 788–812, and chapter 9 is a revision of the article "The Burden of Import Duties with Fixed Exchanges," appearing in the same journal, Vol. XXXVII (September, 1947), pp. 604–632. These articles are reprinted by permission*

of the publishers of these journals. Permission has also been granted by the publishers of the Quarterly Journal of Economics *to quote from the writings appearing therein of A. P. Lerner, E. D. Domar and R. A. Musgrave, and J. M. Keynes; these are identified where used. Similar permission has been granted to quote from an article by Richard Goode appearing in the* Journal of Political Economy *and from articles by M. Slade Kendrick and H. J. Davenport appearing in the* American Economic Review, *and from an article by R. A. Musgrave, et al., appearing in the* National Tax Journal. *Acknowledgments for the specific quotations are made in the footnotes.*

The following publishers of books have kindly granted permission to quote from works published by them: Longmans, Green & Company, J. S. Mill, Principles of Political Economy; *St. Martin's Press, Inc., A. C. Pigou,* A Study in Public Finance, *and F. Y. Edgeworth,* Papers Relating to Political Economy, *Vol. II; The Macmillan Company, A. C. Pigou,* The Political Economy of War; *Harvard University Press, Paul A. Samuelson,* Foundations of Economic Analysis; *Prentice-Hall, Inc., Albert G. Hart,* Money, Debt, and Economic Activity. *Thanks are due these publishers for permission to quote from these works. Acknowledgments for the specific citations are made in the footnotes.*

Several of my colleagues have generously given of their time to read the manuscript. I am particularly indebted to Professor George F. Break for catching many errors and for suggesting improvements. Professor Howard S. Ellis has been very helpful, especially in connection with chapter 5. Professors Norman S. Buchanan, R. A. Gordon, and Maurice Moonitz read the entire manuscript and made many helpful suggestions. Thanks are also due Dr. Arthur Fefferman of the Treasury Department and Professor Joseph Pechman of the Massachusetts Institute of Technology for their criticisms. If I had more often accepted the recommendations of these critics the book would be better, no doubt. None of them should be interpreted as agreeing with any aspect of this work or as responsible for any errors it may contain.

The Bureau of Business and Economic Research of the University of California bore the expense of preparing the manuscript for publication and also aided in meeting the cost of the research. I wish to thank Dorothy W. Haas and Jeanne M. Trahan of the Bureau staff for taking care of the many details incidental to publication.

The traditional acknowledgment of an author to his wife has exceptional significance in my case. The reader may thank her for being spared many a purple passage. More importantly, she deserves the credit for keeping the book from being another hundred pages or so longer. But she, too, should be spared responsibility for the correctness of any of the ideas set forth. Of the remaining members of the family, my sons find the entire project misconceived because it fails to meet the test of profitability. Thus, it would seem, I must bear the sole responsibility for the contents of the study.

EARL R. ROLPH

Berkeley, 1954

Contents

[xiii]

I

Introduction

Fiscal economics concerns the effects of government financial activities on the private sector of the economy. The financial devices employed by government consist of expenditures for services and for currently produced goods and real resources, the making of transfer payments such as subsidies, the receiving of transfer payments such as taxes, and the dealing in old real assets and claims, including its own debt. More succinctly, one may think of government financial activities as purchases and sales of services, goods, and claims, and positive and negative transfer payments. Theoretically any financial action falls into one or both of these two classes. Debt operations, which at first glance may seem to have been left out, are covered because borrowing takes place by the sale of securities and lending by the purchase or retirement of debt.

SCOPE OF THE STUDY

This study emphasizes the implications of government transfers, both positive and negative. Positive transfer payments such as subsidies or interest paid on government debt provide cash to private groups. The method of payment may also attach certain conditions for the qualification of those who are to receive such payments, and these qualifications may affect decisions concerning the manner of employing resources. Similar observations apply to negative transfer payments which, in the contemporary world, consist mainly of taxes. Taxes are financial devices which, to the extent that they have a yield, remove cash from private hands. They too may induce people to behave differently in the management of resources. This "incentive" aspect of a tax or subsidy device depends upon the precise definition of the tax or subsidy base and the rate structure. It is this aspect of taxation that provides the basis for distinguishing classes of taxes.

This is a theoretical study. It is a search for principles that

[1]

may be applied in various epochs of economic development. This purpose precludes close examination of the details of the fiscal structure of any one country. Some theoretical analysis is a necessary prelude to empirical investigation if only to discover what facts are to be examined. No implication is intended that theoretical inquiry is a competitor of empirical investigation in the search for truth in economics, unless empiricism is regarded as denying the possibility of the discovery of general principles.

In the area of theory this work offers only a limited analysis of expenditures. Some attention is devoted to the topic in order to disentangle subsidies in kind from government payments and to suggest the relations between expenditures and revenues. In this regard the method here pursued follows closely that laid down by H. G. Brown, A. C. Pigou, F. Y. Edgeworth, and by their classical forerunners. Taxes are treated as financial devices distinct from expenditures. Since some students of this subject hold that it is theoretically impossible to divorce revenues from expenditures, the topic will be examined presently in some detail.

Government debt operations are also given only incidental consideration. I should like to believe, however, that the theories suggested can be dovetailed into debt-management principles without involving contradiction. The theory of taxes is explicitly developed on the supposition that budgets of governments need not be balanced. Thus there is no necessity for altering in any fundamental way the pattern of thought when debt operations are explicitly taken into account.

No systematic attempt will be made here to define and delineate touchstones or canons to be employed in evaluating fiscal measures. However, where tax or subsidy policies are explicitly or implicitly based on theories regarding their effects, the policies are under criticism to the extent that the theories behind them are ambiguous or merely wrong. Policies may be justified, certain value judgments being granted, even though the theories employed will not stand criticism; the policies may be right for the wrong reasons. In addition, an analysis of government financial affairs may reveal inconsistencies and internal contradictions in the theories employed to support policy measures. Any theory that succeeds in avoiding such errors becomes a method of evaluating government policies.

One final limitation to the coverage of the study relates to the types of taxes examined. The taxes given major attention are excise, import, income, and flat-sum levies. Subsidies examined consist of flat-sum grants and excises. Flat-sum levies are analyzed mainly for expositional purposes; they have little importance as fiscal measures. The others are chosen partly because they are important in many revenue systems, past and present, and partly because they present interesting analytical difficulties. The difficulty test must be understood in relation to the general thesis of this study that tax devices, however they may differ among themselves in their legal characteristics, are fundamentally similar in the sense that they reduce private *money* incomes by amounts quantitatively equal to the revenue obtained by the government. To explain and illustrate this proposition is a major task of the study. The proposition carries the implication that so-called indirect taxation of buyers of goods and services is not a real possibility in an institutional setting characterized by the use of money and prices to ration the output of commodities. Because excise taxes are commonly thought of as burdening consumers more or less, they are studied at some length. If the general theory of taxation here proposed successfully explains commodity taxes without distortion of the evidence, one can readily extend the argument to other taxes, such as income taxes, commonly thought to be shiftable only occasionally.

Similar considerations motivate the detailed study of import duties. These taxes are minor revenue devices in the United States at present, but their effects are not minor. It may be noted parenthetically that import taxes are the backbone of the revenue systems of many small countries and provide large revenues even in Great Britain. But aside from revenue considerations, import levies constitute a challenge to the formulation of a general and consistent theory of taxation. Tariff theory has developed out of a tradition of thought in tax matters which differs in many fundamentals from that surrounding excise tax theories. Tariff theory has been closely associated with the development of international trade theory rather than with tax theory. The pattern of thought in the neoclassical treatment has emphasized general equilibrium analysis rather than the one-commodity-at-a-time approach adopted for internal excise-tax analysis. The clash of differing traditions of thought invites a critical reëxamination of accepted ideas.

METHODS OF ANALYSIS

One method here employed to obtain generalizations may be called, for lack of any better name, the method of clarification.

The opposite of a clear proposition is an ambiguity. Clarification as a method is the attempt to reduce ambiguity. Only occasionally is an economist discovered to be dead wrong on a theoretical issue. Even today it would be difficult to identify the propositions made by Ricardo which are definitely wrong. Yet the departure from Ricardo's ideas on the topics he discussed has been substantial. Some of his ambiguities have been disclosed and clarified.

Clarification means making premises explicit.[1] Differences in economic theories are, I am convinced, mainly traceable to what is taken for granted as "too obvious" to be examined critically. From different premises, radically different conclusions are drawn. Only after clarification of the different but "obvious" propositions can there be an evaluation of the theories constructed on them. Two illustrations may make clear the meaning of this observation.

In that area of thought called "capital and interest" theory, the "roundabout" approach takes for granted that an interval of time exists between the application of resources and the emergence of the product. It is "obvious" that a period of time must elapse between the planting of seed and the harvesting of corn. It is also "obvious" that a house is not constructed in a day. Yet, in the opinion of many, it is "obvious" that there is no gap in time between the application of resources and the emerging product. The roundabout approach leads to such doctrines as "original" factors, wages-fund, discounted marginal productivity, the "average period of production," and distortions in the structure of production—doctrines which are categorically denied as wrong or meaningless by those who find production and product to be simultaneous. Reconciliation of these conflicts requires reëxamination of the initial "obvious" premises.

Those who hold that production and product are simultaneous must mean by "product" whatever results emerge. Seed planting results in planted corn fields, and a planted field is more valuable than an unplanted one. The products of the construction industry

---

[1] Clarification as a method may not give what P. A. Samuelson calls a meaningful theorem defined as a "... hypothesis about empirical data which could be conceivably refuted, if only under ideal conditions." (See Paul A. Samuelson, *Foundations of Economic Analysis* [Cambridge: Harvard University Press, 1948], p. 4.) The critical terms in this statement are "conceivably" and "empirical data." It may be noted that the proposition as stated is, by its own test, meaningless; there are no empirical data to which it applies. Further, the statement condemns as meaningless all relations that are inherently true, such as the equality of expenditures and receipts in a closed system for a given period, since the only method of establishing them is by demonstration that they cannot be sensibly denied. Systematic economic analysis relies heavily on such truisms.

are not merely buildings but buildings in various stages of completion. Product in this sense means not merely what the eye can see or the fingers touch, but any result that people want and that is scarce. The "roundabout" theorists are talking about types of products in a form normally marketed, rather than any product. Immature crops are not ordinarily bought and sold. Thus the apparent "lag" is an incidental feature of some industries, not a basic observation upon which to build a theory.

In tax theory it is common to treat as facts what are, upon closer inspection, really theories. The apparent facts are colored by the implicit theories of the reporter. Thus some take for granted that they are being taxed when they are presented with a bill on which the seller separately itemizes the "tax." The evidence may seem conclusive. Yet if it is studied closely, this "obvious" fact ceases to be very obvious. What the seller pays each tax date to the government may, and often does, have only an incidental relation to the amount calculated by adding the "taxes" itemized on bills. Further, one would need to know what the "price" quoted separately from the tax would be in the absence of the tax, and this is not an observable fact. If the practice of itemizing taxes on bills came into vogue for taxes other than excises, such as personal income taxes, more doubt might exist that the separation of the "price" from the "tax" is evidence that it is shifted. Itemization of bills so as to state taxes separately is a pricing tactic adopted by merchants, often as a result of exhortation or compulsion on the part of tax officials. The fact is that a person is charged a sum of money for what he buys.

Economic sophistication destroys the certainties of man-in-the-street tax theories. Criticism of these theories compels a retreat to more primitive propositions. Clarification as a method is the never-ending process of exposing to critical scrutiny the hidden theories in what has previously been taken for granted.

Another methodological device used extensively in this study is generalizing from the simple case. For certain problems the assumption of an economy producing only two commodities eliminates enormous complexities, and the results reached may readily be generalized to any number. This method of simplification, widely used in economic thinking, has certain dangers.

Simplification may eliminate or grossly misrepresent the pertinent features of the reality to be explained. Not just any simplification will do. Much of economic theory, particularly price theory,

has been developed as if government were excess baggage, to be
sloughed off to get at essential principles. But there is little point
in speculating about the economic characteristics of a society of
any complexity on the assumption that there is no government.
We have no experience with such a world. Likewise, economic
relations of a society consisting of two men and a boy may have
little application to industrial systems.[2] Essential features of economic relations, such as monetary and fiscal facts, the complexities
of large-scale industry, the reduction in personal freedom occasioned by the discipline inherent in large impersonal organizations,
the separation of ownership and control of resources which these
entail, decision-making without access to detailed relevant information—all these are in danger of being lost from sight in a close
study of desert-island economics.

Theories of taxation developed by the simplifying assumption
that taxes are paid in kind, an assumption used by neoclassical
thinkers in connection with import duties, are, it seems to me,
especially dangerous for an understanding of taxes. Fortunately
this practice has largely disappeared in taxation literature. Likewise the emphasis in nineteenth-century English thought on "real"
as opposed to money considerations may from this point of view
be regarded as an improper simplification, and the Keynesian emphasis has not improved matters in this connection.[3] The very
term "real" is pretentious, as if in some sense money valuations
are "nominal," that is, unimportant.[4] It is impossible, it seems to
me, to make sense out of complex systems of economic relations
without treating money as an indispensable feature of the system.

The merits of simplification as a method of analysis need to be
emphasized also. If a problem cannot be resolved under simplified
conditions, there is little point is attempting to solve it for the
complexity which is the real social world. Attempts at realism may
be premature; a possible solution is missed in the hurry to rid
oneself of the charge of being "unrealistic." It is doubtful if a
systematic and consistent theory of sales taxes, for example, could

---

[2] The illustration is Whitehead's, who used it to show that differences in scale are
real differences, and principles applicable to small-scale cases may not be applicable
to large-scale cases. (See Alfred North Whitehead, *Essays in Science and Philosophy*
[New York: Philosophy Library, 1947], p. 157.)

[3] A brief criticism of this element of Keynesian thought, which might also with
equal force be made against a large part of the neoclassical tradition in economic
analysis, is presented in a paper by Howard S. Ellis ("The Rediscovery of Money,"
Money, Trade, and Economic Growth, in honor of John H. Williams [New York:
Macmillan, 1951], pp. 258–259).

[4] I am indebted to my colleague George F. Break for this observation.

be discovered without a previous examination of the tax under conditions of perfectly competitive pricing throughout the system. In any event, if an explanation which makes sense for competitive pricing conditions can be found, some progress will have been made toward the ultimate goal of an explanation that holds for any pricing system.

The risk that a simplification may arbitrarily eliminate a crucial relation indispensable to a proper explanation of a tax must be taken. Some protection against this danger may be achieved if generalizations discovered by attention to simplified conditions are tested by the relaxation of any limiting assumptions initially employed. Some protection may also be provided by close attention to the exceptional case. Exceptions test rules. But there is no certain road to "truth" in fiscal economics, or for that matter in economics generally.

BACKGROUND CONSIDERATIONS

Perhaps the most troublesome problem in taxation analysis concerns the background against which the tax is to be analyzed. Some insist that a tax must be thought of in terms of both the tax itself and the government expenditures presumably financed by that tax. Repeatedly we are told in tax discussions that one should take account of how the government spends the money. Anyone who denies this seems to convict himself of intellectual laziness. A general attack on so-called "classical" tax theory has been conducted mainly upon the premise that its conclusions are vitiated by the neglect of the expenditures of the tax revenue.[5]

Two thinkers who have insisted with some fervor that the background against which a tax is to be analyzed should include how

---

[5] There exists no definite classical theory of taxation in the sense of a distinguishable body of thought. Edgeworth and Pigou are perhaps the two most important thinkers on tax problems in the neoclassical tradition in economic thinking. Neither attempted a systematic explanation of taxes of all kinds, and Edgeworth's thinking exerted little apparent effect upon Pigou's. Marshall directly contributed little to tax theory; indirectly, his influence has been enormous. His formulation of economic theory has been the dominant one used in tax analysis. Pigou strays rather far from the Marshallian fold in the analysis of taxation, being concerned more with aggregative types of problems. In this area he made many important contributions which are periodically "rediscovered." In the United States, Harry G. Brown set forth a systematic explanation of taxation which comes closest to a point of view which is neoclassical in the sense that it is a straightforward application of neoclassical price theory. (*Economics of Taxation* [Columbia, Missouri: Lucas Brothers, 1938].) In recent years, the revived interest in aggregative analysis, traceable in part to the Keynesian influence, has directed attention to fiscal policy theory. Applications of Keynesian theory to the analysis of taxes have not, however, been notably successful.

the government spends the tax revenue are Antonio de Viti de Marco and Duncan Black. An opposing view has been set forth by F. Y. Edgeworth and A. C. Pigou. A consideration of the ideas of these thinkers may be of assistance for clarification of the method of posing a problem in taxation analysis.

De Marco's views on tax incidence emphasize the spending aspects of government finance. According to him, money raised by taxes must be spent by the government in a different way than it would have been spent if left in the hands of private individuals. These shifts in demand resulting from government finance are the important facts in his opinion. Producers of commodities whose demands advance as the result of the government's actions are thought of as having shifted the tax, whereas those producing goods whose demands have fallen or remained unchanged are viewed as paying the tax. If I interpret his views correctly, de Marco holds that a corporation net income tax is shifted by steel corporations in the event the government spends the money for steel products. Corporations that do not supply goods for government use may shift the tax because, for some reason, the private demand for their products rises. This emphasis on the spending features of government finance and the rearrangements in demands for products believed to be associated with government finance seems to be the distinguishing feature of de Marco's point of view.[6]

Duncan Black, an admirer of de Marco, looks upon a tax as having two aspects—the collection of the tax and the disbursement of these moneys.[7] On occasion Black appears to be saying that a tax should be defined to mean a government measure to collect money and a government measure to spend money. Accordingly, the effects of taxation include automatically a study of what is ordinarily called government expenditures. To the objection that a tax (in the ordinary sense) may not be accompanied by an expenditure (in the ordinary sense), Black is prepared to agree that, in this case, tax analysis may proceed by ignoring government expenditures. But simultaneous variation of different taxes to provide the same yield is regarded as an unusual situation. Such types

---

[6] Antonio de Viti de Marco, *First Principles of Public Finance,* translated from the Italian by Edith P. Marget (New York: Harcourt, Brace, 1936), pp. 153–155. I have difficulty in discovering a coherent theory in de Marco's exposition. Henry Simons has indicated a similar difficulty. (See his review of the above work in the *Journal of Political Economy,* XLV [October, 1937]: 712–717.)

[7] Duncan Black, *The Incidence of Income Taxes* (London: Macmillan, 1939), pp. 134–156.

of inquiry are viewed by him as unduly narrow. He therefore favors looking upon a tax as including government expenditures and transfer payments.[8] Throughout much, but not all, of his study he attempts to follow this principle.

Edgeworth disagreed with this view. In a frequently quoted passage he says: "Yet in measuring the burden of a tax to the owner it is allowable in pure theory to abstract its influence on demand."[9] This passage may be interpreted as merely an assumption and criticized for the reason that the kind of inquiry it advocates is an arbitrary one. But in the paragraph of which the quoted statement is the last sentence, Edgeworth makes his meaning more clear: "If a person wears high heels," he asks, "may we not estimate the elevation due to that cause without putting him on a hill?" Addicts of raised heels presumably buy them to appear taller, whether in a subway or on the twenty-seventh floor of a building. Edgeworth holds the sensible view that the effects of a tax should be attributed to the tax and the effects of expenditures to expenditures. Pigou adopts the procedure of separately analyzing the effects of expenditures and the effects of taxes, and in some connections he analyzes their combined effects. In introducing his discussion of taxation, Pigou announces that expenditures and transfer payments are to be viewed as constant.[10]

A technique of analysis is not improved merely by the expedient of attempting to discuss all features of a topic on the same page. Yet the Black–de Marco approach seems to be equivalent to such a procedure. The valuable feature of the taking-account-of-the-proceeds approach is the emphasis on the view that public expenditures should not be ignored in tax analysis. But at this point a distinction needs to be made. It is one thing to hold that a tax and the expenditure of the proceeds are related and another to hold that expenditures are an inherent feature of taxes. On occasion, both Black and de Marco seem to be saying the latter. But expenditures are not taxes. Without a distinction between taxes and expenditures it would be impossible to discuss government budgets sensibly. Economists might attempt to abolish the distinction, but finance officials and legislative bodies could not, even if they tried. Expenditures concern how money is released to

[8] *Ibid.*, p. 142.

[9] F. Y. Edgeworth, *Papers Relating to Political Economy*, Vol. II (London: Macmillan, 1925), p. 70.

[10] A. C. Pigou, *A Study in Public Finance* (London: Macmillan, 1947), p. 40.

acquire goods and services desired by a government. Taxes are devices to extract cash from the public.

What those who follow the de Marco approach have in mind cannot be merely the feeble proposition that the terms taxes and expenditures ought to be abolished in favor of some more inclusive term covering both. What then do they intend to convey? If we take their doctrine seriously, their position appears to embrace the following propositions: (1) government expenditures in any period depend on the tax revenues of that period, (2) the effects of these expenditures should be taken into account in an analysis of the effects of taxes, and (3) shifting of taxes will depend at least in part (for de Marco, altogether) on the specific pattern of government demands for goods and services.

Proposition (1) is a functional one, namely, that expenditures depend on revenues. This is, in one aspect, an empirical issue. If a government obtains cash by means other than taxation, it cannot be true that all expenditures are financed from tax receipts. There is of course nothing unusual about governments financing themselves by selling debt. Taxes are devices used by governments to obtain cash but not the only device. Cash is obtained by borrowing, by selling old assets, by receipt of dividends and interest, and in some cases (rare these days) by profits on government enterprise. Sovereign governments often finance themselves in part by direct creation of money. There is no good reason for assuming that taxation must be the only method of financing government when it is not.

A functional relation may be postulated between tax revenues and expenditures—a propensity of government to spend. Apart from certain logical defects in propensity theories, to be discussed in chapter 5, this issue may be settled by an appeal to well-known evidence. In the United States, the behavior of the Congress in making appropriations and of the executive departments in making expenditures may not be properly described by a theory that government expenditures depend upon revenues. It appears more accurate to describe the process as establishing certain government expenditure patterns and certain tax patterns and letting the chips fall where they may, leaving to the Treasury the task of assuring itself of a sufficient cash balance at all times to meet commitments. Debt management is the technique normally used for this purpose. It has long been a goal of good government to induce legislatures not to make expenditure commitments without at the same time finding the revenue to finance them, but it is an ideal, not an achievement. It is factually wrong to treat government expenditures as rigorously dependent on tax yields.

Propositions (2) and (3) may be admitted however. Government expenditures do occur, and a theory of taxation should not be based on the assumption that they do not exist. Nor need a theory of tax shifting require such an assumption. In the neoclassical tradition of tax analysis as set forth by Pigou, government expenditures are not viewed as nonexistent; rather they are held constant. This method does not imply that expenditures are to be ignored. One variable is held constant to permit the analysis of the effects of taxes. It is a misconception to charge Pigou or Edgeworth with neglecting the effects of public expenditures in their analysis of tax matters.

A more restricted application of the view that government expenditures should be treated as inseparable from a tax has been proposed by M. Slade Kendrick.[11] In those cases where the particular public expenditure can be treated as depending upon a particular tax, the effects of the tax are viewed as including the changes in the demand or supply of the taxed item. Gasoline taxes earmarked for highway improvement are taken to illustrate such a case. According to his argument, the demand for gasoline is increased "by the tax" because the tax proceeds are spent to construct more and better highways. Since, as appears reasonable, gasoline may be treated as complementary to highway use, the demand for gasoline is said to rise "because of the tax," and this permits sellers to increase prices more than would be the case if the demand were treated as unchanging. Sellers, it is alleged, shift more of the tax on gasoline to buyers because the revenue is spent for highways. This argument may be applied to the opposite case. If the earmarked revenues are spent for the enlargement of government facilities which are *competitive* with the taxed item, the demand for the taxed item falls and sellers therefore can, on this account, shift less of the tax to buyers.[12]

---

[11] The crucial propositions in his position are the following: "... if it can be shown that the expenditure of the funds yielded by a tax, changes the supply-demand relationship of the object taxed, a consideration of such effects of this expenditure is relevant to the analysis of the incidence of this tax." "It can scarcely be denied that the expenditure of the yield of a tax is a factor introduced by the tax whenever the dependence of the particular expenditure on the particular tax can be traced." (M. Slade Kendrick, "Public Expenditure; A Neglected Consideration in Tax Incidence Theory," *American Economic Review*, XX [June, 1930]: 227.)

[12] Presumably such a case would be illustrated by a tax on railroad tickets when the proceeds were earmarked for the construction or improvement of highways.

But why not claim that the effects of a particular public expenditure should be taken to include as well the effects of the tax which goes along with the expenditure? Why taxes are so crucial is not as self-evident as is implied. The device of earmarking, now employed even more generally in the case of motor-vehicle fuel taxes than when Kendrick wrote, does not establish a definite functional relationship between tax yields and government expenditures. Pressure groups are not always squeamish about methods used to assure adequate support for their favorite government functions. Earmarking removes such expenditures from periodic legislative and administrative review, a common objective of such groups. Automobile associations together with highway commissions may succeed in obtaining the earmarking of gasoline taxes for highway construction only, leaving maintenance to be financed out of general funds. Earmarking should be looked upon as a political tactic used by pressure groups in the general scramble for government financial support for particular functions. If gasoline taxes were for some reason impracticable, the advocates of paving the countryside would no doubt be able to discover new ways of persuading governments to appropriate large sums for highway construction. Who is to say they would be less successful if earmarking were, say, unconstitutional?[13]

If the political facts are examined, it is evident that the amounts spent for government ends are not functionally dependent upon tax yields in any simple sense. The treatment of particular government expenditures as "financed by" particular taxes is a dubious one even in cases of earmarking. There is no way of ascertaining what tax money is spent for a particular function. Nor is it true that one may think of any additional tax as financing some additional expenditure. Either the expenditure may increase regardless of the tax, or some other expenditure may increase instead. These are questions that are easily answered by assumptions, but even the most astute budget officer would have difficulty answering them in actual political settings. It appears more appropriate for purposes of analysis to treat government expenditures as determined by political and administrative decisions rather than as functions of particular tax yields.

The background against which a tax should be analyzed in-

---

[13] We operate in the United States, as in many other countries, upon the supposition that social security payments are "financed" by social security taxes. In practice, the financing of these transfer payments is indistinguishable from the financing of government interest payments or payments to veterans.

cludes whatever the government policies happen to be for expenditures and transfer payments. Why they are what they are involves a close study of politics. This view implies that budgets may not be in balance; they may be over- or underbalanced. Since these are the usual facts, a theory should conform to them.

TIME ELEMENT

The treatment of government expenditures as determined by political decisions does not tell us in any final way the meaning to be assigned to causation in fiscal measures. There are other problems and perhaps the most urgent of these has to do with that troublesome topic—time. Philosophers tell us that "time" is a general expression for causation. Discussions of tax causation must be explicitly tied to the time dimension.

A beginning may be made by thinking of a tax in the "present." The present involves duration, however short that duration may be conceived. The past is dead except to the extent it is incorporated in the present, whereas the future is yet to be. The future may exert in a sense a "pull" upon the present. This pull in economics is the forward-looking character of all human decisions to take action. The presence of intelligence—final causation—guarantees that the present is not merely the average past all over again.

Many of the generalizations in economics presuppose that the period under consideration is the present. Resources are given only in the present; they are what they are, and an explanation of their present characteristics would involve an indefinite search through all past history. Resources in the present may be used in alternative ways. If a longer period is taken, resources change, or at least may change, and propositions about allocation of resources become vague.

The relevance of the present to tax analysis may be illustrated by attention to a simple tax device. Suppose a head tax of a given number of dollars. Every person, say, above a certain age is required to pay $10 a month to his government. What do we mean by saying that such a tax has effects?

In the present period, the tax liability accrues at the rate of $10 a month for each legal taxpayer. Upon the date of payment this liability is settled with the government by the payment of money. The tax at a certain date each month depletes each person's cash balance to the extent of $10. Therefore he must at some date or dates spend $10 less on goods and services, $10 less on claims,

increase his income by $10, or sell claims including his own debt
of $10, or reduce his bank account by $10. If he merely pays the
tax, that is, reduces his bank account by $10, the payment of the
$10 at any particular date "causes" him to have 10 fewer dollars on
that date. From the point of view of government, the tax "causes"
a revenue equal to $10 per month multiplied by the number of
taxpayers.

A head tax, assuming it is rigorously enforced, confronts people
with the alternatives of spending fewer dollars, getting more dollars, or holding fewer dollars as compared to a no-tax alternative.
If all taxpayers merely hold fewer dollars, the effect of the tax is
to reduce the private inflationary potential; the tax reduces private
financial power to buy things in future periods. In all other cases
the tax is deflationary in the sense of reducing money demands for
products or deflationary in the sense of increasing the supply of
things people wish to sell. We can summarize these observations
by the proposition that the tax liability each month is a reduction
in the net income of the person each month, when net income
means actual income minus tax. Let us call this the *income effect*
of the tax.

But the tax does something else, too. A head tax literally makes
staying alive more expensive. It imposes a penalty upon being
associated with one's head, the base of the tax in this instance. Since,
however, we may suppose that this penalty will not induce a person
to commit suicide, a head tax can be regarded as neutral in its
effects upon human choice. Taxes of this type are unusual. In
almost every instance, the tax formula as set forth in the tax laws
is a conditional one. A person (or organization) is subject to a tax
on the condition that he (or it) is associated with a tax base of
some size, and some freedom exists for the taxpayer to alter the
size of the base. Thus, if income is the base of a tax, a person can
influence his tax liability by influencing the amount of his income.
If total sales of beer are the base of the tax, a seller of beer can
influence the amount of tax to which he is liable by varying the
quantity or the prices of beer sold. The effects of a tax which arise
from the presence of a positive rate of tax upon a base subject to
greater or less control by the taxpayer are what Pigou has called
the *announcement effects* of a tax.[14] These effects follow from the
change in the costs of alternative behavior patterns, a change in-

---

[14] Pigou, *op. cit.*, pp. 55–56. The term is clumsy, suggesting a reference to what may
go on in people's minds in anticipation of the passage of new tax legislation. "Cost

duced by the tax formula itself. The same classification of effects applies to subsidies since they, too, present the potential recipient with a formula which he may be able to influence by his own actions.

The importance of the two concepts "income effect" and "announcement effect" of a tax is just this: any differences that a tax may make can be traced, and must be traced, by these two concepts. The two effects are, however, of very different sorts. The income effect relates to the fact that taxes extract money from people. Whatever else may be said about taxes, this fact should not be missed. No tax theory is complete until it explains who pays the money the government obtains. The announcement effect refers to a tax-induced alteration in the terms of choice. The government, by setting up a tax, describes some base and makes it expensive to be associated with that base. Thus an income tax that exempts some types of gain, such as leisure, from the definition of income for tax purposes makes leisure relatively less expensive by making the obtaining of income absolutely more expensive. For some people this may make no difference; for others it may make a big difference. The causation implied in the announcement effect is "marginal." It is the additional cost for which the activity or item defined as the tax base makes the legal taxpayer liable.

The announcement effect makes the terms of choice different at each moment in the history of a tax law. The effect is present all the time, but it makes a difference only to the extent that legal taxpayers allow their actual choices to be affected by the terms presented in the tax law. The announcement aspect of the tax may be said to "cause" a different pattern of behavior to the extent that it makes some action more expensive and may lead to different choices than would otherwise be made. The expression "would otherwise" is important in this statement. For the question is not how the tax makes the present differ from the past; the question is rather how the present as found differs from another and hypothetical present. For example, in a social system undergoing change—and all do—the present will differ from the past in many ways. Complete information about all these changes would not tell us what the announcement effects of a tax actually are. Ideally, to discover the announcement effects of a tax, we need to know

---

effect" is more descriptive, but cost gets heavy usage in other connections. "Price effect" has the same difficulty. Innovations in terminology are furthermore a nuisance, and since Pigou discovered the idea it is only proper to retain his term.

what a person's behavior would be if he were not confronted with the choice as set forth in the tax base, as compared with what his behavior is when confronted with that choice. In the case of a head tax, it may reasonably be assumed that people are not going to commit suicide to avoid a tax payment. Therefore the tax in question becomes for practical purposes one with a zero announcement effect. Lump-sum taxes of this sort may therefore be treated as neutral with respect to choice.

Neutrality does not, however, mean that the tax does not make a difference in other respects. A person viewed as an income recipient finds that his cash balance is reduced by the collection of the tax and that his income per month is reduced by the tax liability. He must behave differently on this account. He is in a position to buy less, potentially or actually, at any set of prices for products. Thus a person must economize either by buying less or being content to hold a smaller cash balance, or he must work more, that is, earn a larger income before tax. The latter alternative is relevant only for those who are earning less than they might. A person hovering close to the edge of the price system who prefers things which do not involve participating in an exchange economy may be forced, if the tax is rigorously administered, to participate in the price system to obtain enough money to pay the tax. He is thus required to enjoy less "leisure." A tax measure of this type forces a person to work for the government at least in part. In principle, forcing a person to work is no different from forcing him to spend less money or to hold less cash. A system of taxation is a device to force people to work provided a person is not excused from paying taxes by not working. Knight's dictum that people are free to participate or withdraw from a system of monetary organization must be qualified at least to the extent that a government imposes taxes upon them which they cannot avoid by withdrawal.[15]

---

[15] Thus Knight writes: "Everyone is free, as a Crusoe is free, and also enjoys the nearly boundless gain in the effectiveness of action possible through organization. In fact, the individual's range of choice is extended in a new dimension beyond that of Crusoe; he can produce anything he pleases, or make any specific contribution to production, and independently consume anything or any combination produced by anyone anywhere in the economy." (F. H. Knight, "The Rôle of Principles in Economics and Politics," *American Economic Review*, XLI [March, 1951]: 13.)

This conception, even as a first approximation to the characteristics of an exchange system, is dangerous to clear thinking. Even if it were technically possible for any family to produce things without direct coöperation with others—a Swiss Family Robinson—families are nevertheless inescapably tied together by money. Money is one kind of social glue which a person can escape only through withdrawal from the system—a choice which means little in practice. In the presence of money, the con-

The effect of a tax measure viewed only as a device to extract money from people does not differ in any important way from the effect of many other transfer payments made by people. Thus, if a person is required to make alimony payments, his income net of such payments is thereby smaller, and his choices of holding or spending cash and of obtaining more or less money income are affected in much the same way as they would be by a tax. A transfer payment may be viewed as a negative element in the income of those who make such payments and as a positive element in the income of those who receive such payments. Therefore the causation question in connection with the income effect of a tax is a part of the larger question of the causation of income in a money-price system. In chapter 5, the theory is presented that all present income is "functionless" with respect to expenditures in the "present." We shall argue that income can be objectively relevant to expenditures only for future periods.

Our conception of tax causation may be contrasted with the method of speculative history. In some sense economic life in the twentieth century is different, and presumably radically different, because of the use by governments of import duties in the nineteenth century. The speculative history approach is illustrated by a posing of the question of what the world would now be like if Napoleon had died as a child. Although this type of investigation has its uses, it is radically different from what is ordinarily regarded as economic explanation. Causation in our sense must be pinpointed. We look upon any tax in terms of a period of time sufficiently short so that cumulative effects are absent. This period is the "present," a duration that is the smallest possible period for anything actually to occur. This approach means that we shall have to be careful with so-called long-run theories of the effects of taxes. The content of those theories can be expressed without assuming the lapse of special periods of time by thinking of the economy as having a varying degree of adaptability to taxation or to any other measures which may be imposed. Thus a new tax imposed today will have different effects today than will an identical tax that has been in existence for a long period. The effects of taxes depend partly upon their own history.

---

cept of "specific contribution" must be modified if it is defined in real terms as Knight apparently does. The interdependence of persons even in a society of a simple kind, because of monetary transactions, has been stressed by D. H. Robertson (*Banking Policy and the Price-Level* [New York: Augustus M. Kelly, 1949], p. ix).

In a general theory, we try to explain what the effects are whether the tax is old or new, and if old, whether it is to be repealed or continued. Since change in resources and in tastes is inevitable in any actual society, theories as to what the results of taxes would be if the society did not change are not particularly relevant. In principle, the shifting of a particular tax is a continuous and never-ending process. At no date may one stop and observe that certain identifiable people are paying a tax without being prepared to admit that another group of people may be paying this same tax at a later date in history.

TAX THEORY

The theory of taxation to be elucidated in this study is of a fairly simple nature. We look upon any tax or subsidy as a "transfer" involving private groups and government. The concept of transfer, which is discussed in detail in chapter 4, means that taxes are a kind of income from the point of view of the government and subsidies are a kind of income from the point of view of private groups. It also means that taxes are negative income items for private groups and that subsidies are negative income items for government. According to this view, any tax depletes private money incomes by exactly the amount that it increases government income.

A tax or a subsidy may be "shifted" if certain conditions are satisfied. A necessary condition for shifting is that the tax or subsidy has an announcement effect. A sufficient condition for some tax shifting is that the tax formula induces legal taxpayers to behave in such a fashion as to increase their incomes computed before deducting the tax. If the tax gives them no such opportunity, the possibility of their shifting the tax to other groups does not exist. The mere incentive to reduce one's tax liability is not a sufficient condition for shifting. It must also be true that the incentive acts in such a way as to increase a taxpayer's income.

We find that people as consumers do not and furthermore cannot "pay" taxes. The ancient doctrine that some taxes are shifted to consumers appears to be a confusion, traceable to lack of attention to elemental features of a price system. In its place we substitute the theory that any excise tax, or for that matter any tax whatever, reduces somebody's money income, and if he shifts the tax, this occasions a reduction in somebody else's income. This approach also implies that truly general income taxes are not shiftable. Thus orthodoxy is reinforced in this area.

The theory here proposed also implies that a government cannot tax people outside its jurisdiction unless those people own resources within the tax jurisdiction. For example, the view that import duties are devices which tax foreigners is repudiated. It is possible to "exploit" the foreigner by various devices in the sense of making the foreigner suffer, but much as some might wish to do so, we cannot tax the Russians.

Finally, the proposed theory is designed to apply to any money-price system, including socialistic systems, to the extent that taxation is possible in such systems. It is designed to be general in the sense that no unbridgeable gaps are found in the explanation of taxes of different kinds, as is implied, for example, in the distinction between direct and indirect taxes. In fact this ancient distinction might be abandoned in theoretical analysis.

2

Government Ends versus Private Ends

Economics rests upon the fact that the products people want are limited by the resources available to supply them. Governments compete with their own citizens for some of these products, and out of this competition a number of implications emerge. In this chapter, our main concern is the clarification of the concept of government ends or objectives. This task is a necessary preliminary to the discussion of the social costs of government—the topic to be investigated in chapter 3.

In a broad way, government may be conceived as providing services to its constituents. Some of these services are provided for particular people, others are not. In one aspect government operations literally serve people as do private business organizations. Both cater to personal ends. In another aspect, government operations have no parallel in private enterprise. A business cannot force one to take its "product," but a government can. Herein lies a basis for a classification of government activities. Some of these activities are such that people exposed to them have little personal choice in the matter; others of these activities are very similar to those of business enterprise. No great problem of distinguishing these two general classes of government operations would exist if governments kept the two groups of activities clearly distinct. But in fact, they are intermingled in actual government departments and in particular projects. In practice, commercial activities are carried on in conjunction with "pure" government functions, subsidies are mixed together with ordinary expenditures, and taxes are sometimes used in lieu of full payment for services.

In accordance with this basic distinction, government operations which involve the use of resources or the acquisition of products may be divided into the following classes:

1. Operations which promote government objectives directly.
2. Operations which promote government ends that can be achieved only by fulfillment of the desires of particular persons or private organizations.
3. Operations which effectuate money transfer payments by government to private groups and by private groups to government.

Operations designed to promote private ends by the techniques of:

4. Full price rationing of a service or commodity to particular private persons or organizations.
5. Partial price rationing of a service or commodity.
6. Self-rationing of government facilities subject to overuse (diminishing returns).
7. No rationing of any kind (use of facilities not subject to diminishing returns).

Operations 1, 2, and 3 are government functions, and the costs of performing them constitute the costs of government ends. Operations 6 and 7 will also be treated as involving costs of government because these activities cannot be assigned to private groups in any measurable fashion. Operations 4 and 5 will be viewed as "government enterprise" functions which may or may not entail a subsidy in kind to private groups. Their costs are not "costs of government" in our sense because they do not promote government ends.

GOVERNMENT ENDS

1. Some objectives of government are inherent in its position as the ultimate arbiter of social relations. In any complex social system, rules must be established and enforced to provide the kind of order desired by that social group. There is no conceivable method of parceling out rule enforcement to private groups by any rationing system that allows particular members of society to decide for themselves whether or not they want to take the "service." On the contrary, rules must be enforced, if they are to be effective, on the very persons who dislike them. States do not exist merely to benefit particular, identifiable persons; they represent the entire population including those yet to be born. There is no rational basis for assigning benefits from the pursuance of pure government objectives to particular persons; government is indispensable to organized society. Speculation as to whether one group benefits more than another from the existence of government is therefore not a rewarding pastime.

A large part of government expenses arises from the pursuance of pure government functions. Military services, easily the most expensive single aspect of government operations in the contemporary scene in the United States, is such a function. Pure government functions include even such activities as education when it is compulsory. Compulsion rules out assigning the services to particular persons since their likes or dislikes have nothing to do with whether they participate or not. Compulsory education resembles police service; many particular individuals desire to have the service available but they have little choice as to whether or not they take the service. All services of government which are imposed on the group are here treated as promoting government ends.

2. This group of government operations concerns activities which particular individuals are free to take or to leave as they please, but which, from a government's point of view, have consequences that are "good for society." Advanced education, which is not compulsory, illustrates such a category. Here particular students are given the opportunity to expose themselves to higher education. They directly benefit in the sense that they obtain services which they desire. Educational opportunities provided at public expense advance the welfare of the community as a whole by increasing the educational achievements of its members. To accomplish this end, a government has an obligation to provide such services on a scale sufficient to accommodate all qualified persons. A financial test is inconsistent with the presumed objective of increasing educational opportunity and achievement.

An alternative interpretation is to regard government operations which directly benefit particular persons as a subsidy in kind to those who take the service. If a government hands out food, for example, at no charge, it would appear that it is subsidizing in kind some members of the group. Similarly, a student at a university or a child at a public playground may be considered as being subsidized in kind. According to such an interpretation, government activities which directly benefit particular people should be regarded as subsidies rather than as activities which carry out government functions.

The tests here proposed for ascertaining whether or not a public function is being performed when the government provides free services to persons are the following: (1) individuals must have a choice of taking or rejecting the service; (2) the use of a financial device for selecting those who are to obtain the service must be inconsistent with the fulfillment of the public objective; (3) a direct money subsidy to particular persons would not accomplish the public objective. Unless test (1) is satisfied, there is no issue. If people have no choice, the activity falls into our first major classification already discussed. Test (2) applies to those cases in which price rationing would defeat the public objective. If, for example, the government's policy does not involve any selection of the particular individuals who may take the service, the supply could be rationed by price. In this event, the activity is an enterprise function. City water service illustrates such a case. Anyone is free to obtain water. Thus no public objective is defeated by rationing water by price. Educational opportunities provided by government would also be an enterprise function if it were a matter of indifference what persons or how many enrolled. If, however, in the judgment of the community, a financial test would exclude some persons who should be included to accomplish the presumed objective, test (2) is satisfied. In other words, public policy precludes selection by a financial means test.

Test (3) takes account of the distributional implications of publicly provided services. A government might wish to avoid price rationing of a service merely because it believed that some persons could not afford to acquire the service. If this were the only relevant consideration, the operation in question should be classified as a subsidy device rather than as a government function. A clear case of such subsidies is found when a government gives away food and clothing to individuals selected on the basis of some means test. These particular individuals could also be assisted by direct money payments. If money subsidies were provided instead, government stores or other facilities for making gifts in kind might be abandoned or, alternatively, operated according to ordinary commercial rules. Thus the practice of subsidizing restaurants provided for members of the United States Congress implies a judgment that such people should have higher incomes. The same result could be achieved by paying congressmen higher money salaries and raising their restaurant prices to competitive levels.[1] Test (3) is satisfied if a system of money payments would not accomplish the government objective. In the case of higher education, the question becomes whether gifts of money to prospective students instead of "free" services or nominally priced services would effectively achieve the social objective. Flat grants of money do

---

[1] Subsidies in kind have the advantage of being tax-free income. They also conceal the amount of income being granted to those who qualify for the subsidy in kind.

not, however, assure attendance at a university which charges tuition to ration its service. Some young persons would prefer to spend their money in other ways. Gifts of money to parents with children do not assure that the children are kept from playing in crowded streets. Therefore provision of free government services to selected groups implies in such cases that the government treats the acquisition of the services by these particular groups as an indirect means of achieving some public end. The government is not merely substituting a group judgment for the judgment of particular persons concerning what is good for them; it is making a decision that the promotion of certain ends of individuals provides results which are good for society in a more general sense. Even in a society in which inequality of wealth is negligible, there would be occasions for the provision of free government services to accomplish some public objectives.

3. Money transfer payments by government require administrative machinery for their accomplishment. The cost of providing these facilities is a part of the costs of government. The transfer payments themselves are not costs in any proper sense—a point which will be elaborated in the following chapter. Transfer payments do not involve the use by the government of scarce resources to promote its own ends. Individuals subsidized are free to spend the money so obtained in accordance with their own desires. Any resources used to provide the things they want belong in the private sector of the economy in the sense that the results of production are taken by private groups.

Transfer payments made to government, such as taxes, also involve administrative machinery, and the value of the services involved is also a part of the costs of government. As in government subsidies, taxes, which are their negative counterparts, do not measure the costs of government—a point which may be less obvious. The mere relinquishing of money by private groups to their government does not imply that private groups are relinquishing real things. Taxes in their aspect of money redistribution have no direct bearing on the costs of government. Government costs concern the use of resources to accomplish government ends or objectives and involve a burden on private groups in the sense of reducing the things they may obtain through the exercise of choice, irrespective of the financial machinery employed.

GOVERNMENT ACTIVITIES SERVING PRIVATE ENDS

The classes of government operations numbered 4 through 7 above are devices to supply products to people with the government acting as an intermediary. Because of certain special problems it is impossible, even if all relevant information were available, for private groups to value these resources, and therefore some of these operations (classes 6 and 7) are grouped together with government functions for lack of any better solution.

4. Where the government decides to provide some service and to use the price mechanism for selecting those who are to obtain the service, no peculiar public ends are being pursued, and the activities should be classified as enterprise functions. Any costs to government in connection with the supplying of such services are costs of promoting the ends of private groups. According to this test, postal service involves costs of promoting private ends rather than government ends. The service in this case is fully rationed by price. Anyone is free to use the service in any quantity he pleases. The worth of the service to those who acquire it is what they pay for a unit of the service. Private valuation of government-provided commodities involves no differences in principle from the valuation of products provided by private enterprise.

The above statement that no public end is served by government enterprise must be interpreted with care. In one sense all enterprise, whether publicly or privately managed, may be presumed to promote the general welfare. A government has an interest in the economic well-being of its members. Certain types of business activities may be prohibited, such as the production and distribution of narcotics. Failure to take such action with regard to any product implies that government policy endorses private effort to produce the things that people want, although in some cases evidence may be available that these things are not "good for" the persons using them. Government enterprises, such as the supplying of water or of postal service at a price, are not necessarily more important than the supplying of milk or of railroad transportation. Some government enterprise falls into the category of "natural" monopolies, which would require close regulation if left in private hands. Some are managed by government for no cogent reason; they were started by government in the past, and effective private competition has been disallowed or has failed to develop because of government competition. Government management of resources therefore gives little information as to whether or not public ends are being promoted.

Whether an enterprise should be under government or private management is to be decided by a comparison of the relative efficiency of private and public management, the socially demanded amount of public regulation of private enterprise, and similar considerations. The proposition that public enterprise need entail no public objective should be interpreted to mean, therefore, that public enterprise is similar to private in the sense that it provides people with certain goods for which they are willing to pay money. No further value judgment need be made about the social desirability of such uses of resources.

The treatment of a government operation as an enterprise function may appear to be somewhat strained in cases where the government incurs a loss. The loss might seem to imply that some special government function is pursued in conjunction with the supplying of the service to private groups. The much publicized heavy losses of the United States Post Office Department may be and often are construed to mean that it is subsidizing those using the mails. But this view offers difficulties. It is not usual to think of ordinary business losses as subsidies made to the customers of such enterprises. There is of course the possible difference that a loss incurred in a government enterprise may be deliberate whereas this is not usually true in private enterprise. Such considerations support the theory that customers of government enterprises are subsidized to the extent of the loss.

Although it is true that losses on government enterprise are similar to subsidies paid to private enterprise, it is not true in either case that those who buy the services or goods in question are those who are subsidized. Rather, such policies increase the money incomes of those whose resources are employed to produce the subsidized products and those whose resources, although employed in other fields, are competitive with those in the subsidized industries. This point, which is discussed more fully in chapter 6, may be readily seen if either the government operated all industry at a loss in a socialistic system or provided uniform subsidies to private enterprise in a decentralized system. In either event, buyers as a class would not obtain more output than they would obtain if no products were subsidized. It may not be assumed that subsidies increase the efficiency of the economic organization as a whole.

Government enterprise losses may alter the pattern of resource allocation, especially in a system in which many privately produced products are subject to taxes. Presumably the operation of a government enterprise at a loss, such as the postal system, is intended to make the commodity more abundant relative to other forms of output than it would otherwise be. Theoretically, postal services could be made equally abundant, but also profitable, if heavy excise taxes were placed upon all remaining commodities. There is a system of excise taxes on some commodities which is equivalent in its allocation effects to a system of subsidies (or government enterprise losses) on others. Whether a government happens to make a profit or a loss on its postal operations provides no information germane to the classification of these operations as one that serves government ends or one that serves private ends. The Department of State may similarly be looked upon as incurring a loss. We do know, however, that postal services are rationed to the public by price. This evidence is sufficient to establish that the operations are of an enterprise character.

5. The government may provide a service to members of the public but charge less than the value of the service as determined by the amount which people would pay if full price rationing were employed. Many enterprise activities of government fall into this category. It is common practice, and even more common belief, that certain types of government services should be supplied at "cost" by the government. Government irrigation projects, for example, may provide water at such a low price that other rationing devices need to be employed to select those who are to obtain the water. We do not raise the issue as to whether the specialized facilities should have been constructed in the first place or even whether the government should take the initiative in providing the service. Our problem is, given the facility as it now stands, what interpretation should be placed upon the nonprice techniques used to determine who is to obtain various quantities of the commodity. The practice of charging on the basis of cost, as that concept is commonly interpreted for government enterprises, may result in a price that prevents full utilization of the facilities—alleged to be true in the case of the Alaskan railroad. "Cost" pricing may lead to overpricing. The disposition of governments to charge monopolistic prices is disturbingly common. A cost policy may also result in prices that are unduly low. Some public power enterprises

charge prices well below the price that rations the service to the
capacity of the facilities.[2]

In cases falling within this class, the government, by undercharging for the service, provides a subsidy in kind for those who qualify
as customers. The amount of the subsidy may be measured by the
difference between the value of the service as measured by a price
that fully rations the service and the price actually used. This
amount is a subsidy to those obtaining the service because they
get something for nothing. There is no difference in principle
between the outright gift of money and grant of services at nominal
prices.

There are difficulties which should not be concealed in distinguishing in any particular instance whether a government is attempting to promote its own ends by promoting private ends (class
2) or merely engaging in an enterprise without charging all the
traffic will bear, consistent with the full use of the facility. The
critical test would seem to be whether only certain groups are to
be treated as qualified to obtain the service and whether their selection is made on grounds other than the desire to provide them with
extra income. Some illustrations may be helpful to reveal how one
may judge whether the underpricing is merely a subsidy or whether
it indicates a foregone gain of the government to achieve its own
objectives.

To clarify the cost issues arising in the subsidy-versus-govern-
ment-ends interpretation of government operations, let us examine
a hypothetical case of a government irrigation project. A government is assumed to own facilities which will provide a certain
known number of acre-feet of water for a given agricultural district
which depends upon irrigation. The government, let us suppose,
rations this water partly on the basis of the rule that no water shall
go to any farm in excess of 360 acres. However, the demand for
water by those who qualify on an acreage basis is assumed to be
sufficiently large to take all the water available. The government,

---

[2] Unlike certain types of consumer subsidies in kind, government gifts of services
of an instrumental nature are reflected in higher money incomes of those benefited
and become therefore a part of the statutory income of those obtaining the service.
The comparative cheapness, because of nonprice rationing, of government-supplied
water for irrigation need not reduce prices of the products in question. Costs are
relevant to prices to the extent that they affect supplies. It is a mistake to suppose
that even under competitive conditions marginal cost must always equal price. This
theorem requires, among other conditions, that money cost measures the value of a
unit of the instrumental service to the enterprise. This is not true when the instrumental item is rationed partly by methods other than price.

we suppose, adopts a policy of rationing the water exclusively by price to those who qualify. Those who do not qualify cannot buy water from the government on any terms. Furthermore, the price is just sufficient to cover all "costs" of the operation of the facility. Is anyone subsidized in kind, and if so who?

In the absence of the acreage restriction, which in the present instance is the only nonprice rationing feature of the scheme, a clearing price for the water would be a higher one, since the over-all demand would be greater in the absence of restrictions. There-fore, qualified owners obtain water at a lower price than they otherwise could. Yet from their point of view, a unit of water-flow is worth exactly its cost to them, that is, the price, since by assump-tion they are free to buy whatever quantities they please. On the other hand, owners of acreage in excess of the critical amount have their money costs of production increased. If their costs would be increased by acquiring government water at a price which would just clear the market, they would not demand the water at all. If these two groups of farmers are in competition with one another in the sense of producing crops for the same markets, the prices of products would not reflect any differences in the costs of acquiring water, whether from the government for acreages of 360 acres and less, or by pumping or other methods for acreages exceeding that amount.

As long as some incentive exists to own excess acreage, because, for example, of economies of scale, the government should not be regarded as paying a subsidy. Rather, it is bearing a hidden ex-pense, theoretically measured by the difference between the income which would be earned by the project if the rationing were wholly by price and the income obtained under the rationing system actu-ally employed. This expense is the cost of obtaining the supposed social benefits arising from a community consisting of many small farms as compared with one consisting of large farms.

The empirical test of the efficiency of the government's social objective is the continued existence of the foregone income of the project. Complete success occurs when all acreage is broken into ownership lots of 360 acres or less. In this event, pursuance of a policy of rationing the water wholly by price would result in a higher price for the service and a profit or a smaller loss on the government operation. No nonprice rationing would then be pres-ent. The test of owning the critical acreage or less would no longer be relevant. Complete failure means no reduction in the size of holdings, in which case the government is getting no social return for its foregone income.[3]

In the example just considered, it would, I believe, be incorrect to claim that farmers who are entitled to government water are subsidized. Rather, the foregone gain of the government is a part of the cost of promoting the government objective of a community of "small" farmers. In the absence of this objective, water could be sold to any buyer at a higher price without allowing supplies to go unused.

The illustration needs to be altered to reveal a case of subsidies in kind. Let us suppose that the government places no restrictions as to which landowners may acquire government water, but a price is charged which is below the clearing price for the available supply. The demand at this price exceeds the supply, and therefore other methods of rationing automatically come into play. If the nonprice rationing method used is some limitation rule as to the amount of water-flow permitted per acre, each holder of acreage may be considered to be subsidized by the difference between the price actually paid for the amount delivered and the value of the water if price were employed as the exclusive rationing device. Owners of the land are subsidized in this case. The financial advantage which this group obtains is reflected in the added profitability of their operations. With the rationing system based on water-flow per acre, this gain becomes reflected in higher rentals, if the land is rented. Land carrying such rights becomes on that account "better" land. The added income may also be reflected in higher capital values. The relevant social issue involved in such

---

[3] The particular illustration raises the question as to whether a more sensible public policy, granted the objective involved, would be to prohibit, outright, holdings in excess of the critical number of acres, or, alternatively, to make excess holdings subject to a special tax with the rate increasing as the number of acres held increases. In either of these cases, the social objective of promoting small holdings might be achieved without the social waste involved in denying water to some land. Government water, given the restriction on large acreage, is marginally more productive on the larger than on the qualifying farms. Thus in addition to the government costs in the form of foregone income, the practice entails a wasteful use of resources. A general presumption exists against policies granting special favors in the distribution of government services. If the general conviction exists that a particular objective is of sufficient importance to justify government action for its accomplishment, the direct and simple method is either outright prohibition of the practice or direct money subsidies to encourage the desired private action. In the case of acreage limitation policies, a policy of outright prohibition of acreage under control of one person or family in excess of some given amount would make the issue at stake clear and definite instead of directing public attention to what are essentially side issues. The use of roundabout methods to accomplish an objective may occasion considerable expense and in many cases be a failure.

cases is whether these particular landowners should be subsidized. If it is social policy to raise the level of their money incomes, yet another issue arises. Why should this particular group have any special claim to government funds? If it is public policy to subsidize certain landowners, a more open and definite policy would be outright grants of money to the group accompanied by full price rationing of the public service in question.

When a government service is final rather than instrumental and when other rationing devices in addition to price are used, the government provides a "consumer subsidy." This case is illustrated by government-managed housing projects when the rationing of the service is partly by price and partly by other means. Suppose the government selects tenants on a first-come-first-served basis—there being no public policy involved in the selection of tenants. If the housing service is provided at a rental of $25 per month and the competitive rental is $75 per month, a subsidy in kind is provided the tenants equal to $50 per month. This observation holds even if there is a profit on the housing project at the actual rentals charged according to ordinary accounting methods of computing costs. There is an actual loss to the government in the sense of foregone income of $50 per month, and this measures the amount of the subsidy per unit.

But it could be claimed that a public function is being performed by this practice, and therefore the foregone income measures the cost of the public end accomplished. What would the public end be in such a case? An answer often given by supporters of low-cost housing ventures is that certain groups in the population are provided better housing facilities, and this benefits the community at large. More adequate housing may produce better citizens, healthier children, and lower crime rates. To evaluate this type of claim, a number of distinctions are necessary. If people in general are believed to be benefited by more housing, an appeal is made to the conception of some ideal allocation of resources. An increase in the output of some things in a society which must husband its resources means a sacrifice of the output of others. A government policy of increasing the output of certain items which are to be taken by the public presupposes therefore that the changed allocation of resources is an improvement over the allocation that would result in the absence of the specific policy in question.

If housing is judged to be inadequate in quantity as compared with other things, the end of increased housing can be accomplished by government construction of housing units, subsidies to builders, special financing arrangements provided by government to enable people to finance more housing compared with financing other things, taxes on the production of commodities which compete with housing for resources, special rules other than taxes which place obstacles to the production of goods which compete with housing, and the like. This list of possible measures emphasizes two points: (1) the entrance of government into the real estate business is only one of a number of devices to increase the supply of new houses; and (2) subsidies are not necessarily involved in changing the allocation of resources among different products. The implication of measures adopted to change resource allocation are different from those of government rationing of the services of facilities it operates.

The foregone income of government-managed resources is the cost of pursuing a public end provided that full price rationing would defeat a public objective. Is a public objective defeated where a facility is rationed to the public partly by price? There would appear to be no public end involved if the selection of those who are to get the service is a matter of indifference to the government as implied by the adoption of a first-come-first-served method of rationing. In this event, it would be hard to believe that a public end is promoted which could not equally well be achieved by rationing the facilities entirely by price. In cases where people are free to take or leave the service, a public function is implied only if the selection policies are deliberate rather than random.

Returning to the case of public housing, let us assume that instead of selecting tenants on a first-come-first-served basis, the condition is laid down that a tenant's income must not exceed $3,000 per year. The illustration is now similar to that discussed in connection with the rationing of water based on size of acreage. The partial rationing of housing service by reference to the size of a tenant's income places a penalty upon the attainment of income beyond the critical point. The equivalent "tax" rate of such a system of selecting tenants exceeds 100 per cent for a range where the loss to tenants from having to move and find other dwelling accommodations exceeds the value of the subsidy to them. An increase in a tenant's income before taxes of one dollar beyond the critical point would mean a loss of subsidy worth several dollars. Thus, unless a person finds an income opportunity that permits him to leap the gap, the practice places a heavy penalty upon tenants who may wish to work more or find better-paying jobs. The incentive effect is highly adverse.

A government policy directed to preventing people from working more need only be made explicit to justify the conclusion that it could not be supported in any sensible way. The motivation for the use of size of income as a rationing device is therefore to be found elsewhere. Presumably the reason must be to assist people with low incomes. If this is the rationale, the policy is discriminatory unless everyone in the low-income group can become a tenant in a low-cost housing project. But even in this case, the method itself is defective because it reduces the incentives of the persons concerned to increase their incomes.

In addition, a subsidy in kind is wasteful of resources as compared with a money subsidy of equal monetary cost if the desires of the group in question are respected. An outright grant of money to tenants in amounts equal to the income loss by the government from the adoption of a policy of extra-price rationing would permit a tenant to continue to take the service if he chose to do so. If the subsidy is $50 per month, the payment of this amount in cash to any tenant would permit him to pay $75 in rental without reducing his expenditures in other directions. Some might prefer to take less elaborate housing quarters and more of other things—a choice which is denied them by the method of subsidy in kind. Subsidies in kind are, therefore, a type of economic waste from this point of view.

6. There is a further class of government-operated facilities where the service is taken by individual members of the public but where for technical reasons price rationing is impossible. This class of public management of resources may be distinguished as follows: (1) no peculiar public function would be defeated by a price system of rationing the service; (2) the facilities are subject to overcrowding; and (3) no feasible method is available to ration by price.

Highways are a conspicuous illustration of such a case. Although transportation on highways is obviously of some public concern, this holds true for private transportation systems such as railroads. As mentioned above, no case exists for government provision of a service or a product merely because in some sense it is socially desirable. Highways are provided and maintained by governments mainly because they cannot be provided on any adequate scale by private enterprise. General recourse to tolls for highway use would

lead to enormous expense for collecting tolls and preventing sur-
reptitious use. Where it so happens that the collection of tolls is
feasible, price rationing *may* be socially justified.

No problem exists if the facilities provided by government are
demanded at a zero price in a quantity which is smaller than the
capacity of the facility. In this event no rationing of any kind is
needed, and a zero charge for the service by the government is
proper. Although there are government facilities which do not
require any formal rationing device to prevent overuse, highways
do not seem to fall in this category. On the contrary, overcrowding
is typical in and about heavily populated areas and between such
areas in many cases. The strong demand for continued expansion
of road networks suggests that overcrowding is the rule rather than
the exception.

H. Hotelling, however, argues for a contrary view, suggesting
that even where price rationing of a public facility is practicable,
such as, for example, on bridges, such a policy defeats the optimum
use of resources.[4] Hotelling's main argument is a simple one. If a
facility is not subject to overcrowding and there are no variable
expenses in connection with its operation, the marginal cost of any
unit of service taken is zero. By definition, an additional unit taken
by one person does not reduce the units available to others. It
follows that proper pricing is zero pricing.

The argument is correct granted the premise that no overcrowding would exist if the facility were open to all on a zero-price basis.
The question is a factual one. A bridge, for example, may at certain
hours of the day (or more probably night) accommodate more
traffic without additional cost to any user, and thus a zero price is
indicated. At other hours, the addition of cars increases the cost
or reduces the quality of the service to all users as the volume of
traffic reaches the saturation point. The theoretically correct solution of the issue is pointed out by F. H. Knight as well as by Allyn
Young and D. H. Robertson in the discussion of A. C. Pigou's
celebrated contention that industries subject to increasing costs
push output beyond the socially optimum point whereas the re-

[4] See Harold Hotelling, "The General Welfare in Relation to Problems of Taxation
and of Railway and Utility Rates," *Econometrica*, VI (July, 1938): 242–269. We are
not presently concerned with the issue of whether the rule of equating price to marginal cost is a theoretically correct statement for optimum resource use. The criticisms
by Ragnar Frisch of Hotelling's argument are mainly directed toward this problem.
(Cf. Ragnar Frisch, "The Dupuit Taxation Theorem," *Econometrica*, VII [April,
1939]: 145–150, and further comments by Hotelling and Frisch in the same issue.)

verse holds for industries subject to decreasing costs.[5] Knight maintains that optimum pricing of a facility subject to overcrowding calls for a charge equal to the marginal foregone cost of using the facility. In Pigou's illustration of a straight, narrow road and a broad but rough road connecting two points, the proper price for the use of the narrow road is one that satisfies the condition that the cost to a trucker including toll on the narrow road just equals the cost of using the free but rough road. Knight's criticism demonstrates that Pigou's illustration does not justify the proposition that industries subject to increasing costs push output too far. It does not demonstrate that there could be cases in which competitive pricing would give less than optimum solutions in terms of the welfare test of economic efficiency being employed.

Because price rationing of highway service is not feasible except in special circumstances, the prevention of overuse and social waste by a price system is ruled out. Consequently, highway facilities may be used to the point where incremental returns even become negative. A social policy to prevent avoidable waste therefore calls for alternative rationing devices. One method of rationing is the enforcement of rules which exclude from the highways certain types of vehicles, for example, heavily loaded trucks. Another and common method is taxation of commodities which are complementary with the use of highways, mainly motor vehicle fuels.

Where public facilities are provided to people on a free-for-all basis and no price-rationing device can for technical reasons be employed, no guidepost can be found to measure the amount people would pay for the services. Although there is no question that people in their private capacities obtain such services, a valuation of them by private groups is theoretically impossible. For lack of any better solution, services of this kind provided by government are here treated in the same way as pure government services.

7. Some government-provided services do not need to be rationed at all. Their use by some does not exclude use by others—the ancient lighthouse illustration. Public services may be provided in sufficient quantity so that the demand never exceeds the supply at a zero price. Thus a sewage system may for technical reasons be built to accommodate any demand placed on it. Price rationing would accordingly be irrelevant. Public agencies may for some reason build facilities for which there is little demand, such as

[5] See F. H. Knight, "Fallacies in the Interpretation of Social Cost," reprinted in *Ethics of Competition and Other Essays* (New York: Harper, 1935). See references therein.

airports where there is little air traffic or highways in sparsely settled regions. A rationing system which excludes any potential user involves a social waste in such cases.

In cases where rationing is unnecessary, the private marginal valuation of the service of the facility is zero. The item is "free" in the sense that competitive pricing policies would call for a zero price. These cases raise serious difficulties in connection with whether or not the facilities should be maintained, or, if not in existence, whether they should be constructed. The "benefit" is not susceptible to measurement by financial tests, and we are forced back on some form of common sense. Like class 6 above, facilities which require no rationing of any kind are treated as serving public objectives. The valuation of the services can, in principle, only be made by government itself. To private groups, their marginal money value is by definition zero.[6]

IMPLICATIONS OF THIS CLASSIFICATION

The foregoing classification provides a method of distinguishing between those activities of government which serve its own ends and those which serve the ends of individuals and organizations viewed in their private capacity. The basis of the distinction rests upon whether or not in principle the "something" resulting from government organization can be rationed by price to private groups. If it is not rationable, government expenditures for the activity in question are regarded as serving the ends of government. All others in principle should be classified as serving private ends. But as has been stated, in some cases a service cannot be rationed for technical reasons. Private valuation of the services is impossible, and for this reason they are classed with pure government functions. In other cases facilities provide services which do not need to be rationed. Only the group as such can decide whether these services are worth while, and this means that government must make the valuation decisions.

The above classification separates subsidies in kind from public functions. It seems reasonable to hold that giving people goods and services is not fundamentally different from giving them money. In either case, particular persons get something for nothing. But where a government decides to ration a service partly by

---

[6] Economic analysis reaches its limits in cases of this kind. There are many activities which are "worth" something to people but which are not susceptible to valuation in money terms. This is only saying that economics does not cover all phases of human relations.

price, some criterion must be found to determine whether any gift is involved. In the foregoing discussion, the main criterion is the price that would result from competitive pricing. This criterion appeals to the clearing function of a competitive price. It is the price that values a unit of a service when all the service is taken.

Government activities involve costs to the public. These costs are the value of services government takes for its own ends. If government organizations were merely business devices engaging in selling goods and services to demanders, only costs of producing particular products would be relevant. There would be no cost of government as such if this were the case. In fact, if such an interpretation were valid, government might be eliminated altogether merely by placing all enterprise in private hands. A more reasonable view, however, seems to be that some government is inescapable in any social organization. Accordingly, government must be viewed as having ends of its own which cannot be broken down into the ends of individuals. It is meaningful and important to ascertain the costs to private groups of providing for these ends.

3

Social Costs of Government

Government uses resources which it hires and products obtained from private enterprise to accomplish its ends. The procurement of services and products involves costs. Some preliminary observations about the interpretation of the costs of government may avoid unnecessary controversy. There exists a long history of debate between those who favor and those who oppose the expansion of government activity. Regardless of what position is taken on this question, there are costs of government. The concept of costs does not imply any judgment of the benefits derived from government activities. A military program which costs $50,000,000,000 annually may or may not be regarded by particular citizens as yielding benefits to the country equivalent to the cost. Debates about the scale of operation of any government activity concern the assessment of the benefits to be obtained in view of the costs. Intelligent judgments about the desirability of government functions require a concept of costs and their measurement.

A MONEY-PRICE SYSTEM

Government procurement operations always occur in a particular social setting and must be studied against this setting. The salient characteristics of economic organizations in much of the civilized world, and in the United States in particular, are the institutions of money and prices.

In societies of any complexity, those who acquire title to output do so through relations with those who undertake to combine resources which give rise to production. Except in cases where owners of resources take the products of their own resources, some kind of rationing system must be employed to determine how the products emerging from the productive organization are to be parceled out among persons and organizations, including government. Theoretically any number of rationing systems is possible;

in practice many different kinds have been used in various historical periods, and many different kinds are contemporarily being
used in any one country. The dominant rationing system found in
Western societies is a money-price system. In such a system prices
of products and money payments for those products determine
what people or organizations obtain the products and in what
quantities.

Commonly, those among whom products must be rationed are
called "consumers"; hence the frequent observation that the end
and aim of all production is consumption. Such a position could
be correct only if all items currently produced were final in the
sense of providing an enjoyment or satisfaction. Actually the history of Western societies during the modern era is dominated by
the growth of resources through production and discovery. In any
given period, people and organizations as investors have, through
their demands for products, something to say about the character
of output. Furthermore, governments take products from the productive organization, and these activities cannot be called consumption without stretching that concept beyond recognition.
We shall use the neutral term "takers" to characterize those who
obtain the output emerging from the system of resource organization.[1]

A money-price system of rationing output carries with it an
income-incentive device for the organization and management of
resources. An income-incentive system means that persons and
organizations having the power to manage resources do so to obtain
money gain. Private ownership of resources requires some system
whereby the owners have an incentive to manage them. If all resources, including even human labor power, were owned by the
government, income incentives would have little relevance although a money-price system of rationing output might nevertheless be employed.[2] A money-price system of rationing output is
part and parcel of an income-incentive system for the management
of resources. With money and prices operating as rationing devices

---

[1] The term was suggested by Ragnar Frisch in his article, "The Interrelation between Capital Production and Consumer-Taking," *Journal of Political Economy*,
XXXIX (October, 1931): 646–654.

[2] A 100 per cent socialized economic system employing money to ration products
allowed private groups would require some device for paying out cash to persons to
prevent a complete drain of cash from the population. Under such a system of socialism, if it were dominated by equalitarian objectives, the payments would be in equal
amounts per head with perhaps special treatment for children. Income obtainable by
management of resources would be relevant only for the government itself.

for output, money gain may be achieved by those who control resources by producing the things which people are willing to buy.

A money-price system therefore exhibits an irreducible dualism. On the one hand people desire output and compete with their dollars for what they want. On the other hand people and organizations own resources and compete among themselves for the dollars of buyers by offering current production for sale. In any actual system, competition among people as takers of output and among people as owners of resources is highly complex. The nature of these interrelations can be made more understandable and definite by close attention to a pure money-price system. Such a system also permits a definite calculation of the costs of government.

Pure economic systems are imaginary; actual systems are always mixtures of various types of activities. Yet the salient characteristics of actual systems can be more readily understood by comparison with this logical extreme. A pure money-price system means a system of organization in which every valuable item is continuously priced in terms of money. All products are priced as they appear on the scene, all services are priced as they are performed, and all resources are priced in each moment of their life span. Products are priced in such a way that takers can acquire all they desire at that price. This condition means that all alternative devices of rationing other than money and prices are excluded. Exclusive rationing by price is a minimum condition for perfectly competitive pricing (or purely competitive pricing—the terms are here treated as synonymous). A single price rules for all groups of buyers and sellers of any particular item at any given time and place, and that price is a clearing price for any particular quantity of the item available.

The meaning of these conditions can be made more clear by contrast with ordinary markets. Actual market results only approximate at most a competitive price in our sense. A perfectly competitive market may require testing the potential decisions of each buyer to discover how much he would buy if the price were any given amount. Actually, a person is not apt to know what he will do until he is confronted with an irrevocable decision; otherwise he may vacillate or mentally experiment. At any actual price, he makes such a decision, but only at actual prices, and then it is too late for an observer to know definitely what he would have done at some other price. The usual assumption that competitive conditions require each buyer and seller to accept the going price as given is not a sufficient condition for perfectly competitive pricing. The going price must be initially set at the point where, for the period in question, it remains, and all participants can succeed in buying or selling all they want to buy or sell at the one price so established. The closest real approximation to a perfectly competitive price as here conceived would be a market where some outside agency sets the price based on as complete information as it is possible to obtain, and yet is completely flexible in its price-making role in the sense of altering the price for every change either in the quantity produced or in the demand for the product. Multiplicity of buyers and sellers is not required for competitive pricing as here defined.

Such a price system of rationing is pure also in the sense that all considerations other than price are irrelevant in the selection of how much each taker obtains. Any discriminating monopoly or monopsony power in pricing is excluded. We also exclude cases where the prices established differ for various sellers or buyers. Likewise, multiple prices which occur because buyers have special attachments to some sellers are excluded. A perfectly operating money-price system is compromised to the extent that such factors are relevant; other rationing systems are operating in conjunction with price. A pure money-price system of rationing is an impersonal system. One dollar counts the same as another, regardless of who owns the dollar, whether he is rich or poor, influential or insignificant, an organization or a government.

In a pure money-price system of economic organization, the prices of resource services must also be at the competitive level. Competitive price means in this case also a uniform price which clears the market. Any owner of resources, whether of labor power or of nonhuman resources, can always sell the amount of services he desires to sell at the competitive price. Involuntary unemployment is ruled out by this condition. Unemployment exists in actual systems because of imperfections in the pricing mechanism—imperfections which may be aggravated in actual conditions by declines in the demand for products over time.[3] Clearing prices are

---

[3] Much attention has been given to the monetary and fiscal conditions of full employment. The view is often adopted that a unique (high) level of aggregate demand for products is a necessary condition for full employment. The monetary conditions necessary to obtain this level are then regarded as crucial. This approach is meaningful and relevant in a social setting where all prices do not adjust immediately and fully to changes in demands. There is no "right" level of aggregate spending in a social setting where prices, including of course wages, are established under perfectly competitive conditions. In this event, absolute or money prices adjust immediately

a sufficient condition for full employment in the sense that resource owners can sell all the services they wish to sell. Employment in this context refers to the use of nonhuman as well as human resources.

As concerns production, a pure money-price system implies that the output of any commodity is also continuously priced so that the market is cleared. As Davenport suggests, the "supply" of any product may be thought of as a physical quantity instead of in terms of "supply prices."[4] If the organizations responsible for the production of any commodity choose to retain some part of it, they are treated as demanding their own product. When there is a choice of selling or retaining an item, intelligent choice requires information concerning what the item is worth in money terms. Under ordinary conditions, the worth of an item can be only estimated, and some vagueness surrounds the choice actually made. An organization which chooses to retain its own products is acting as a taker, and presumably the choice takes account of the alternative of selling the items for money.

According to this approach, production may be viewed as the combination of resources giving rise to a particular, identifiable product. The concept of firm as ordinarily used to mean an organization under one management is too big a unit for analytical purposes. Only rarely does one business organization produce one product; multiple products are the rule, single products the exception. This is true even if product is used to mean only those items which are sold to outsiders. If product is defined in the more general sense of any emerging valuable result, it is doubtful that any actual business organization produces only one product. In place of the concept of firm as the elementary producing unit, we may substitute "production center." A production center means the combination of resources producing one product under one management. Thus a fender-stamping machine, its operator, floor space, supervision, electric power, and flat sheets of steel illustrate a production center—the product being stamped fenders. Any business organization is an organization of production centers, each with a product. In practice, a large part of such products become resources

and fully to all variations in demand and supply circumstances, and one level of spending is "just as good" as another. The aggregate of money expenditures is a completely arbitrary magnitude and so are money prices; their significance arises from their interrelations. For a contrary view, see A. P. Lerner, "The Essential Properties of Interest and Money," *Quarterly Journal of Economics,* LXVI (May, 1952): 191–193.

[4] Cf. H. J. Davenport, *The Economics of Enterprise* (New York: Macmillan, 1923), pp. 48–52.

of other production centers. In each center, production (the application of resources) and the products (the emerging valuable results) are simultaneous in time in the sense that production and results are aspects of a composite service.[5]

Production must compromise the idea of completely general and continuous pricing. In each center, there must be some resources, the services of which are not explicitly priced. This follows because the money value of the product would not necessarily be equal to the sum of the prices times quantities of resource services used to produce that product, if all the latter prices were explicit. At a clearing price for the output of any center, the value product of the center is given by the amount produced. This value product equals the aggregate value of the services of resources giving rise to that output. This equality holds because the returns of some resources are residual. An escape from the necessity for implicit "pricing" of some resources can be made by the assumption of perfect foresight. Only in this event would the possibility of some "profit" or "loss" be eliminated, when "profit" or "loss" means the difference between the money value of resource services and the money value of the product. Assumptions of perfect foresight are both dangerous and unnecessary; human beings are not supernatural in their powers. Lack of accurate knowledge of future events is an inescapable feature of human affairs.

The characteristics of the particular resources not explicitly priced within any production center depend upon institutional organization. On one occasion, the nonpriced service may be human labor power; on another it may be all resource services except human labor power. In practice, business units own and control substantial portions of the nonhuman resources employed. Profits as here defined mean the residual returns in any production center or in any combination of production centers belonging to one organization.

The inclusion of government in a pure money-price system has certain difficulties. Some activities carried on by government cannot be rationed by a price mechanism without defeating a government objective. Nevertheless, following the suggested distinctions in chapter 2, we may think of government as having objectives

---

[5] This conception of simultaneity between production and output should not be confused with the curious idea of timeless production. (Cf. Wassily Leontief, "Interest on Capital and Distribution: A Problem in the Theory of Marginal Productivity," *Quarterly Journal of Economics*, XLIX [November, 1934]: 150.) Production is valuable activity and activity implies duration.

which involve the use of resources or the taking of products for its own ends or for the ends of private individuals where these products cannot be rationed by price devices. We only exclude at this point any underpricing of government services provided they could technically be rationed by price alone.

DEFINITION OF COSTS OF GOVERNMENT

The money cost of government may be tentatively defined as the value of the services and products taken by government. "Value" in this context means the prices paid by government multiplied by the quantities taken. The computation of the money prices of products taken by government in this sense does not depend on whether the government or private groups own the resources. If all services and products are explicitly priced at competitive levels, the prices of products do not depend upon the identity of the owners of the resources producing them.

The money costs of government as defined may be compared to the private sacrifice or "social cost" involved in the fulfillment of government objectives. By social costs of government, we mean the value of the things foregone by private groups because of the procurement of products and resource services by government. Generally no divergence between money and social costs exists provided that the prices of the resources used by government and the products taken by government are independent of government demands. In this event the money costs of the things acquired by government measured by market prices would also measure the foregone gain of private groups viewed as takers of products.

But even under the special circumstances assumed by a pure money-price system, there can be a divergence between money costs and social costs of government objectives. Some resources used to produce items for government account may be completely specialized to government ends. Where specialized facilities have been constructed, for example, to produce munitions, the cost of using these facilities in the sense of the foregone gain to private groups may be zero. Thus if the services of such facilities were continuously priced, their prices would be zero in times when the demand by the government for munitions is zero and would be some high price in times of war. In such cases the social cost is zero, or if some maintenance is necessary to keep the facilities in existence, it is identical with the maintenance outlay. Such facilities are ordinarily owned by government, or if privately owned some system of compensation is arranged to provide for maintenance during peacetime. However, social cost is equal to the maintenance cost even in times of war, since by definition the resources in question have no private use and therefore entail no private sacrifice.

Divergences between money costs and social costs may also occur if resources used for government account carry with them positive or negative by-products because of their employment for government objectives. For example, in the absence of a pure money-price system some business groups may regard a government as a less attractive customer than some private buyer. The condition of the government's obtaining the products of such sellers becomes, in the absence of the use of force, the payment of a price higher than the prices paid by others. Likewise if government employment is considered by people to carry with it by-products of an unattractive sort, employees will require a higher payment as a condition of government employment. This divergence may also work in the opposite direction. If owners of resources regard government as a more attractive customer for the sale of services, the government may pay less than the value of these services in private employment.

Divergences between the money and social costs of government may also arise in cases where the government hires resources directly, but the value of resource services as measured in terms of their market prices differs from the value of resources as measured by the market price of their output in private employment. This divergence would not occur in a pure money-price system. These circumstances may be illustrated by the example of general monopoly pricing of products in the private sector of the economy. Following a line of reasoning developed by J. S. Bain and A. P. Lerner,[6] one can show that hired resources will obtain lower money incomes, given the level of national income, because of the presence of monopoly in the pricing of products. Monopoly power implies an ability on the part of some strategically placed groups to restrict output and raise prices as compared with the absence of such power. This incentive to restrict output generally is translated into a reduction in the demand by such employing groups for all hired resources. This lowered demand requires a lower set of prices for hired resource services relative to the prices of prod-

[6] Cf. J. S. Bain, *Pricing, Distribution, and Employment* (New York: Henry Holt, 1948), pp. 168–172, and A. P. Lerner, *Economics of Control* (New York: Macmillan, 1944), p. 101.

ucts. Therefore in such a situation anyone who hires resources outright obtains them at a relatively lower set of prices than he could if no monopoly power existed in any part of the economy. To the extent that government hires resources outright, the money costs in the sense of the payments made for these services will be less than the value of the output these resources could produce if left in private employment. The government overcomes or offsets some of the monopoly power of private groups by direct employment of resources. It would be accidental if it should overcome this monopoly power altogether. Therefore the foregone gain of private groups, in the sense of the value of private output not obtained because of government's direct use of resources, may be greater than the money payments made by government. If there are some by-product disadvantages of government employment, the monopoly element in private enterprise may result in the underpricing of resource services by an amount which just offsets the overpricing occasioned by the assumed disadvantages of government employment. If people, however, regard government as a "better" employer, these two factors may combine to understate the social costs of government functions even more.

Divergence between money costs and social costs may occur because of taxation. If government forgives a tax in connection with a government purchase, there is on that account an understatement of the social costs of government. An illustration may be helpful to clarify this point. Suppose that income taxes are levied on corporations at a rate of 60 per cent of their net income. Government procurement agencies are, we also suppose, instructed to adopt the rule that sellers to the government are to have their income-tax liability canceled on all sales for government account. If, then, Corporation X sells $100,000,000 worth of goods to government at market prices at a profit of $10,000,000 on those sales, a rule that permits the forgiveness of a tax liability ($6,000,000 in this case) means that the government need pay only $94,000,000 for the goods in question. The theoretically correct method of computing the cost of these goods to the government calls for adding back the forgiven tax liability. Private individuals would pay $100,000,000 for the same goods in the assumed case, and therefore they do not obtain goods of this value because of the government's procurement action. Such cases depart from the general rule of a pure money-price system because both a money and a tax device are being used to ration products among takers. The government, in this illustration, uses its power to discriminate among taxpayers as a procurement device.

The position that the costs to the public of the government acquisition of goods and services should include any forgiven taxes may be questioned. It might even be claimed that the foregone-value sacrifice imposed on private groups should be measured by the total government payments computed at market prices minus the tax liability on private suppliers because of government sales. Consistent application of this rule would require in principle the subtraction from government expenditures in any period of the tax liability traceable to those expenditures. The question is whether the social costs of government should be measured by what might be called the "net cost," defined as the government expenditure minus any tax liability occasioned by that expenditure, or whether the social costs should be measured by what private groups have to pay for the same items.

The latter conception appears to be the valid one. The net conception gives absurd results. Suppose, for example, the government owns some oil-producing property, acquired in years past, and uses the oil to operate naval vessels. How should the "cost" of this oil be computed? To make the illustration even more simple, we assume that the money cost of obtaining the oil is zero—it simply flows out of the ground at an unchanging rate. If one adopts the "net cost" conception, it would appear that the social cost of burning this oil in naval vessels is zero. Even if the government should charge itself the going market price for oil of the same specifications, it should, according to this theory, at the same time deduct the income which it obtains as an owner of oil-producing facilities. Such accounting also gives a zero cost. Such a conception of social costs distorts the facts. Oil is actually taken by government. This oil could be made available to private groups. They obtain less oil than they would if it were made available to them at going prices. Just as in any case where a person takes the product of his own resources, provided the commodity is valuable to others, the use entails a cost, namely, the money sum he could realize by selling it to others. A process of canceling the income against the value product, if carried out consistently throughout the economy, merely results in a zero-value product.

No difference in principle arises if, instead of the oil property being owned outright by government, it is owned privately, and the private groups are obligated to pay taxes on the income obtained. If the tax is 60 per cent of the income obtained, the government has the equivalent of a property interest in the real wealth. Deduction of the tax liability from the payment understates the costs of the government's acquisition of the product in question.[7]

The practice of forgiving an income tax in government procurement is not a common one. But it is common for the government to use other tax devices to reduce its money costs. Many government units forgive a sales tax levied on private sellers on any products purchased. The presumed rationale of this procedure is that the tax is "really" levied on the buyer anyhow and therefore the government, by forgiving the tax in cases of sales to itself, is simply avoiding putting money in one pocket only to take it out of the other. This practice is a variety of price discrimination in favor of government; the money payments by government in such cases understate the social costs. If cigarettes are sold to private buyers at $1.70 a carton and the federal excise tax is $.80 a carton, the purchase of cigarettes by the government at $.90 a carton understates the social cost to government of its acquisition of cigarettes. The market value of cigarettes provides the objective evidence as to what they are worth to private groups.

The practice of tax-induced price discrimination in favor of government makes its operations seem less costly than they really are. Theoretically a widely used tax-forgiveness program would make the cost of government, in terms of actual money payments made, a mere fraction of present government expenditures. If all income taxes were forgiven on incomes obtained by government employees, if all corporate income and excess profits taxes were forgiven on corporate sales to government, if income taxes of employees of private enterprises working for government account were forgiven, and if a substantially larger portion of the government tax structure consisted of sales taxes of various kinds which could be forgiven, the money costs of government as measured by outlays would grossly understate the social costs.[8] The practice of

---

[7] The illustration is factual in the sense that the United States government does own oil property and does not charge itself the market value of the oil. The illustration is not factual with respect to the assumed large tax liability on private owners of oil property.

[8] Economists have sometimes employed questionable arguments in this connection, especially during the Great Depression, to persuade the public that fuller use should be made of the government's financial power to put resources to work. To allay fears of financial "unsoundness," the argument was advanced that additional government expenditures would be virtually costless to the government because they would gen-

giving tax concessions to government suppliers, even aside from the handicaps such procedures create for a systematic and equitable tax system, does not commend itself.[9]

Underemployment of resources offers another possible source of divergence between the money and social costs of government. This observation is of course an old one. In a pure money-price system, underemployment is ruled out. In fact "full" employment is rigorously definable only in terms of such a system. Underemployment of resources means that people have services for sale which they cannot sell at prevailing prices. This statement has definite meaning in a system of pricing where resource owners can sell all they wish to sell, that is, in a competitive pricing structure. Where underemployment exists because of some defect in the money-price system, government, by employing these resources, apparently does not force any sacrifice on private groups. Thus in a deep depression, the expansion of government demands for resources appears to be socially costless to private groups. But this point of view is valid only on the hypothesis that no feasible method can be devised to reduce unemployment except by increased expansion of government demands. If, for example, the government, by increasing transfer payments to private groups or by reducing tax liabilities or both, can succeed in increasing private demands for products, cost considerations would again become relevant in government procurement programs. There is little reason to suppose that private expenditures are less efficient than government expenditures in overcoming underemployment of re-

erate sufficient increases in income to provide the tax revenues to offset them. The cause was a good one but the argument less so. Even in the highly unlikely case that a dollar of government expenditure would increase tax revenues by two dollars, no case exists for the additional government expenditure on this account. If in fact the alternative to government employment is unemployment, the social cost is zero regardless of what additional tax revenues occur; under full employment conditions, the social cost of expenditures by government is independent of any additional tax revenues arising from these expenditures. Tax revenue does not offset the costs of government. Likewise no consideration should be given to possible losses in tax revenue arising from a government economy campaign. If government can become more efficient, the release of resources is a gain to private groups even though tax revenues may be lost on this account.

[9] In a democratic society, people should be aware of what their government is costing them. Such information is indispensable for intelligent judgments about the desirability of expanding or contracting particular government functions. People need to know the presumed benefits that will accrue to the community from the government expenditure and what it will cost them to obtain these benefits. Public accounting should, ideally, provide this cost information in an unambiguous manner. A correction of government accounting for the understatement occasioned by tax-forgiveness practices would be an important reform in this connection.

sources. Thus a decision to use resources for government account does then entail a social cost. The comparison of relevance is not between the situation existing before an expansion of government expenditures and the situation after the expansion; the proper comparison is between what is and what might be. The government's decision to take more output this month may lead to more employment this month, but if financial policies could have been devised to allow private groups to take more output this month, private ends are being sacrificed for government objectives this month. This view implies that government projects involving the use of resources should be made to pass economic tests even during threatened depressions provided that corrective fiscal and monetary measures are available to be used to increase employment.

COSTS AS CONTEMPORANEOUS

The previous analysis presupposes that cost in either the money outlay or the social sense involves a comparison between two contemporaneous situations, one actual and one hypothetical. The doctrine that social costs are contemporaneous arises directly from the observation that resources existing at any moment can be used in various ways. To the extent that they are used for one purpose, they cannot be used for others. It is now commonly, but not universally, held that costs of public objectives are inherently non-postponable. Pigou takes the position that the costs of war activities are *in part* postponable.[10] In principle, Pigou holds that resources which are destroyed, undermaintained, or simply not produced at at all because of the large government expenditures during wartime entail a loss to future generations. Foregone consumption, when not disguised as human disinvestment in the sense of reducing the length of people's working lives, is treated as contemporaneous economic sacrifice for war procurement programs. His position is consistent with a theory of capital as congealed waiting. The concept of waiting suggests present uses of resources yielding products of significance only in the future. Therefore, the groups who would engage in waiting anyhow have no additional sacrifice imposed on them because their waiting offsets government expendi-

---

[10] The summary passage of Pigou's discussion of this topic is the following: "... we may reasonably assert that, whereas resources obtained by using up existing capital or by refraining from the creation of new capital wholly hit the future, resources obtained by augmenting production or by diverting resources from the service of personal consumption, at all events in large part, hit the present." A. C. Pigou, *The Political Economy of War* (New York: Macmillan, 1941), pp. 45–46.

tures. The issue is whether a reduction of investment resulting from expansion of government military activities involves a present sacrifice on private groups.

The position here adopted is that all costs of government involve contemporaneous sacrifice. There can be no postponement of the costs of achieving government ends, including war ends, if private investment is looked upon as a demand for things which people and organizations desire here and now. Investment decisions necessarily take the form of demands for concrete things just as do consumption decisions. The term "future goods," meaning capital items, is a form of poetic license. Investment actions result in present (actual) goods. Thus a policy of government use of resources which involves the sacrifice of private investment items is a sacrifice of real things—machines, buildings, and the like—in the present. In this sense there can be no postponability. *This sense is the economic sense.* Why people and corporations desire particular real assets may be investigated, and the rationale may or may not be the same as the rationale found for people's desire for consumption items.[11] But it can hardly be maintained that desires for real assets do not exist. Perhaps people are injured less in some sense in the present by policies that require their giving up real assets instead of consumption items. Investment items may be social luxuries. A corporation that is prevented from expanding its productive capacity during wartime has its desires frustrated. An ethical defense could be made for giving less weight to desires of organizations than to those of persons.

On economic grounds, government policies which frustrate persons' desires for new real assets involve a social cost in the present. Undoubtedly postponement of private investment may have adverse repercussions on future generations. But failure to use resources for current government objectives may have adverse repercussions on future generations as well. Cost is inherently contemporaneous, and postponement is impossible.

[11] The theory of investment seems to be moving toward the treatment of the desire for real assets in the same fashion as the desire for final services. Uncertainty in people's projections of what an asset may yield to them in the future makes propositions in terms of equalization of rates of return on investment inapplicable unless uncertainty can, somehow or other, be reduced to certainty equivalents—a highly questionable procedure. Unless then uncertainty can be rationalized in some defensible manner, one must accept the bare facts that corporations and individuals have various "tastes" for assets. See G. L. S. Shackle, *Expectation in Economics* (Cambridge: University Press, 1949), and C. F. Carter, "Expectation in Economics," *Economic Journal*, LX (March, 1950): 92–105.

The principles used to assess the social costs of promoting government ends are no different from those applicable to the ends of any group considered as opposed to another group when both depend upon the same body of resources to satisfy their desires. If there are two groups, A and B, the costs of satisfying the demands of Group A from the point of view of Group B are measured by the contemporaneous value of the products that Group B is forced to give up on that account. If Group A has tastes which are a more or less perfect sample of both groups, Group B gives up products of the same type which it is already obtaining. Thus if Group A's spending power were transferred to Group B, Group B would buy the same things as would have been bought by Group A; therefore the money costs of those things is a proper measure of the social costs of Group A's desires to Group B. At the other extreme, if resources used to produce goods for Group A cannot be used to produce goods wanted by Group B and if the products of these resources are likewise not desired by Group B, the contemporaneous social cost of the presence of Group A to Group B is zero.[12] Since in practice resources are more or less adaptable, the social costs are certain not to be zero. If government is substituted for Group A, the same observations hold.

GOVERNMENT COSTS AND TRANSFERS

Government financial activities are reducible to buying and selling, and to positive and negative transferring of income with private groups. In the previous discussion we have noted some of the complexities of the buying activities of government. In general as a buyer of services and of products, government competes with its own citizens for output. If this competition is "perfect" and if no resources are specialized to government ends, a dollar of government expenditure measures the foregone gain of private groups. A special problem in this connection arises only when government procurement policy is tied in with its monopoly of force.[13] Conscription of resources by government, with or without compensa-

---

[12] Costs in this sense are unlike those involved in international trade because any national group must be viewed as possessing resources not available to other groups except by trade.

[13] Local governments are scarcely in a position to use the threat of force to obtain current output. But except in real peace times, the threat of force is important in United States government procurement. In wartime, steel companies could scarcely insist on serving their old customers first, and the United States government last, and hope to get away with it. The use of the threat of force in procurement policies has not been explored to the extent that its importance would seem to warrant.

tion, involves a social cost. The money payments would only accidentally reflect this cost. We should need to know what the resources would produce for private account to make such a judgment. Government procurement tied to its tax powers likewise may give a distorted picture of the social costs of government ends. Divergences may occur for many reasons when the system is not operated altogether along pure money-price lines.

One of the main peculiarities of government in its economic aspects concerns its role as a transferrer and a transferee of money. The government makes large transfer payments to private groups. Some of these are contractual, such as interest payments, which are similar to those made among individuals and between organizations and individuals. Others are gratuitous transfer payments. Although there are private organizations which make gratuitous payments also, governments do so on a vaster scale. Government also forces people to make transfer payments to it in the form of taxes. This power rests upon its monopoly of force. The compulsory transfer of income from one person to another is extortion unless ordered by government. The closest private, legal parallel to a tax is an alimony payment. Even such a payment may be construed as the fulfillment of a past contract, although perhaps not always very convincingly.

Taxes do not in principle or in practice measure either the money or the social costs of government. Although in any particular period tax revenue may equal government expenditures, we must look to government expenditures for evidence concerning costs in the sense of what private groups are forced to give up as takers because the government acquires the use of resources. This proposition raises some doubts concerning the conception of taxes as constituting an independent burden on private groups. Taxes, being financial devices, involve payments by private groups to their government. Whether these payments entail a cost to the people who make them is a question to be explored; an affirmative answer may not be assumed. If a government could operate without imposing taxes (a situation that may be plausible for a socialized system where the profits from government enterprise yield adequate revenues), the people of such a community would bear a cost of government functions in the sense of not obtaining goods and services for their private use because of the appropriation of goods and services for government ends. In a system dominated by private management of resources, the burden of government is present also irrespective of whether the financing of government involves taxation, money creation, or sale of debt. The common-sense conception that a person's tax liability in some way indicates the share of government costs borne by him is by no means self-evident.

How then should the financial-burden aspects of taxation be interpreted? The theory here adopted, and to be explored in more detail in chapter 4, views a tax as a transfer payment from private groups to government. The function of taxes in this respect is twofold: (1) they reduce money incomes of private groups for any given level of national income, and (2) they rearrange the pattern of income distribution among families and individuals, except in the special case of a tax system that is distributionally neutral. The first function carries with it the implication that taxes are defla-tionary devices with respect to private demands for products and old assets. This is the monetary function of taxation. The explana-tion of the effects of taxation in this connection is applied mone-tary theory. The second function of taxation, the rearrangement of the pattern of money-income distribution, is relevant to the equity question: what kind of pattern of income distribution do people, speaking through their government, want? But there are economic constraints upon income redistribution because of the inherent limitations of tax and subsidy devices to effectuate some desired pattern. These limitations necessarily exist in any society in which people have rights and responsibilities to manage them-selves and their wealth.

4

Government and Social Accounting

The purpose of the present chapter is to examine the principles inherent in the logic of social accounting with special attention to government activities. We wish to learn whether this logic provides insights into the effects of government expenditures, transfer payments, and taxes. Social or national accounting requires that definite judgments be made concerning the specific classification of government financial activities. These judgments involve theories, and a close examination of these theories should be revealing for analytical purposes.

A few general observations about this topic may be pertinent. Although social accounting is an ancient topic in economic thinking, its present important position in economics is traceable to developments during the past two decades. In this period a vast literature has appeared concerning national-income conceptions, empricial estimates of national income as variously defined, and theories of changes in certain income and product aggregates. We are presently concerned only with the conceptual aspects of this topic—the questions concerning the meaning and content of the social accounts—rather than the explanations of the specific magnitudes that may be found at any particular period. In reviewing the literature, we find an increasing definiteness in the development of thought in this field. National-income estimators must make decisions concerning the treatment of any specific item. Shall interest on the government debt be looked upon as a transfer payment, or shall it be regarded as a payment for a service? How such questions are answered makes a difference in the resulting aggregates. Before the development of official estimating of national income, such questions were of theoretical interest only.

The critical issues concerning the treatment of government financial activities in the social accounts are centered mainly around government outlays for goods and services, changes in the government debt, interest payments on such debt, subsidies and other gratuitous payments by governments, and, of course, taxes. Many of these issues may be discussed in connection with the concept of transfer payments, and consequently our main attention will be given to this topic. On the product side, issues arise concerning the classification of government expenditures and the computation of the costs of government. The latter will be an application of the distinctions already set forth in chapters 2 and 3. We ignore conceptual problems connected with the international features of an economic system. Some attention will be given to these problems, however, in connection with the discussion of import duties. We also ignore problems of the proper treatment of financial institutions.

SOME DEFINITIONS

Aggregates associated with the term "national income" reflect a product side and an income side. The product side relates to the value of what is currently produced in a society. The income side concerns the gain of persons and organizations in a society. Following accepted procedures, I shall treat the product side as necessarily equal to the income side; any gains of a person or organization which are not traceable to the production of goods or services are ignored. Changes in the value of securities and the gains or losses of the holders of securities are therefore omitted. This neglect is arbitrary in the sense that it distorts, more or less, the accurate measurement of the gains of individuals and organizations. The distortion is perhaps justified by the convenience of an income concept which is necessarily equal to the product side of the accounts.

Persons and organizations may be looked upon as takers of products. From this point of view the product side of the accounts may be classified into consumption, private investment, and government-purchased goods and services. We may also look upon persons and organizations as producing units. The resources under the control of any identifiable person or organization may be thought of as generating output and as providing gain to their owner. Ownership is, however, a complicated notion. In some sense a corporation owns the physical plant and equipment carried on its balance sheet as assets. Yet in some sense stockholders and bondholders of such corporations own something also. Complicated organization gives rise to what has often been described as separation of ownership and control. Out of this fact a number of problems in connection with transfer payments emerge.

Government roles may be divided into enterprise functions and "taker" functions. All enterprise functions of government are theoretically to be valued in terms of market prices if price rationing is employed, and in terms of what the clearing price would otherwise be if rationing devices other than price are employed. Thus if the government limits by decree the amount of services that may be taken by anyone, the value of the government's output is to be computed in terms of what the price would need to be to eliminate all nonprice rationing. Such a price is theoretically measurable only if the demand for the service in question can be known in the neighborhood of the clearing price.

The money payments of government for services of resources and for output produced under private management may be considered as the value product acquired for government ends. However, in those cases where the government reduces its money payment by making a special tax concession to the seller, the value of this privilege should be added back to compute government costs. The reasons for this procedure have already been discussed. Where the government owns resources, the value of their services should ideally be included in the computation of the value product taken by government—the cost of government should not be affected by the ownership of the resources it uses. In a pure money-price system the estimation of the value of these services would present no great difficulties. In such a setting, the price of every service would be objectively known. In practice the value of such services must be estimated, and in many cases there is little objective evidence to provide nonarbitrary figures. This difficulty is not peculiar to government, of course. The rental values of owner-occupied dwellings can at best be only roughly estimated. Such estimates are not, however, theoretical problems in national-income measurement.

The main difficulties in consideration of government are found on the income side of social accounts. Shall we think of government as being an income recipient at all? Much national income literature provides a negative answer. For reasons to be discussed later we shall treat government as an income recipient. The general formula for defining the income of any group, including government, is the earnings of the resources under the control of that group plus all transfer payments made to it minus all transfer payments made by it. Earnings, in this context, means the money gains, excluding capital gains and losses, arising from the use of real resources including human labor power. Control means effective decision-making as to how resources are to be employed. Thus a person is viewed as controlling his own labor power; a corporation controls the real assets reported on its balance sheet. The critical feature of the above formulation concerns a definition of transfer payments.

CONCEPT OF TRANSFERS

Transfer payments may be preliminarily classified as contractual, voluntary, and compulsory. As applied to government, we include under contractual transfers all interest payments on government debt and all pensions receivable as a matter of enforceable right. Under voluntary transfers we include all government payments in the form of relief, unemployment insurance, and social security payments, and all subsidies. Under compulsory transfers we include all taxes and fines. All these suggested classifications are controversial in national-income literature and therefore need to be investigated in some detail.

Transfer income may be formally defined as any income either in money or in value in kind accruing to persons or groups which is not in payment for any current service, product, or asset provided by them. This definition is similar to that ordinarily used in national-income literature. The crucial negative feature of the definition—that transfer income is not in return for services or products—appears to be generally held, whether the definition is stated as "no contribution to social product,"[1] "no specific quid for the specific quo rendered,"[2] or a failure to "enhance the production of economic values."[3] Similar definitions of transfer income are given by Kuznets, Copeland, Lindeman, Clark, Stone, Hicks, Bowley, and Keynes.[4] General agreement about the formal definition of the concept of transfer income has not resulted in agreement about the specific types of income to be classified as transfers. Further-

[1] Gerhard Colm, "Public Revenue and Public Expenditure in National Income," *Studies in Income and Wealth,* Vol. I (New York: National Bureau of Economic Research, 1937), p. 200. In the following citations the title of these volumes will be abbreviated to *S.I.W.*

[2] G. C. Means, "Problems in Estimating National Income Arising from Production by Government," *S.I.W.,* Vol. II, pp. 269–270.

[3] R. W. Nelson and Donald Jackson, "Allocation of Benefits from Government Expenditure," *S.I.W.,* Vol. II, p. 319.

[4] Simon Kuznets, *National Income and Its Composition, 1919–1938,* Vol. I (New York: National Bureau of Economic Research, 1941), p. 11; M. A. Copeland, "Concepts of National Income," *S.I.W.,* Vol. I, pp. 27 ff.; John Lindeman, "Income Measurement as Affected by Government Operations," *S.I.W.,* Vol. VI, pp. 14–15; Colin Clark, *National Income and Outlay* (London: Macmillan, 1937), pp. 9–10; Richard Stone,

more, even when a particular kind of income is treated as a transfer, often very different reasons are given in justification for this treatment. Official United States estimates treat interest on government debt as a transfer, but interest on personal and business debts as a nontransfer income.[5] It is not obvious that the differences between government debt and private debt are such that they justify such a radically different treatment of interest payments. At one time Gilbert, for example, held that government bondholders provided the service of letting the government use their money.[6] Stone regards interest as a payment for lending service.[7] Yet it is the official British position that interest on a national debt is transfer income mainly because, with unimportant exceptions, such debts have come into existence in connection with the financing of wars. Unlike the usual definition of transfer income that relies on the negative test that the payment is not in return for some valuable item, this historical criterion relates to the productivity of the assets acquired through debt financing.

Gratuitous payments by government are commonly treated in two ways. Subsidies that are regarded as reducing the costs of production are deducted from both the product and income sides of the national accounts, whereas other subsidies are treated as transfer payments. This classification of gratuitous government payments into "direct" and "indirect" parallels the treatment of taxes. Canadian and United States experts have adopted the long-established British practice of viewing direct taxes in a manner consistent with their being transfer income and of viewing indirect taxes as deductions from both sides of the accounts. This nonparallel treatment of gratuitous payments and taxes obscures the

---

"Two Studies on Income and Expenditure in the United States," *Economic Journal*, LIII (April, 1943): 65–66; J. R. Hicks, "The Valuation of the Social Income," *Economica*, VII (May, 1940): 115; A. L. Bowley, "The Definition of National Income," *Economic Journal*, XXXII (March, 1922): 10; J. M. Keynes, "The Concept of National Income: A Supplementary Note," *Economic Journal*, L (March, 1940): 61.

[5] U.S. Department of Commerce (Bureau of Foreign and Domestic Commerce), "National Income," *Supplement to Survey of Current Business* (July, 1947), p. 11. A discussion of the reasons for the present procedure is presented in a paper by E. F. Denison, "A Report of Tripartite Discussions of National Income Measurement," *S.I.W.*, Vol. X, pp. 9–10. A defense of an earlier United States Department of Commerce treatment of interest on a national debt as nontransfer income is provided by Milton Gilbert, "U.S. National Income Statistics," *Economic Journal*, LIII (April, 1943): 81–82.

[6] Gilbert, *ibid.*, p. 81.

[7] Richard Stone, "Functions and Criteria of a System of Social Accounting," *Income and Wealth*, Ser. 1, International Association for Research in Income and Wealth (Cambridge, England: Bowes and Bowes, 1951), pp. 22, 61.

issue as to whether they should be viewed in general as transfer income. Other types of payments by government, such as repayment of its debt, are also sometimes regarded as transfers. This view has the support of Shoup and Kuznets.[8]

It is here proposed to treat all interest payments whether by government or by private groups as transfer payments. "Interest" in this context means that part of a series of payments called for in a debt contract, net of repayment of principal. It is important that the term interest as used here not be confused with the concept of the earnings of real resources other than human beings. Such earnings would of course exist in a society with no transfer payments at all. In discussing types of income, we shall refer to this category as the earnings of nonhuman resources. *Interest in our sense relates solely to payments in connection with debt contracts.*

The basis for the claim that all interest income is a transfer arises from the very nature of debt. If an inventory of all assets were taken for an economy as a whole for the purpose of obtaining a nonduplicating total, all claims such as bonds and short-term debt would cancel out. Debts are assets to some because they are liabilities to others. If all debts were wiped out, the community's net assets would remain unchanged because liabilities would be wiped out along with evidence of indebtedness. A consolidated balance sheet for the community as a whole, leaving international considerations aside, would show as assets only those which are sources of earning power, that is physical real resources, including human beings as well as nonhuman types of wealth. This point of view is, of course, very old and has been defended ably and in detail by Fisher.[9]

For example, if A possesses a farm worth $50,000 and B holds a mortgage of $10,000 against the property, A and B together own the entire underlying real resources—the land, equipment, and buildings—which together are worth $50,000, not $60,000. The mortgage, being an asset to B and a liability to A, cancels out if we look at the value of the claims of A and B taken together. They can own no more, since by assumption the real wealth to which they

---

[8] Carl S. Shoup, *Principles of National Income Analysis* (Boston: Houghton Mifflin, 1947), p. 274. Kuznets states: "They [domestic transfers] may be in the nature of payment on government debt—either interest or principal." ("Government Product and National Income," *Income and Wealth,* Ser. 1, p. 235.)

[9] Irving Fisher, *The Nature of Capital and Income* (New York: Macmillan, 1906), pp. 66–98. O. C. Stine in commenting on E. F. Denison's paper (*S.I.W.,* Vol. X, p. 64) also suggests, without offering explicit reasons, that all interest be treated as a transfer.

have claim is worth only $50,000. If we apply this same reasoning to the income aspects of their relationship, the transfer character of the interest payment becomes clear. Suppose the farm earns at a rate of $6,000 per year, and suppose the interest on the mortgage is $500 per year. The income of A and B is clearly $6,000, rather than $6,500. B shares in the income generated by the use of the real resources to produce farm products to the extent of $500, which is treated as a deduction from A's apparent income of $6,000.

Either of two theories may be adopted to explain why B obtains the $500 income. It may be argued that B performs a service for which A pays $500. But since the service is instrumental, rather than final, it is deducted in computing A's income. By this line of reasoning, interest becomes a payment to be viewed in the same manner as if A hired B to work for him on the farm, paying him $500 for his human services. This reasoning, if extended, logically requires that interest income wherever found be treated as non-transfer income, that is, as a payment for a service. A holder of public debt, then, must be supposed to provide some kind of service for which interest is paid to him, since it is difficult to maintain that private debt holders perform services and public debt holders do not. Furthermore, it is clearly incorrect to treat interest on public and personal debt as a payment for an instrumental service. The basis is thus laid for claiming that these interest payments represent payments for final products. Thus the greater these interest payments, the greater are gross and net national product. In short, how we explain B's income, whether as a payment for a service or as a transfer, establishes the basis for the treatment of all types of interest payments.

Our position is that the only logically sound reason for deducting B's income of $500 from the $6,000 earned by the farm, and for counting A's income as $5,500, is that B, having a claim to the assets represented by the farm, is entitled to income as a matter of contract as a part owner of the farm itself. A does not own the entire farm; he has an equity interest only. The entire farm is owned by A and B together. Thus B obtains income, not because he is selling a service to A, but merely because he owns something. The particular payments which are interest income to B are the money mechanism of respecting B's right to income established by contract. This proposition means only that income is obtained by both parties because they own something, namely a farm, but the nature of the ownership relation calls for A making payments to B as a recognition of B's claim to the earnings of the underlying wealth. From the point of view of national-income analysis, interest is not a payment to be looked upon in the same way as a payment for a product or a service. The latter is an exchange transaction, that is a purchase and a sale. An interest payment is simply a method of permitting some owners to share in the income of assets to which they are entitled by contract.

Another way of looking at the same facts is to describe transfers in the form of interest payments as arising because of the separation of the ownership and control of real resources, including human beings. If every piece of wealth and every human being were owned without encumbrance, there would be no contractual transfers. Under such conditions, the people in control of the use of resources would obtain the income from their employment directly and in full. In such a society, contractual interest payments would not exist, and the problem of transfer payments would not arise.

Actual interest payments may be a redistribution of the earnings of physical resources, or of human beings, or of both. In the case of corporate enterprise, the assets under the control of the corporate management generate whatever earnings are realized from the organization of these assets combined with services hired from outsiders. Income thus generated may in part be redistributed in interest payments to creditors. In this case the income of the creditors is a transfer of earnings generated by the employment of nonhuman resources. A redistribution of the earnings of human resources occurs when an individual who owns nothing but his own earning power has incurred debt in the past. The interest paid on this indebtedness is a transfer of income arising from human services. It does not matter, as far as the transfer element is concerned, what the purpose of incurring the indebtedness may have been in the first instance, whether, for example, it was made to finance the training of that person for some particular occupation or to accomplish some frivolous purpose. A person under such an obligation against his earning power transfers part of the income arising from the employment of himself to people who have a claim against him. It so happens that the mores and legal system of contemporary societies limit the extent to which one may successfully contract away the earning power of his person. People are not forced to fulfill contracts where their income net of such interest payments would leave them nothing or very little, and bankruptcy proceedings are available to slough off excess claims of overmortgaged people.

The same argument for the treatment of interest as a transfer payment applies to dividends, when dividends may properly be viewed as income at all. They are transfers of income for the reason that no services are rendered in return for the income in this form.

There are a number of possible objections to the position that interest (and dividends) should be treated as transfer income. In spite of occasional criticism, both national-income computers and economic theorists in general treat contractual interest as nontransfer income like wages. Several arguments are used to bolster the view that creditors provide a service for which interest is paid. Of these, the propositions that interest is the price for the use of loanable funds or that interest is paid on productive debt seem to be the criteria most commonly used.

The description of interest as the price for the use of money (or of loanable funds) for a given period of time need not be inherently wrong. The danger lies in considering the "use of money" as similar in character to the use of a building or the use of manpower. If taken literally in this sense, it is a misleading statement. In an actual loan contract, A, the borrower, agrees to pay B, the lender, a specified sum of money at a specified date or a series of sums at specified dates. B agrees to pay A a sum of money for A's promise to make the future payment or payments specified. Every loan contract can be described, therefore, as a purchase and sale. The borrower is offering to sell something, namely, his promise to pay a sum or a series of sums of money in the future; the lender is offering to buy this promise at a price. But a loan is a capital, not an income, transaction. Each party gives up something which, from the point of view of the other, is an asset. This view is implicit in the practice of national-income computation. None of the current series provide for a larger national-income total merely because of an increase in the number of loans being made.

The "use-of-money" argument for the justification of interest as a payment for a service may be regarded by some as looking beyond the date of the loan transaction itself to the relation of borrower and lender as interest accrues and payments are made. The lender allegedly provides a service, over the period of the contract, in the nature of a rental of money previously handed over to the borrower. Interest, then, is the payment for this service. How else, it may be urged, is it possible to explain why a borrower is willing to pay interest at all?

In reply to this theory, certain irrelevant considerations must first be cleared away. One of these is that the borrower is better off in some sense by having entered into the loan contract, and hence the lender may be described as the fountainhead of this betterment. This view is admissible, but incomplete. Presumably, in a loan contract, as in other voluntary contracts, the borrower as a seller of a promise to remit sums at specified future dates is better off by entering into the contract than he otherwise would have been. By the same token, the lender as a buyer of an asset is also better off. This presumption follows from the fact that the parties are able to get together and, according to their own lights, consider the contract as better than none. The presumption, it may be emphasized, is that *both* parties, not merely the borrower, are better off. Any implicit assumption that the lender is doing the borrower a special favor in lending money has little basis in fact. A mere inspection of the manner in which banks are prepared to seek the business of corporations of excellent credit standing should suggest that they are not providing special favors contrary to their own interests as they see them.

Equally irrelevant is the ethical argument sometimes advanced that the recipient of a transfer income is "unproductive," and hence not entitled to the income as is a recipient of nontransfer income. Gilbert, for example, objects to placing bankers in the same class as persons on relief.[10] There is, however, no ethical issue involved at all as far as the particular person who obtains transfer income is concerned. As previously argued, a person obtains income because he owns resources. A lender has a kind of ownership right in these underlying assets. People as owners get income arising out of the services of real resources, including human beings. Failure to make a distinction between the ownership of resources and the rendering of services by resources is the source of confusion behind this ethical argument. A singer with an excellent voice may command a substantial income. If a part of this income is shared with a banker to whom he is in debt, it is improper to conclude that the singer is ethically entitled to the entire income on the grounds that he himself is more productive than the banker. The voice produces the service and both have claims to the income

_____
[10] Gilbert, *op. cit.*, pp. 81–82.

arising from the service. The relevant ethical question should be posed in terms of what is the ideal distribution of wealth, including human earning power, in the society—a question that cuts across the transfer issue.[11]

The only relevant aspect of the use-of-money argument is the claim that a service is performed by debt holders for which interest is paid. When the argument is stated in this way, there appears to be no alternative but to insist that it is fallacious. If it means that a debtor at the time of a loan contract gets a service from the creditor, it is confusing a capital transaction with an income transaction. One asset, cash, is exchanged for another asset, a promise to pay. As of this moment of exchange, no income or service feature is present. If the use-of-money argument means that the debtor obtains a service by paying interest to the creditor, it is a denial that a firm debt contract exists. Debtors do not have the right to refuse to pay interest to creditors on the ground that they no longer desire the "service" provided by the creditors. Depending upon the type of debt contract, they may have the right to extinguish the debt by repayment or by simply offering to buy back their own liabilities. Such an exchange is again a capital, not an income, transaction. Statements that interest payments made by governments, for example, are in exchange for the service of letting the government use one's money are likewise unwarranted. Such an argument is no more compelling than the proposition that the government performs a service by letting people use its debt.[12] The literal facts suggest that debt holders obtain interest because they own something, and like others in our society, their ownership of sources of earning power (including human earning power) is the basic explanation for obtaining income of any sort. This is one of Irving Fisher's important contributions to this subject.

---

[11] This argument is of course not new. Knight, in particular, has forcefully argued that the social issues as to what persons should be entitled to the earnings generated by the use of nonhuman resources apply equally to the use of human resources. (F. H. Knight, "Interest," *Encyclopedia of the Social Sciences*, reprinted in *The Ethics of Competition* [New York: Harper & Brothers, 1935], p. 255.) By the same token, the issues are no different with regard to people who obtain income by owning claims.

[12] We must therefore reject the view urged by Carl S. Shoup (*loc. cit.*) that repayment of government debt is a transfer. Shoup's conclusion either assumes some other definition of transfer income than the one ordinarily used, or he is treating a capital transaction as an income transaction. If a government repurchases debt, it wipes out a security which was an asset to its holder and provides him with another asset, cash. No income payment is involved; the receipt of the cash arising from debt repayment is not income at all. On this point, the orthodox treatment of debt cancellation in national income accounting appears superior to Shoup's proposed innovation.

The suggestion that contractual interest income should be universally treated as a transfer from debtors to creditors is not a new idea in economic thinking. In accounting theory, certain schools of thought have long urged that contractual interest be viewed as a distribution item, rather than as a cost of production.[18] The concept of distribution of earnings in enterprise accounting appears identical with the concept of transfers in national-income accounting. The accounting rationale for treating interest as a transfer, rather than as a cost, is based upon the theory that costs have to do with the use of something, such as the prices of services hired from outsiders or the depreciation of resources owned within the enterprise. The financial structure of a business is relevant to the determination of the manner in which the income generated within the enterprise is shared among various claimants, and it is relevant to the likelihood of bankruptcy proceedings, but it is not relevant to costs of production.

TAXES AND SUBSIDIES

The treatment of taxes (compulsory transfers) and subsidies (voluntary transfers) in national-income accounting may be considered together. The position here adopted is a simple one. All taxes including so-called indirect taxes and all gratuitous government payments including subsidies should be treated as transfer payments. In other words, the government's income is to be computed by adding tax yields and by subtracting subsidies and other gratuitous government payments. Taxes should, in our opinion, be viewed as transfers because they are a clear and definite case where income is obtained which is not in payment for services rendered. Government tax revenue or income arises from the exercise of the government's coercive power to force its members to make contributions to it. A tax is a transfer because of the nature of taxes, namely that they give rise to tax yields which are income to governments and are not paid as a condition of obtaining any particular commodity or service. A legal taxpayer, by meeting his tax bills, is only accommodated to the extent that he is not liable to be prosecuted for tax evasion, which can scarcely be deemed a kind of government service. The fact that governments do provide services to citizens does not directly depend upon the taxes, if any, which those citizens pay.

Likewise, subsidies should be viewed as transfer payments because by definition they refer to payments by government for which

[18] W. A. Paton and R. A. Stevenson, *Principles of Accounting* (New York: Macmillan, 1918), p. 613.

the government receives no product, service, or asset. A person who obtains a subsidy does so because he conforms to the requirements set down in the subsidy legislation, such as having been a member of the armed forces, producing certain commodities for sale, or being unemployed. Subsidies are essentially similar to taxes except for the difference in sign. Therefore if a rationale can be provided for the treatment of all taxes as transfer payments, the same rationale can be used to justify the treatment of subsidies as transfer payments. To conserve space, we shall therefore concentrate on taxes.

Our proposed treatment of all taxes and subsidies as transfers of income between private groups and government is not used in any of the current national-income estimates. At one time Kuznets argued that government should be treated in the same way as business organizations. Taxation, according to this view, becomes the price of government services sold to individuals or to business.[14] He has more recently suggested another method of treating taxation.[15] His new approach is much too complex to be summarized here.[16] He does, however, retain the theory that the valuation of some government activities is in principle determined by tax revenues. Both British and United States official estimators employ a different basis. They distinguish between direct and indirect taxes, deducting the yield of indirect taxes but not of direct taxes from both the product and income sides of the accounts.

Four main reasons are used to justify the deduction of indirect taxes from both the product and income sides of the social accounts: (1) indirect taxes are costs of production; (2) indirect taxes affect relative prices directly; (3) the incomes computed by deducting indirect taxes measure the returns to the "factors of production"; and (4) indirect taxes are shifted to consumers. None of these arguments turns out to be compelling upon close examination.

(1) It is frequently argued that indirect taxes are chargeable as a cost of doing business. This point of view is emphasized in the British White Papers.[17] The view of indirect taxes as costs of pro-

---

[14] Simon Kuznets, *National Income and Its Composition*, pp. 31–34; also his comments, *S.I.W.*, Vol. 2, pp. 296–306.

[15] Simon Kuznets, "Government Product and National Income," *Income and Wealth*, Ser. 1, pp. 178–244.

[16] A summary is provided by I. M. D. Little in his review of *Income and Wealth*, Ser. 1, in *Journal of Political Economy*, LX (April, 1952): 172.

[17] British White Papers (Cmd. 6623), *Federal Reserve Bulletin* (August, 1945), pp. 735–736. The following illustrates this view and also the "factor" argument. "This means that from the total actually spent indirect taxes are deducted since this amount

duction in some significant sense becomes a basic reason for this special treatment. The labeling of a tax as a cost of production does not of itself add anything to the sum total of human knowledge. One can search in vain for a theory of costs to justify the special treatment of indirect taxes. The significant question is the proper meaning of cost and its implications for taxation. In one sense, all taxes are costs, if by costs we mean any money payments made in connection with doing business. A tax on property, called indirect in British usage for example, is a cost in this sense. Any corporation owning property must meet its tax liabilities. In this sense a corporate net income tax is a cost; such a tax must also be paid. But such a definition of cost makes it impossible to distinguish between transfers and business expense. To do this we need a more restricted definition.

In economic theory, cost is often used to mean foregone gain. Thus the marginal cost of producing a unit of X is the amount of Y which could be produced instead. The foregone-product conception of cost does not permit the treatment of a tax as a cost. The conception of cost used in connection with a firm means the amounts paid for services hired from outsiders plus the value of resources owned within the firm which are used up, that is, depreciation. Where a particular firm can produce several products, the use of equipment to produce one product means the sacrifice of the alternative gain of producing other products. Since taxes are not a payment for a service or a product, it is improper to consider indirect taxes as costs of acquiring the use of resources. A business must pay them, to be sure, assuming that it satisfies the tests laid down in the tax law, just as it must pay interest on any outstanding indebtedness. We recognize this fact by computing the income of business in the sense of the amounts accruing to the residual claimants by deducting all taxes and interest payments. The argument that indirect taxes require special treatment because they are costs of production is not a compelling one.

(2) It is often claimed that taxes classified as indirect affect relative prices, whereas direct taxes do not, and for this reason indirect taxes should be subtracted in computing the national income.[18] It

---

of the sales proceeds is taken by the taxing authority and is treated as a business cost and not as a part of income, while subsidies are added on since they represent a source of income available to producers in addition to the proceeds of sale. The resultant, or 'factor cost,' represents what producers and distributors, their employees, landlords and creditors, in a word the factors of production, receive for the sale of their products and services after duplication has been removed." *Ibid.*, pp. 738–739.
[18] *Loc. cit.*

may be admitted at the outset that some taxes do affect relative prices. Import duties, for example, undoubtedly do allocate resources away from export production and change the composition of imports. Actual prices will reflect this fact. Taxes classified as direct in British estimates may likewise affect relative prices. A personal income tax may induce some people to take more leisure. Partial income taxes upon particular occupational groups may reallocate resources and alter product prices. However, many factors other than taxes change relative prices. Obviously, no effort is made in social accounting to allow for those changes in relative prices occasioned by changes in the public's tastes. Nor is there any attempt to allow for changes in relative prices resulting from the change over time in capital equipment. Hence one may ask why only the prices of those products upon which certain taxes are levied should be adjusted, when it is obvious that many other circumstances (including direct taxes) affect relative prices. National-income totals, to be meaningful, should be computed in terms of the community's actual experience with prices. There is no occasion for arbitrarily changing these prices on the ground that they may be affected by the presence of certain taxes.

(3) The "factor-of-production" argument is more frequently repeated in British studies than is any other. National income computed by deduction of indirect taxes from gross gain gives, it is asserted, the returns of the "factors of production."[19] This concept may give the impression that national-income totals thus computed yield results which correspond to functional income distribution in economic theory.

If by the "factors of production" is meant literally all the various kinds of labor power, tools, equipment, buildings, and soil existing in the economy, the factors thus defined generate the total income of the community. The value placed upon the output of these resources, computed net of duplication and depreciation, becomes the income of the community. This income would accrue entirely to private individuals and groups in the absence of taxation or of government-owned real resources. Because of taxation, some part of this income will accrue to government, whether the taxes employed are personal net income, property, import, or excise. Taxes divert income to governments in some amount. The omission of the yield of indirect taxes, on the ground that they are not part of the income generated by the resources in the economy, does not

---

[19] *Loc. cit.*

give a result that includes the total returns of the factors of production in this sense; it omits a part of those returns.

This difficulty might be surmounted by the advocates of the "factor-cost" doctrine if they defined the factors of production to mean private individuals and groups who own something, such as labor power, other real resources, or claims to these resources, and whose incomes are computed after the deduction of certain taxes labeled "indirect" but without the deduction of other taxes labeled "direct." In this way, a factor of production is defined according to the method of computing income. The result is correct but meaningless: the factors of production are those private groups who obtain private income computed before deducting direct taxes but after deducting indirect taxes. Such a method of defining the factors of production does not help the argument that the deduction of indirect taxes gives a meaningful aggregate.

(4) The argument that indirect taxes are shifted to consumers appears to have great weight among those who urge special treatment of indirect taxes. If it is held that excise taxes increase prices paid by consumers, a case exists for treating such taxes differently from those which are not believed to be shifted. Pigou holds that excise taxes should be treated differently from, for example, personal net income taxes, because excise taxes increase the price of a taxed article whereas income taxes presumably do not.[20] According to those who accept the view that incidence is directly relevant to national accounting, the amount of each tax shifted to consumers should be deducted, because otherwise a change in the tax system toward the more extensive use of indirect taxes would give an arbitrary increase in national income. Thus, if a tax on a commodity is instituted and if sellers of the commodity raise prices by some amount, buyers are said to be paying the tax. Therefore in computing the value of output, prices should mean net prices to sellers. Failure to follow this rule according to this point of

[20] A. C. Pigou, *Economics of Welfare* (London: Macmillan, 1932), pp. 40–42. Professor Pigou's discussion of this point is a highly confused one. He does not make clear whether he thinks that both value product and incomes should be computed net of such taxes, or only one of them. However, at this point Pigou finds his theory of incidence clashing with his views on social accounting; and, unfortunately for tax theory, he assumes that conventional incidence theory should be given intellectual priority. In general, a similar point of view is endorsed by a large number of students of national income accounting. Cf. M. A. Copeland, "Some Problems in the Theory of National Income," *Journal of Political Economy*, XL (February, 1932): 30; Lindeman, *op. cit.*, pp. 7–11; Blough, discussion of Shoup's "The Distinction between 'Net' and 'Gross' in Income Taxation," *S.I.W.*, Vol. I, p. 286; Clark Warburton, "Accounting Methodology in the Measurement of National Income," *S.I.W.*, Vol. I, pp. 89–92.

view means that national income is shown at a larger figure than it should be. Thus, a rationale is established for treating indirect taxes as deductions because they are believed to be shifted entirely or nearly so, whereas direct taxes are not treated as deductions because they are presumed not to be shifted. This argument seems to be the dominating one for special treatment of indirect taxes.

This theory confuses causation with computation. In national income accounting, the issues at stake are conceptual rather than causal. The main problems are what categories should be established, what distinctions should be made, and what methods of estimation should be employed. Another, but different, set of problems pertains to the fact that some or all of these components may change over time. Prices may fall or rise and production may increase or decrease. No summary statement in itself can give the reasons for these changes, nor is this its purpose. To explain why prices change requires an investigation of determinants, such as demands for products, production techniques, labor union policies, and business price policies. When it is argued that indirect taxes may be shifted to consumers through increases in prices, the discussion concerns these determinants rather than the meaning or content of what is determined. Over time the imposition of sales taxes may be accompanied by higher prices. The opposite may also occur. Taxes do remove money from someone; and sales taxes, like income taxes, can induce a smaller expenditure upon output and thus lower rather than raise prices. (See chap. 6.) Either development is possible; the first when monetary expansion in demands for products occurs in a setting when employment approaches its maximum; the second, especially when deflation is developing. Even if one believes, which I do not, that the preponderance of evidence suggests that increases in excise taxes will be accompanied by price increases over time, this view is not a justification for defining national-income categories in such a way that these increases are disguised rather than revealed. Yet many students of this problem assume that indirect taxes will increase prices and that this, in turn, will increase national income; but for some unexplained reason, this result is deemed improper. National net value product and national income, being stated in money terms, increase when a general rise in prices occurs, whatever the reason may be for the rise.

If it is real income that is to be measured, the results obtained by using a deflator constructed from actual prices give evidence as to the changes in the quantities of real product. An attempt to take out some part of the price increases first, on the ground that they are attributable to certain kinds of taxes, is not only unnecessary but actually invites error. For example, suppose that during two successive periods the quantities of each kind of output are the same. This means that real national income in both periods is the same by assumption. Suppose that prices in the second period are 10 per cent higher than in the first period, and that all the increase is attributed to new excise taxes. If indirect taxes are deducted, the money value of production for both years is the same. But if national income so computed is deflated by an index of actual prices, it will appear that real income has fallen, which is ruled out by assumption. It is, of course, possible to avoid this error by using a price index "corrected" for indirect taxes in the same manner as the money value of output is corrected for them. But it is wholly incorrect to suggest that any error in computing national income is introduced by counting prices at their full amounts, rather than at amounts computed by deducting indirect taxes.[21]

There is furthermore a distortion of fact if indirect taxes are deducted from prices. The action of a person paying, for example, eighteen cents for a package of cigarettes cannot be described so simply if the indirect tax deduction view is adopted. His action must be reinterpreted to mean that he really pays only ten cents and the other eight cents is a donation to the government. Prices are no longer simply prices, but are mixed results of what a person "really" pays for the commodity and what he contributes to his government as a kind of gift. People's decisions are guided, of course, not by the fictitious price of ten cents, but by what they pay to get a package of cigarettes. It might be just as proper to say that he pays even less than ten cents, because some part even of this amount goes to the cigarette industry and to the people employed in it to help them pay their income taxes. There is no occasion for such distortion. The total amount that a person spends for an article is the price he pays.

The treatment of indirect taxes, wholly or in part, as a deduction from prices paid also has its counterpart on the income side of the accounts in the refusal to count the yield of indirect taxes as part of government income. But what valid reason is there for ignoring the yield of indirect taxes? From the point of view of governments, the dollars these taxes provide are just as good as

_____
[21] For an excellent statement of this argument, see Shoup, *op. cit.*, p. 265.

dollars provided by direct taxes. Both yield revenue and both are included in budgetary decisions. Perhaps this refusal, especially in British practice, to view indirect taxes as government income is traceable to a reluctance to think of governments as income receivers at all, except in cases of government-operated enterprises. The yield of direct taxes can, for purposes of obtaining aggregates, be recognized by not deducting these taxes from the incomes of taxpayers. Such a practice does not directly make the yield of these taxes government income. Theoretically, indirect taxes might be shown in the same way, that is, as a part of the income of legal taxpayers computed before deducting such taxes. But no one seems willing to follow this practice.

Perhaps the reluctance to adopt the simple expedient of treating the government as an income receiver is traceable to the factor-of-production approach to the explanation of incomes which implies that government cannot be viewed as a factor of production. But the government may be treated as an income recipient without implying that it is a factor of production. Income accrues to particular persons or organizations because they *own* something. People obtain income in the form of wages because they own themselves. In a particular institutional setting, services of resources generate income which accrues to particular persons or groups because they own or have claims to these resources. It is the services that function, not the owners of the resources that give rise to services. In the case of government, the power to tax is an important type of ownership right in resources under the control of private parties, as Fisher has indicated.[22] A government, however, does not limit itself by contract as to the amount which it collects. It can assert its power to divert money income to itself in the form of tax revenue by devising new taxes or increasing the base or rates of old ones. Governments do obtain income. This fact should not be ignored or obscured because a government is not deemed to be a factor of production. All taxes and all subsidies may be treated simply as transfer payments involving government. A distinction between "direct" and "indirect" taxes and subsidies is unnecessary for social accounting.

AGGREGATION

Transfer payments may be treated in either of two ways to obtain an aggregate of incomes. The computation may be based on the

[22] Fisher, *op. cit.*, pp. 30–31.

income of each recipient when income means the net gain excluding capital gains and losses accruing from the use of resources under his control. This treatment may be called the *omission* rule. Any person or organization responsible for managing real resources is necessarily the first recipient of the gains arising from their employment. Correct totals can be found merely by adding the incomes so generated. A hypothetical illustration may be used to clarify this method. Suppose in a given period the government acquires $10,000,000,000 worth of goods and services for its own ends. Subsidies in kind and government enterprise are assumed to be absent. Private groups acquire $90,000,000,000 worth of goods and services during this period. Thus the value of output is $100,-000,000,000. We assume this to be a net figure by treating depreciation, depletion, and inventory disappearance as negligible. The gross income of private enterprise is therefore $100,000,000,000 after deducting for any instrumental services provided by one enterprise to another. To compute the net income of enterprise according to the omission rule, we deduct the value of instrumental service supplied by persons outside of enterprise such as owners of labor power, and these sums are then counted as their income. If, for example, wages amounting to $70,000,000,000 are the only payments made by business organizations for instrumental services, the income of enterprise is $30,000,000,000. No further deductions from business incomes, such as interest, dividends, or taxes whether direct or indirect, should then be made. Likewise no interest or taxes paid by owners of labor power should be deducted. Consistent with this rule we should not add any transfer payments made by government to private groups such as interest or subsidies in computing the incomes of private groups. The sum of incomes of business organizations and of labor so computed gives a correct total on the income side of the social accounts. Since by definition transfer payments are irrelevant in computing the value of output, no adjustment need be made on the product side of the accounts. The sum of incomes so computed equals by definition the value of output computed at the prices actually charged for goods and services produced.

The omission rule does not give a correct picture of the income of any segment of the population, except in the special case where the segment neither makes nor receives transfer payments. For example, the "income" of the government according to the omission rule would always be zero by definition in the absence of government enterprise. Likewise the income of a worker required to make alimony payments to a former spouse would be treated as belonging entirely to him when in fact the court has decided otherwise. Although the omission rule correctly measures the earnings of the real resources under the control of a corporation, this method incorrectly treats any incomes obtained by people as owners of its stocks, bonds, and short-term securities as zero. Consequently the incomes of financial intermediaries would be zero or negative.[23]

If, therefore, a correct picture is desired of the money gain accruing to particular persons or organizations, account must be taken of transfers paid by them and to them. The same total for all incomes, $100,000,000,000 in our illustration, can be obtained by consistent application of what is here called the *deduct-add* rule. This rule means that any transfer is shown by deducting the amount of the payment from the income of the transferrer and adding it to the income of the transferee. Since every transfer payment carries both a plus and a minus sign in a closed system, this treatment guarantees that the total of incomes cannot be affected by the amount or complexity of transfer payments.[24] Thus the income of a divorced man is computed by deducting any alimony payments made by him. The amount of such payments is added to the income of his former spouse. The employment of the deduct-add rule requires that the income of government be computed in the following fashion (ignoring subsidies in kind): the positive

[23] We are not concerned in this study with issues involving the proper treatment of financial organizations. It does appear incorrect, however, to view commercial banks as financial intermediaries as is now done in official estimates. It is simply not true that commercial banks lend the money of their depositors. Banks lend demand deposits which are created in the process of making loans. Neglect of this elementary point largely vitiates the rationale presently used in official estimates for commercial banks. Cf. Dwight B. Yntema, "National Income Originating in Financial Intermediaries," *S.I.W.*, Vol. X, p. 36. The same peculiar theory of banking is adopted by Richard Ruggles, *Introduction to National Income and Income Analysis* (New York: McGraw-Hill, 1949), p. 56.

[24] The qualification of a closed system is important in this connection. When any country's transfer payments add to zero, it is an accident or occurs by deliberate government policy of disallowing its members to become involved with outside groups. Transfer payments involving members of more than one national group take the form of interest, dividends, gifts, and, in certain cases, taxes and subsidies. If an aggregate national income figure is computed by reference to the income generated from, or arising out of, the use of resources physically located within one country rather than to income of resources wherever located owned by residents of the country, the net value of output of the resources, if exports are treated as a part of such output, need not equal the aggregate of incomes obtained by people within the country. Equality between net value of output and the aggregate of incomes can be restored by the adoption of certain conventions, although somewhat artificially.

elements consist of all profits (or losses) from government enterprise, all tax revenues (including fines), and all interest and dividends paid to government by private groups; the negative elements consist of all interest payments, pensions, relief payments and other voluntary transfers, and any compulsory transfers made by government to private groups. The resulting figure for government income or net revenue may be positive or negative. In practice, however, the figure is usually positive; taxes ordinarily exceed transfer payments made by government.

This method of computing government income is much less complicated than that used by some investigators of this topic. Shoup in his study maintains that income totals computed according to what he calls the "after-tax rule" require the addition of certain government expenditures and the subtraction of any government borrowing, money creation, or increase in the government's cash position. These results, which he finds uncongenial, are traceable to the overstating of national income in the first instance and the deduction of items which should not be treated as income transfers at all.[25] The point can be illustrated by the use of our former example with some modification. To follow Shoup's dictum that only capital expenditures by government are to be treated as final, let us suppose that the government spends $10,-000,000,000 for this purpose. We assume the absence of all other types of government expenditures and any transfer payments in money or in kind by government. Let us suppose that tax yields for the period in question are $6,000,000,000. Factor incomes before deduction of taxes are $100,000,000,000 and after deduction

---

[25] Shoup, *op. cit.*, p. 280. Some possible ambiguities in his treatment of government arise from the theory adopted that what he calls "general-purpose" services of government are not to be treated as final product (*ibid.*, pp. 266–270). A somewhat similar point of view is adopted by Kuznets, "Government Product and National Income," *Income and Wealth*, Ser. 1, pp. 184–199. Kuznets, unlike Shoup, is willing to treat the output taken by government during a major war but not, I presume, during a cold war as final product. Both regard the characteristic governmental functions as "not final," a point of view which seems to imply that these services are instrumental to something, but what this something is, is not always clear. Shoup's position is based upon the welfare argument that a country that requires more of what are called "general-purpose" services is worse off on that account. Thus, if people were generally decent and willingly respected the rights of others, a community could get along with fewer policemen. The observation is plausible, but is it relevant? If it did not rain on houses we might not need roofs, and if we did not become ill we might not need doctors. But violence and the threat of violence are facts which must be dealt with. Likewise military preparedness as well as war itself requires the use of resources to accomplish a public objective. It seems improper to reject such objectives on so-called welfare grounds as Shoup does.

of taxes are therefore $94,000,000,000. The Shoup rule calls for the addition of the $10,000,000,000 of government capital expenditures to the $94,000,000,000 of factor income after deducting taxes—or $104,000,000,000. He then proposes to deduct the sum of the following: government borrowing, government money creation, and the increase in the government's cash balance.[26] Since the last three necessarily equal the difference between government expenditures as defined and tax yields—$4,000,000,000 in our illustration—the result is the correct total of $100,000,000,000. But to make this treatment meaningful, it is necessary to regard a loan made by a bank or a private individual to the government as negative income. This is a distortion of fact. A person who buys government securities in a period does not have a smaller income on that account; he has merely changed the form of his assets. In contrast our method applied to the above illustration would show the income of private groups computed after taxes as $94,000,000,000 and government income as $6,000,000,000. This gives the correct total of $100,000,000,000. *No attention need be given to how the government finances its deficit in this computation.* Our method has the advantage, among others, of avoiding the error of treating government borrowing as a transfer payment. The purchase of a security fits the requirement that the payment be in return for some valuable item. These are capital transactions and not transfers.

ILLUSTRATIONS OF PROPOSED METHODS

The method here proposed for computing the income side of the social accounts is set forth below.

PROPOSED METHOD OF COMPUTING NATIONAL INCOME

Personal

1. From *Use* of Real Resources.
   a. Salaries and wages.
   b. Net earnings of unincorporated enterprise and "personal" corporations.
   c. Net rentals.
   d. Imputed net income (net value of services of owner-occupied houses, etc.).

2. Transfer Incomes.
   a. From business to persons.
   Less: b. From persons to business.

---

[26] Shoup, *op. cit.*, p. 280.

Personal (Continued)

c. From government to persons.

Less: d. From persons to government (personal taxes).

3. Total Personal Net Incomes (1 + 2).

Corporate

4. From *Use* of Real Resources.

a. Corporate net earnings from current production (computed before deduction of taxes, interest, dividends, or gifts).

5. Transfer Incomes.

a. From government to corporate.

Less: b. From corporate to government (taxes).

c. From persons to corporate.

Less: d. From corporate to persons.

6. Total Corporate Net Incomes (4 + 5).

Government

7. From *Use* of Real Resources.

a. Net profits of government-operated enterprise.

b. Net implicit income of government wealth.

8. Transfer Incomes.

a. Yield of all taxes.

b. Other transfers to government.

Less: c. Contractual transfers (to corporations and persons).

d. Voluntary transfers (i.e., pensions, subsidies, social security payments, relief, etc.).

e. Subsidies in kind to corporate.

9. Total Government Net Income (7 + 8).

10. National Income (3 + 6 + 9).

In this presentation the economy is divided into three sectors: personal, corporate, and government. The distinction between personal and the corporate is somewhat arbitrary. Ideally the corporate sector would be restricted to those corporations which are "impersonal" types. An impersonal corporation is one in which the controlling group is guided by the desire to promote the interest of the corporation as such. The small, closely held corporation where the controlling group treats the organization as a personal instrument should, according to this conception, be classed in the personal sector. These distinctions are admittedly in the nature of degrees. A person who owns only his own earning power is in one sense in the business of selling services, and he may have certain costs in connection with obtaining his income. The same is true of a farmer conducting the characteristic family-farm operation. At the other extreme there are the giant corporations where ownership and control of resources are almost completely divorced.[27]

The totals computed by adding 1, 4, and 7 could provide the figures for national income as indicated by the omission rule for a closed system. Each of these categories refers to earnings of real resources classified according to the characteristics of the groups controlling their employment. The net income of any sector as indicated by 3, 6, and 9 is computed according to the deduct-add rule. It will be observed that the method of computation of transfer incomes is identical for each sector. In all cases transfer income paid to the sector from others is added and transfer income paid by the sector is subtracted. Transfer incomes are defined in the same way for every sector; thus interest is a transfer payment whether made by government, corporations, or persons.

In the government sector the item 8a, yield of all taxes, requires no distinction between different types of taxes. Any item properly definable as a tax, whether in the form of an excise levy, import duty, or estate levy, is treated in the same fashion.

The government account could be subclassified in any degree permitted by the data. Ideally complete information about incomes, subject to the limits of the income concept used in national income computations, would be provided by a classification listing every income-receiving unit separately. The income of each person and impersonal organization identified by name would be shown. The statistical data on income lack this degree of refinement.[28]

SOME IMPLICATIONS

We have claimed above that the product side of the social accounts should be computed at market prices rather than at market prices

---

[27] The distinction between the private and corporate sectors here proposed should not be confused with that used in the U. S. Department of Commerce estimates. A "person" according to their categories is not necessarily a real human being. For example, a "person" whose income arises entirely from ownership of real estate is a "business." Our method avoids the circularity involved in defining person or business by the characteristics of the income received.

[28] The problem of defining the income-receiving unit permits of no easy theoretical solution. A family presumably constitutes a unit for income purposes provided that its members practice communism within the group, assuming this word may still be used in its literal meaning. Actually communism and individualism even within the harmonious family are a matter of degree. In some respects products taken by the family are shared in common, yet even young children exhibit areas of independence within the sharing. It is doubtful that any nonarbitrary solution of the problem of defining an income unit can be achieved.

less certain taxes. This point of view was supported by the argument that a market price total fits the evidence of actual experience whereas the "factor-cost" conception does not. In addition, the arguments that have been employed to support a factor-cost conception have been found deficient. There should be nothing surprising about this result. Students of public finance have attempted for many decades to find a meaningful distinction between direct and indirect taxes and have failed. The failure itself is instructive. At best the distinction has rested upon preconceptions about shifting, and any theory that has yet been systematically proposed has found that shifting of taxes is a matter of degree and depends upon circumstances other than the legal characteristics of the tax itself. Students of national income accounting, feeling obliged to take cognizance of fiscal theories, grasp the distinction between direct and indirect taxes, and for want of any better solution, treat each class as different in kind. This is a needless error.

Social accounting does not rest upon conceptions having to do with causation; rather it is a conceptual device to recognize the inherent dualism of economic relations. This dualism arises from the nature of money-price methods of economic organization and not from mere conventions of double-entry bookkeeping. A participant in the exchange system is at once a taker of products and an income recipient. This dual aspect does not exist in a Robinson Crusoe economy. A Crusoe takes what he and his equipment produce. Income is a superfluous notion in such a system. When people employ exchange systems to organize their economic lives, it becomes necessary to separate those aspects having to do with the acquisition of valuable things from those having to do with the getting of income. It is true to be sure that this separation is not 100 per cent complete in any actual society. Such products as leisure cannot be separated from the resources supplying them. But the great bulk of economic activity does involve such separation. Thus what a person takes from the economy in the form of valuable services and products may differ from the size of his accruing gains arising out of resources under his control plus net transfers made to him.

The method of computing the value of output at the market prices actually paid means that the income of some private groups computed according to the omission rule must reflect the yield of any taxes regardless of how classified. The income of the liquor industry so computed will be greater than the income retained by it or transferred to other private groups by an amount equal to the total tax liability imposed upon it. This tax liability will of course include any liability in connection with liquor excise taxes. This observation does not imply that the liquor industry—the legal tax-payers in this case—cannot shift the tax to others. It does mean, however, that the liquor industry must somehow or other obtain a larger income from the resources under its control because of the presence of certain types of tax liabilities.

The dualism of the money-price system indicated above raises the issue of the function of income. How shall we view the differences that income makes to particular persons or private organizations? How shall we view the function of government income? It is traditional in fiscal theory to assume that tax revenues impose a sacrifice on private groups. A large body of literature has developed on this premise. Utilitarian hedonism as applied to fiscal policy presupposes that taxes can impose sacrifices in various degrees on individuals. But if taxes are viewed as transfer payments from private individuals and organizations to government, there is a real sacrifice only if it can be shown that this transfer implies a reduction in the amounts which people obtain as takers of products. To learn the revelant facts in this connection, we must explore the implications of income in relation to individuals' and government's expenditures.

5

Monetary Basis of Fiscal Theory

Fiscal analysis requires a theory of money to explain how various government financial measures affect private expenditures. Of the four types of government financial activities—purchases, sales, negative transfer payments, and positive transfer payments—only a part of one, namely, government purchases, *directly* impinges upon the demands for current output. Taxes, subsidies, and debt operations are relevant to the rate of expenditures for goods and services only through their indirect effects on private decisions. If there were no such influences, a government might confine its financial activities to expenditures alone and eliminate thereby the political difficulties associated with the enactment and enforcement of a tax system. But taxes are needed to offset the inflationary effects of government expenditures. They induce a reduction or prevent an increase in the level of private expenditures. Taxes are also necessary to offset inflationary private monetary expenditures arising from government doles, subsidies, and interest payments. As far as I am aware, no school of thought is prepared to deny these propositions. But there exist important differences in theories of the causal steps by which these effects are believed to be more or less achieved.

In speaking of the monetary basis of fiscal theory, I do not wish to beg any questions about the relative importance of fiscal as distinct from monetary weapons, judged from the point of view of government influence on private expenditures. Tax devices, no less than central bank operations, involve money. A theory is needed that permits an analysis of the effects of either set of devices without contradiction. Our investigation serves to emphasize that the unifying core of all government financial devices, including central bank operations, is their connection with money in some way or other.

Our study of monetary theory is restricted to the determinants of the flow of expenditures through time. This is the area in which differences in views are critical. No effort will be made here to study systematically the relation between the level of expenditures and the prices of products and instrumental services. Different theories of the determinants of private expenditures need not involve differences in views of the causal relations between aggregate expenditures and the price level.

There are a number of monetary theories presently vying for the role of explaining how taxes, subsidies, government expenditures, debt-management operations, and central bank techniques affect the level and changes in the level of aggregate expenditures for current output. Easily the dominating point of view in contemporary thought is the Keynesian approach. A basic tenet of Keynesian doctrine is the negative one that the quantity of money is not a significant factor affecting private expenditures in a direct way and may or may not be a significant factor indirectly through effects upon security prices and rates of interest. Although there continue to be differences in views concerning the crucial positive features of this approach, as I shall attempt presently to point out, there is the minimum common ground that income is regarded as an important consideration affecting people's consumption expenditures. This feature of Keynesianism is portrayed through the use of propensity-to-consume and propensity-to-save concepts. There are differences of some importance in the precise meaning given to these concepts by those who wear the Keynesian label.

A second general approach to the explanation of the level of aggregate private expenditures for current output is the quantity-of-money theoretical tradition. Whatever the differences among the many versions of this approach, and there are many, the common denominator is the theory that the quantity of money is directly pertinent to private expenditures on current output. Of those whose views on money appear to fall into this category, Robertson is a major contributor.

The monetary theory here adopted is a variant of the quantitative approach. The capital value of a person's assets is taken to be the dominant objective determinant of his expenditures for consumption and investment items. The rate of his consumption expenditures is the outcome of a choice between holding assets and consuming. In choosing among the kinds of assets including cash that he wishes to hold, he determines his demands, and to some extent others' demands, for new real assets. This theory has the important negative implication that current income is not an objective determinant of current expenditures. It is this negative finding that makes it necessary to repudiate the Keynesian emphasis almost entirely, along with its applications to taxation, debt management, and other fiscal and monetary policies. This position that income is not a determinant of expenditures is based upon the principle that contemporaneous events cannot be mutually causal. The violation of this principle gives rise to "magical" theories of which the Keynesian investment-multiplier concept is a conspicuous example.

The presentation will first be confined to an exposition of the asset-flow theory of expenditures. After this has been done, some attention will be given to the income theory of constraints as found in the several versions of the Keynesian theory of expenditures and in equilibrium price theory. Finally the theory here adopted will be applied to the financial actions of government, with special attention to taxation.

For a closed system, and we shall neglect international repercussions, the aggregates to be explained in each period of history are the left-hand items of the equation

$$E_g + C + I = Y_p + Y_g$$

where E_g is government money expenditures for current output, C is consumption expenditures, and I is the value of current private capital formation computed net of depreciation, obsolescence, and inventory disappearance, Y_p is private net income computed by adding transfer payments made by government and deducting any transfer payments made by private groups to government, and Y_g is government net revenue, similarly computed.

Government expenditures require no special economic explanation. These expenditures are viewed as determined by the political complexion of the society and its government, by political attitudes and beliefs, and by the needs that people believe the government should meet. Those who adopt the de Marco theory that taxes and expenditures are inseparable may be interpreted as holding that expenditures of government are a function of tax yields. Reasons for rejecting this interpretation of government financial actions have already been given in chapter 1. The crucial aggregates to be explained are private rather than government expenditures.

STOCKS AS EXPENDITURE CONSTRAINTS

The need for economy reveals itself to persons, in a money-price system of economic organization, through the constraints limiting the services and goods they might like to have. That some sort of constraint on personal expenditures exists can scarcely be denied. If a person tries to behave as if he had unlimited means, he is disciplined by facts beyond his immediate control. In a financial system of social organization, money prices, as everyone seems ready to agree, act at least in part as such constraints. Buyers select what they want at prices stated in money terms. But prices can act as constraints, and hence as rationing devices, only in the presence of limited financial means. With an unlimited amount of money to spend, prices are not an obstacle to the acquisition of commodities. What then determines the amount of money a person has to spend? Is it his current income or some fraction thereof, past income, expected income, future income, resources (as Marshall seemed to hold on some occasions), the quantity of money owned by a person, the total value of all the assets under the control of a person, or some intermediate amount between the latter and the quantity of money he owns, such as his "liquid assets"? Or is it some combination of these, perhaps to be discovered by our tossing them together in one bag, grabbing out the ones which happen to suit our purpose at the moment, hoping in this fashion to discover the correct answer?

The question has two aspects: the nature of the constraints (1) on one person, and (2) on the entire community. It does not necessarily follow that the constraints on a community are merely the sum of the constraints on each person. We shall first consider the nature of the constraints on a person (or family).

At any given date in time, there is some upper limit to a person's expenditures for consumption and investment items during the ensuing moment of time. This moment of time may be looked upon as the "present." Such a period is not arbitrary; it is the shortest duration for anything to happen at all. The absolute limit to a person's expenditures during that period would appear to be given by the total cash value of all assets owned by him at that date in time. Cash value means the amount of cash he owns plus the total money value others are willing to place on his assets plus the cash value others are willing to place on any obligations he may create. The date in time refers to the cross-section date at the opening of the period—not to the duration itself.

This upper limit may be discovered more readily if initially securities are banned from the scene and if all real assets are thought of as having definite market prices. The absence of securities eliminates the possibility that a person may partly capitalize his personal earning power by becoming indebted to others. By banning claims, we also temporarily eliminate a troublesome and difficult topic, namely, the relevance of rates of interest in a financial system. But we do wish to keep commercial banks in the scene. To do this, it will be necessary to think of them as dealing in real assets, such as buildings, which they rent to others. Demand deposits are treated as money for the usual reasons rather than as debt instruments.

The maximum amount that a person can spend, in such a setting, is the market value of his real assets and the amount of his cash inherited from the past. Whatever a person's tastes, the quantities of goods and services he can acquire depend upon their prices, his cash holding, the kinds and quantities of physical resources he owns, and the prices of those resources. In money terms, the maximum amount of net investment and consumption by a person is equal to the quantity of cash he owns. This is a definitional relationship. Net investment is the difference between the value of any real assets sold to others and the value of any real assets acquired from others. A rearrangement of a person's asset holdings, other than cash, does not constitute net investment by him. It remains true, however, that the maximum amount that a person can spend for consumption items equals the present value of all his assets and his cash holding; a person can disinvest to obtain cash to finance consumption expenditures. His actual decisions concerning the amount to be spent for consumption are to be examined in view of the actual alternatives confronting him. Any consumption expenditures involve giving up cash. Any net investment expenditures likewise involve giving up cash. At a given point in time, therefore, a person must reconcile his desires for real assets of various kinds, for consumption items of various kinds, and for cash. "Freedom of choice" is meaningful only in terms of what he may do within the limitations of what he owns.[1] Unlimited freedom of choice is an impossibility.

---

[1] The range of freedom of a sovereign government is not fixed by its ability to obtain cash, which is theoretically infinite. Its power to promote government ends is determined by the potentialities of the resources found in that society.

A theory is therefore needed to explain (1) the variety and quantities of inherited real assets a person will continue to hold, (2) the variety and quantities of other real assets he will acquire, (3) the quantity of cash he will continue to hold, and (4) the variety and quantities of consumption items he will acquire. The first three of these topics may be discussed initially, ignoring consumption.

Let us assume that a person has inherited from the past real assets X and Y, which are the only marketable resources he owns, and also some given amount of cash.[2] Competitive markets are assumed to exist for X and Y; the prices of these assets are given to any buyer or holder. In figure 1, CD shows the various amounts of assets X and Y which a person could hold without drawing upon his cash balance, and point P indicates the actual quantities of X and Y inherited from the past. The slope of CD is given by the relative prices of X and Y, and its position is given by P—the physical quantities of inherited resources. A person may or may not be content with his inherited asset holdings. If indifference curve I shows his preference for the two assets, he sells X and buys Y, placing him at point R, which is his preferred asset position in terms of X and Y.

A person may prefer types of assets other than X and Y. He may buy such external assets from other owners or order them directly from production centers. The choice between other assets and the types he happens to own initially is pictured in figure 2. The vertical axis represents composite units of his inherited assets, at given prices, and the horizontal axis represents types of assets owned by others and those being currently produced. The assets X and Y

---

[2] It may be observed that cash holdings of persons are here taken as given. To the question—where does the cash come from?—our answer must be that it comes from "all history." The quantity of money existing at any date in time cannot be explained except in historical terms. We can select some date in the past and show what changes in the assets of banks and their liabilities other than deposits require the observed change in deposits plus currency. These changes in assets and nonmonetary liabilities can in turn be explained by appeals to evidence of why banks did change their asset holdings. But no complete explanation is possible unless one goes back to the beginning of money, if such a date can be found. This limitation in explanation applies to all stocks of a society. The stock of physical resources, including human labor power, at any given date is an inheritance from the past. Changes can be explained by selecting some earlier date as a starting point, but this is always and inevitably arbitrary. Likewise the "stock" of tastes existing at any date is the cumulative effect of the prior history of a society, its mores, and its economic and political organization. These are all given for the present in the sense that they are what they are. It is a function of analysis to explain *changes* in these items, and in this respect the theory of economic development is a by-product of pure theory.

may be viewed as a composite unit provided their prices are invariant. The slope of the constraint line *EF* (fig. 2) is given by the
relative prices of internal and external assets, from the point of
view of the person or organization in question, and its position by
R, which now represents the market value of his old assets corresponding to *R* in figure 1. If other assets are preferred, he will sell
old assets. His choice in this regard depends upon the relative
prices of owned and other assets, and upon the relative "gain"
which he associates with owning assets. In figure 2, his maximum
position is shown as *Q.* At this point he equates gain per dollar
for inherited and external real assets.

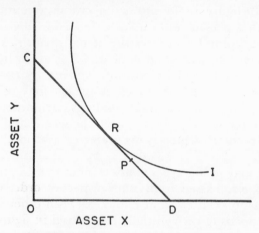

Fig. 1. Choice between two classes of inherited real assets.

A person, having arrived at the best combination of real assets
he wishes to hold, may or may not be content with his money
holdings. He may wish to part with cash to acquire more real
assets or to acquire cash by selling part of his asset holdings. His
preferences in this case are shown by figure 3. The horizontal axis
measures composite units of real assets, and the vertical axis measures money. The slope of *GH* is given by the assumed price of a
composite unit of his real asset holdings. *Q* is the combination of
real assets represented by point *Q* in figure 2, and the quantity of
cash inherited from the past is assumed to be the amount represented by *OL* (fig. 3). Whether a person will rearrange his asset
position by releasing cash or absorbing cash in exchange for other
assets cannot of course be determined a priori. The case in which
a person prefers to hold more cash is illustrated by the position of

indifference curve I_1 and the preference for less cash by I_2 (fig. 3). In a world without securities, the desire to hold some cash rather than all real assets corresponds to the idea of liquidity preference.

Thus a person inheriting a certain asset combination from the past may or may not wish to continue to hold that asset combination. The alteration in his asset holding depends upon his choices among assets, in a setting of known prices for the assets he owns and those he might care to acquire. These choices may be ration-

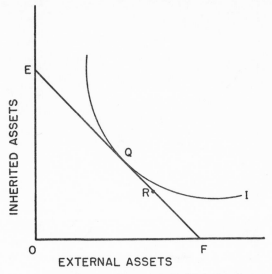

Fig. 2. Choice between external and inherited real assets.

alized, and typically have been rationalized in economic thinking, by the employment of the concept of rate of return. A person is viewed as attaching future "gain" to an asset holding thought of as "net income," and the ratio of this net income to the price of the asset is the rate of net return on the asset. Accordingly, a person buys or sells assets so as to equalize the marginal rate of return on each type of asset holding and thereby maximizes the total net gain to be obtained from an asset combination. This method of statement is avoided here, not because it is believed to be necessarily wrong, but mainly because it involves the employment of the assumption of perfect foresight or the identification of possible gains or losses with some unique or certainty-equivalent amount of future net gain, and we do not wish to make these special assumptions.

A minimum theory of asset holding may be constructed merely by supposing that people do like certain types of assets, perhaps for reasons best known to themselves. Unless they wish to hold only one kind, they have a problem of choice. These choices among types of assets may be interpreted in terms of indifference maps. Thus our statement is a type of minimum theoretical proposition to which more precision may be added if investors' actions may properly be interpreted in terms of rates of net return.

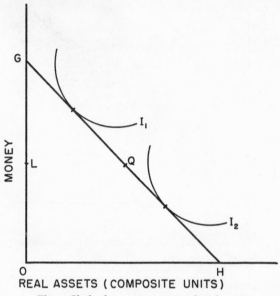

Fig. 3. Choice between money and real assets.

People do not of course live by admiring their assets alone. It is well known that people, with few exceptions, do consume, and therefore the previous comments must be modified to take this important fact into consideration.

We now propose the following theory of consumption expenditures: *The amount of a person's consumption expenditures depends upon the value of his asset holding, including cash. The greater his asset holding, the more he spends on consumption but the smaller is the proportion of these expenditures to his asset holding.* This is our substitute for the "psychological law" as proposed by Keynes. This hypothesis is offered as a statistical generalization in the sense of applying to groups on the average, or to "typical" persons, rather than to every person. The proposition rests on the necessary fact that a person cannot spend for consumption amounts greater than the capital value of his asset position plus his cash holding. Therefore the less wealthy he is, the less he can spend for consumption ends. But the maneuverability which persons have in this regard is large when consumption is viewed for a very short period of time. A few desperate individuals may exhaust their asset position; any general attempt to consume on such a scale would occasion a breakdown of organized economic relations. A more specific theory must therefore look to empirical

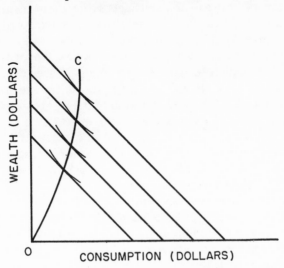

Fig. 4. Relation of wealth to consumption.

evidence regarding behavior. Observation suggests that rich people spend more than poor people. It also suggests, however, that the rich consume less in relation to their wealth position than do the poor. Although data on wealth distributed according to persons is even less satisfactory than similar data on income, empirical findings in this area appear consistent with the suggested hypothesis.[3]

The generalization that a person's consumption depends upon his wealth position, increasing with wealth but by amounts less than the increase, is graphically represented by *OC* (fig. 4). At a zero wealth position, consumption is zero. As the amount of wealth increases, consumption is greater. At some high point, a person

---

[3] See, for example, "The 1953 Survey of Consumer Finances," *Federal Reserve Bulletin* (September, 1953), pp. 940–947.

may not increase his consumption at all. Thrifty persons would reach such a point earlier than profligates; in fact one measure of the thriftiness of persons is the habitual relation they maintain between wealth and consumption expenditures.

ASSETS AND SECURITIES

We may now apply and modify the proposed theory to situations where securities of various kinds are present. Securities or claims are institutional features of social organization. Securities permit the separation of control of real assets from their ownership. A person owning a claim, government securities excepted, owns a right to real assets considered at a point in time, and owns a part of the earnings of those assets considered as a flow over time. The money payments which recognize these rights in the form of interest, dividends, or royalties are, as shown above, transfer payments. These payments are the implementation of the rights which holders of claims possess to the underlying resources.

Securities perform important functions in complicated economic organizations. There is the well-known fact that resources can sometimes be made to yield more gain in business units too large to be owned outright by a few persons. Securities provide divisibility of ownership. They also provide more opportunity for catering to different tastes for prospects of gain (and loss) than would be possible in their absence. Bonds can be sold to conservatives and common stock to the less timid. In a world where everyone had the same tastes for securities, illustrated by the special assumption of "perfect foresight," meaning no conscious risk, there would be no reason to have the variety of corporate-stock shares and short-term and long-term debt contracts we now have.

In a social organization that permits the existence of securities, the constraint on a person's ability to finance the acquisition of real things is no longer limited to the value of his real assets and cash. Debt contracts allow the partial realization of the capital value of human earning power. Thus we need to amend the previous statement of the over-all constraints on a person's ability to finance consumption expenditures so as to include that part of his future earning power which he can induce others to capitalize in the form of debt contracts. The ability to borrow or, more generally, to sell securities also permits a person or a business organization to obtain cash without giving up control over real resources. A person can have control of a house although the mortgage company owns a good part of it. A corporation controls enormous aggregates of real assets while others own its securities.[4] Thus the constraint on a person must be redefined as the net value of the assets inherited from the past including securities when "net" is computed by deducting the present value of any claims held by others against the assets under his control, including himself, plus the amount of cash he can obtain by selling new securities.

What is the specific limit, if any, to the amount of cash obtainable in this fashion? This limit is the dollar valuation that others are willing to place on the assets under a person's control. It is, in other words, the net realizable present value of his inherited asset position, including himself, viewed as a resource. This sum is the absolute constraint on his ability to finance consumption expenditures. In selecting the asset combination a person wishes to hold, he needs to take account of his power to sell securities against his own earning power. A person who refuses to become indebted, when he might do so, makes a choice to do without other assets or consumption expenditures.

The principles previously laid down need not be modified except in detail when account is taken of securities. A part of a person's wealth position is the potential earning power of himself viewed as a resource. There are apt to be in many cases wide differences between the capital value which the person himself places on this prospect and that which a commercial lender places upon it. It is what others are willing to spend on his debt, not what the person in question thinks they should spend, that matters.[5]

There is a long tradition in economic thinking which teaches that the amount of cash realizable by a person or an organization is theoretically unlimited. This theory has developed implicitly as a by-product of attempts to explain "the" rate of interest under simplified conditions. The emergence of a unique rate of interest requires many conditions, one of which is that all securities be viewed as perfect substitutes. This assumption in turn is possible only if buyers and sellers project the same gain for each type of security. Only in this case are all securities homogeneous in the sense of being reducible to the common denominator of dollars of

---

[4] There are exceptions here especially in connection with so-called "nonprofit" organizations which often do manage assets to obtain gain, but the gain cannot be distributed to persons. In such cases, organizations become ultimate ownership units.

[5] The value of a person's debts to potential lenders may be based on any factor that "goes along" with the person including, for example, prospects of inheritance as well as expected personal earning power.

future net income. Once this assumption is made, it is an easy
next step to make the competitive assumption that each buyer or
seller assumes that he can buy or sell any amount of securities at
any particular interest rate—the "price" in question.[6] This competitive assumption gives the apparent result that in the absence
of uncertainty a person could sell any amount of securities at
"the" rate of interest. This simplification is, however, improper if
it is interpreted literally. It involves the implicit assumption that
the capital value of a person's or organization's position could be
indefinitely large if perfect markets for securities existed. Although
some students of this topic are prepared to qualify such generalizations by invoking the idea of "credit rationing"—a term which
seems to imply that perfect markets do not exist—this is an understatement of the actual limitations involved.

Even if potential lenders are very sure of the relevant facts, there
is an absolute limit to the amount of cash any person can obtain
from outsiders by selling securities. That such limits exist in fact
can scarcely be denied. Even with perfect markets, a potential
lender would lend only up to the amount which would divert all
the income from the assets under control of the borrower to himself. (Actually the limit, even aside from risk, is much lower than
this because society cannot tolerate the condition where a person
can mortgage himself completely to others.) Lenders do take account of the underlying earning power of a borrower's assets
through tests of credit worthiness. Such tests are not mere institutional details. A banker who intends to engage in banking and not
in making gifts cannot afford to ignore the future earning power
of the assets under the control of the borrower. The assumption so
commonly made that "the" interest rate or a pattern of rates
uniquely defines the willingness of lenders to buy securities, even
under competitive pricing conditions, is not merely a simplification; it is an erroneous theory. I suggest that this oversimplification
explains the limited success of the many attempts to solve the so-
called "interest problem."

---

[6] It appears to be misleading to regard an interest rate as a "price" of something—
loanable funds or whatever. The prices emerging in fact are the prices of securities—
present values. A rate of interest is then computable if certain assumptions are made
concerning the size of expected future net income. These assumptions involve certainty postulates and as such have serious limitations. In the case of a security of
uncertain yield, one may not validly speak of one rate of interest attached to it.
There are a number of possible rates of return definable only subjectively. This
observation applies even to many debt contracts. The presence of "risk" cannot be
ascertained merely by looking at the form of the security.

The maximum supply of securities exists when every real asset has been mortgaged to the hilt and when every new asset is born with a mortgage wrapped around it.[7] The demand for securities in this sense is given by the total value of all assets that can be mortgaged. In other words, this merely visualizes a world where the maximum degree of contractual transfers exists.

The maximum amount a person can spend is limited to the value of inherited real assets, his inherited cash, the value of claims which may be sold against his wealth and earning power minus the value of claims outstanding against him. This sets the limit to the actual amounts of real assets and of consumption items he can acquire from others. This over-all constraint together with the actual prices of the items he might wish to acquire provides the financial environment for the operation of a money-price system of rationing.

EXPENDITURE CONSTRAINTS ON A GROUP

The constraints on a community as a whole differ from those on a person. Prices are not given for the entire community; rather they are the results of the exercise of choice on the one hand and the physical facts—stocks of resources and their possibilities in production—on the other. Individual constraints cannot simply be generalized for a community as a whole. The first qualification necessary to the foregoing analysis when applied to a group concerns the capital value of wealth inherited from the past. The amount that a person can, for example, spend for consumption items depends upon the willingness of others to buy assets other than cash from him. But a general effort to liquidate assets results in lower prices of assets and therefore reduces the amount that anyone can spend for current output. The community's expenditures for things other than old assets is limited by the quantity of money found in its possession plus the amount of money the banking system is prepared to create, or minus the amount of money it is prepared to destroy. These factors determine the objective liquidity of asset holdings. Thus we arrive at the old-fashioned view that the quantity of money in the sense just defined establishes the upper limit to the community's rate of spending on current output.

The actual limit is, however, well below even this point except

---

[7] Again a sovereign government is an exception when dealing with its own members. Government securities, unlike private ones, need occasion no concern about the "quality" of the underlying assets because the government cannot go bankrupt in the narrow technical sense of not meeting its obligations in cash. There are limits to a government debt but this topic will not be pursued here.

when hyperinflation is in prospect. In a financial system where physical exchange of goods and services is not literally paid for in money at the precise moment of exchange, people's present cash holdings are in part earmarked to settle past obligations. This earmarking of cash to settle obligations incurred in the past is counterbalanced by the fact that some products may be obtained in the present without immediate parting with money.

There is the further limitation that a substantial part of the cash held at any date is committed to the financing of instrumental services, transfer payments including interest and dividends, interchange of inventories among business organizations, and other payments not directly germane to the taking of products. An advanced industrialized society will exhibit a monetary behavior different from a society in which each person is a firm in his own right. This is another way of saying that in a monetary economy, money has more work to do than merely financing current output; this additional work limits the capacity of persons and organizations to finance the taking of products.

The over-all objective constraint on the rate of a community's expenditure on current output may therefore be taken as the uncommitted quantity of money in the sense just discussed, plus or minus the change in the amount of money which the banking system is prepared to make. Although any particular person or organization may spend more money than is inherited from the past, the group as a whole cannot finance expenditures by selling assets or securities. The ability of some to obtain cash by parting with securities implies that others are willing to buy them. The specific demands for assets, old and new, for consumption, and for cash itself depend upon the quantity of money as defined above and upon the relative desires of people for various kinds of assets, consumption services, and cash. The specific prices for each type of output depend upon these demands in conjunction with the alternative costs of producing various commodities by employing the existing resources. Thus the categories to be explained are the prices of old assets, the prices and the quantities of both currently produced assets and consumption items, and the money gain of resource owners. The stocks which are given by the past consist of the varieties and quantities of real resources, including labor power, the stock of money, the "stock" of tastes, and the pattern of social habits or institutions. The stocks or potentials become the flows under the influence of human purpose and direction.

The desires of each person and organization for consumption items, new real assets, and cash together with resources and their production possibilities determine the actual prices and quantities produced. To reveal these interrelations, let us suppose that the prices of real assets are such that each person is content with his real asset holding. His choices are now holding cash, buying new real assets, and buying consumption items. For simplicity, consumption and investment may be viewed as composite commodities.

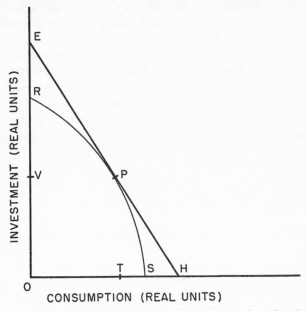

Fig. 5. Relation between investment and consumption in a closed system.

Existing resources can be used to produce consumption items or new real assets. The production possibilities for investment and consumption items ars represented by *RS* (fig. 5). Point *P* is taken to indicate the relative demand for consumption and new assets.[8] This point must satisfy two conditions: (1) the prices of consumption and real assets shown by the slope of the price-expenditure line, *EH*, must exclude any nonprice rationing of output; *P* may

---

[8] The point *P* might be established by the employment of a community indifference curve tangent to *RS* at *P*. The temptation to do so is resisted because of the doubtful meaning to be assigned to a community indifference curve in any connection and because, even if this objection could be overcome, it is not a legitimate device to depict relative demands by a group of people. *P* may be thought of as summarizing the relative demands for consumption and capital items and, in a more detailed analysis, as the outcome of the tastes and capital positions of each buyer in the group.

not be to the right of RS, (2) the prices of consumption items and real assets must exclude any nonprice limitation upon output; P may not be to the left of RS. The latter condition means that prices must be such that sellers can sell all the potential output of the system. This is the full-employment condition (EH must touch RS). Given the demands and the production alternatives of resources, the outputs of consumption and investment are OT and OV (fig. 5) at the prices shown by the slope of EH.

In a money-price system of rationing, prices and quantities of consumption and investment items depend, therefore, upon the quantity of money, banking and fiscal policies, and the relative desires of people for various kinds of consumption and investment items and for cash. The prices of old assets are a determinate rather than a determinant in this over-all view, as indeed are all prices. Given the quantity of cash, prices of new assets will be higher the greater the demand for them, unless the production possibilities curve should be linear. Thus the more some people prefer assets, the more others can spend for consumption purposes. A profligate is better advised to live in a community characterized by strong preferences for assets because this preference augments the value of the real assets he can dissipate and because the relatively lower level of consumption demands keeps down the prices of consumption items.

FUNCTIONS OF INCOME

The foregoing comments relate the flow, expenditures on output, to stocks, the inherited past. Nothing has yet been said about the functions of income, a main purpose of our inquiry. This omission has been deliberate in order to reveal, if possible, that people's expenditures do depend upon stocks. But our analysis has not proved that expenditures may not depend upon current income as well. Indeed, there have been several attempts to resolve controversies on this subject by a judicious combination of both stock and income theories of over-all demand for products.[9]

A main function of income in a money-price system is to offer people positive incentives for management of resources. People employ their resources including their own labor power to obtain

---

[9] The writings of Albert G. Hart illustrate this variety of eclecticism (see *Money, Debt, and Economic Activity* [New York: Prentice-Hall, 1953], pp. 167–263). His position is succinctly put: "When we allow for the effects of uncertainty . . . we find that both the 'propensity to consume' and the willingness to invest will be affected by the stock of cash even though interest is unaffected." (*Ibid.*, p. 192.)

gain in money terms. Allocation of resources to the production of various commodities occurs partly because of potential differences in prospective gains. Ideal allocation, from this point of view, occurs when resources of each homogeneous type are distributed in such a way that the marginal gain is equal in every actual method of use. Ideal allocation occurs only if money gain is the one relevant consideration to resource owners. If considerations other than gain in money terms, such as differences in working conditions, are relevant in selecting where to place resources, ideal allocation must be stated in the vaguer terms of "net advantages."

In practice, allocation of resources is based on the *hope* of gain. There can be, and in fact is, a difference between hope and achievement. Resources are often employed in ways which result in losses rather than gains. Although presumably no one would deliberately employ resources in such fashion, losses are real facts which should not be assumed away in a general theory.

A second function of income arises from the nature of income itself—namely, net gain over the period in money terms. The net gain of a person from the use of resources owned by him is the increase in the value of his assets when the value of consumption services taken is not deducted in computing net gain. Consumption in this context means final services—which is not to be identified with using up of stocks. Any final services taken by the person when the resource is owned by him should be imputed to him in a complete accounting. In a pure money-price system, all services would be priced separately, and only in this case may the income of a person be ascertained without some imputation. The concept of income here used is essentially identical with the usual interpretation of Simons' concept as the value of consumption plus the change in net worth over the period.[10] Income is the increase over

[10] See Henry C. Simons, *Personal Income Taxation* (University of Chicago Press, 1938), p. 50. The concept of income has many perplexing difficulties which will not be pursued here. The Simons approach differs substantially from the Marshall-Pigou approach to income as a "... flow of so much goods and services." A. C. Pigou, *A Study in Public Finance* (London: Macmillan, 1947), p. 77. This concept of real income, which is only one of many such definitions, is adopted by Pigou mainly because of the alleged superficiality of money income. But against this point of view, two considerations appear to be conclusive. (1) The Pigou definition permits no sensible way of distinguishing between what a person takes in the form of services and goods in a period and what a person obtains by management of resources. His money gain need not equal the value of goods and services he acquires. This is a basic fact and should not be obscured by a definition. (2) A collection of "stuff" per se has no economic significance unless it is tied to human interests, and in this event a valuation problem is inescapable. This difficulty is particularly evident when

the period in the net value of assets plus consumption when income is positive and the decrease in the net value of assets plus consumption when income is negative.

This view of income has been severely criticized as inappropriate for scientific analysis. It is sometimes claimed that such a definition of income gives an *ex post* concept and as such has no relevance to economic analysis. This criticism is explicitly made by Hicks[11] and is implicit in much of the *ex ante–ex post* approach. Despite the weight of opinion to the contrary, this type of criticism appears to be based on a confusion. A person may, for example, expect to eat lunch tomorrow, but this does not mean, as Hicks implies, that lunch must be defined as an *ex ante* concept to make it significant for conduct. Rather, to make such a statement meaningful, lunch must be defined apart from a person's expectations, or else we shall have him expecting an *ex ante* lunch. To state that a person expects to become wealthier next month is a meaningful proposition because "wealthier" can be defined independently of his expectation of enjoying that state. Becoming wealthier describes a change in a state of affairs which has happened and will happen again. Hicks' criticism that *ex post* concepts of income are irrelevant for conduct and only interesting for history cannot be supported in either semantics or logic.[12]

The total of all incomes in a society, aside from changes in asset valuations, is equal to and determined by expenditures upon current output. Given these expenditures, incomes in the aggregate

---

depreciation and obsolescence are under discussion. Pigou now holds that obsolescence occurs only when the equipment is discarded (Pigou, *Income* [London: Macmillan, 1946], p. 5). This wholly arbitrary procedure is justified on the grounds of convenience. Pigou's writings illustrate an extreme case of emphasis upon real magnitudes, a point of view which characterizes a large portion of English economic and legal thought. In this connection, see Lawrence H. Seltzer, *The Nature and Tax Treatment of Capital Gains and Losses* (New York: National Bureau of Economic Research, 1951), pp. 25–46.

[11] J. R. Hicks, *Value and Capital* (Oxford: Clarendon Press, 1939), p. 179.

[12] There may be something good to be said for the *ex ante–ex post* approach to economics, although I have not been able to discover what it is. Swedish economists, quite improperly in my view, believe it to be an improvement on Wicksell's analysis. The posing of plans versus results and calling equilibrium a situation in which people's plans are not disappointed adds up to nothing that can be called an explanation either of the plans or of the results. The basic behavior concept for economics, it seems to me, is the Marshallian concept of a *schedule* to which *ex ante* qualifications are redundant. A statement that a person will buy various quantities of a commodity at various prices is merely made ambiguous by adding plans. Plans are just plans until choices are made. A schedule is a series of "if-then" propositions of great explanatory power, showing how an actual outcome emerges from potentialities.

are then determined. They are the effects of expenditures in the sense that spending, a positive act of choice, values the quantities of goods and services made available during the period. Personal income, leaving income transfers aside, may be explained by the determinants of the magnitudes of each of the items constituting income: any increase in the value of old assets, the value of services and products sold, the value of any instrumental services purchased, and any depreciation in the value of old assets.

During any period, the process of generating income through expenditures will not, except by the most remote accident, leave the distribution of asset holdings unchanged. At the end of any period, however short, some people have spent more money than they have received and some have received more than they have spent. No mechanism exists to make these spendings and receivings balance for each person during the period, although by definition they always balance for a closed group. Consumption expenditures reduce asset holdings; income increases asset holdings. Hence some groups find their cash position larger and some find it smaller. The same observation applies to asset holdings other than cash. In the following period, people again decide to spend, and there is again another redistribution of assets, and so on indefinitely through time. In each period people spend cash which they own at the opening of that period and during each period people obtain cash through sales to others.

This point of view stands in marked contrast to one of the most common observations in economics, namely, that people spend their income. As a rough approximation, the statement is harmless enough, but when it is made a cornerstone of a general theory it creates confusion. Literally, a person does not spend income, cannot spend income, and never will spend income. It is impossible to spend a flow. The spending of money is a flow and the money spent comes out of a stock. A decision to spend is a decision to part with assets, and in order to part with assets a person must have assets in his possession. This point is fundamental to price, monetary, and fiscal theory, and indeed to all economics. Failure to pay close attention to the differences between stocks and flows has been the source of many erroneous doctrines.

The proposed theory of expenditures that treats cash holdings as a determinant of the rate of expenditures for a closed group is closely related to, and directly inspired by, the writings of Robertson. A few salient similarities may be noted. Robertson treats the

income of the present period as functionless in the present with
respect to present expenditures. This interpretation follows directly from his refusal to regard *saving,* defined as the difference
between simultaneous income and consumption, as something
which can be successfully determined by individual savers, and
from his employment of the alternative conception of *saving* as the
difference between past period income and present period consumption expenditures.[13] Robertson's scheme of thought is an important contribution to monetary theory of the stock-flow variety.
The great weakness of that approach, as set forth by Irving Fisher
for example, is the absence of an explanation of why people spend
the money they do. Choice is only casually examined. Reliance is
placed on the assumption that people normally spend money in a
constant proportion to their stock of money. Fisher did admit that
some people spend relatively more than others. During transition
periods, furthermore, the rigid relation between money and expenditures is relaxed.[14] The absence of any systematic theory of behavior toward money is a weakness of Fisher's work which Keynes
himself noted in his review and which Fisher acknowledged as an
important criticism in the preface to the second edition.[15] By contrast, Robertson's theoretical structure is specifically designed to
permit analysis in terms of individual choice. The concept of a
"day" is defined as the minimum time that can elapse (not the time
that does elapse) between the acquisition of cash assets (income
receipts) and the expenditure of those assets. This would be a ques-
tion-begging definition if in fact people could simultaneously
spend the particular dollars they receive during a moment. In such

[13] Robertson first introduced the concept of a "day" in a somewhat casual fashion
in the Appendix to chapter 5 of *Banking Policy and the Price Level* (London: P. S.
King & Son) in 1926. He extended it to a more general setting in his article, "Saving
and Hoarding" (*Economic Journal,* XLIII [September, 1933]: 399–413) and in several
later articles. Keynes' early criticisms of Robertson's distinctions were directed
toward the alleged arbitrariness of the "day" concept (see the discussion of Keynes,
Robertson, and Hawtrey in the December, 1933, issue of the *Economic Journal*). In
the *General Theory,* Keynes gives Robertson's views the questionable distinction of
being a "first approximation" to his own theory of causal analysis (John M. Keynes,
The General Theory of Employment Interest and Money [New York: Harcourt, Brace,
1936], p. 78). He later dismissed Robertson's technical criticisms by the observation,
"... both he [Robertson] and I differ more fundamentally from our predecessors
than his piety will allow." ("The General Theory of Employment," *Quarterly Journal
of Economics,* LI [February, 1937]: 210.) This attempt to include Robertson in the
"revolution" was a notable failure.

[14] Cf. Irving Fisher, *The Purchasing Power of Money* (New York: Macmillan, 1920),
pp. 55–73, 167–169.

[15] See J. M. Keynes' review of *The Purchasing Power of Money, Economic Journal,*
XXI (September, 1911): 395.

an event a "day" would be zero in length and therefore nonexistent. The positive nature of the "day" concept in this context is the
implication that the expenditures of a person cannot be financed
by his receipts at the same time, or, in other words, that one person's expenditures cannot simultaneously finance another person's
expenditures.

INCOME THEORY OF EXPENDITURES

The Keynesian concept of a propensity to consume and its accompanying concept, the multiplier—both different ways of stating the
same supposed relation—are a standing criticism of the Robertsonian view that current expenditures do not depend upon simultaneous income. It is also the basis for the denial of the view
adopted here that asset holdings determine expenditures. Criticisms of the income theory of expenditures as developed by Robertson, Haberler, Ellis, and others stress the point that a person cannot
decide the relation between his expenditures and other people's
expenditures for his services or goods. The Keynesian theory presupposes that people have more freedom of choice than is possible.
The issue is identical with the question of whether people can
"decide to save" or merely "attempt to save," a point with which
Keynes wrestled and decided to solve by dropping the expression
"propensity to save."[16] If he had taken the next logical step and also
dropped the propensity to consume, he might have reached a more
satisfactory solution.

The persuasiveness of the idea that a person's expenditures depend upon the size of his income should not be underrated. Among
laymen few economic ideas are as commonly held. Why some
people live in hovels and some in mansions is commonly attributed
to differences in income. Statistical studies often involve the same
premise. Income easily outranks all other measures of relative economic status. Budget studies take for granted that income is the
guiding factor in people's expenditures. It would be a great mistake to suppose that Keynes invented the idea that consumption
depends upon income. He took what he believed, apparently, to
be an intuitively obvious observation about people's behavior and

---

[16] Keynes, *The General Theory of Employment Interest and Money* (New York:
Harcourt, Brace, 1936), pp. 64–65. At this point Keynes asks himself the question of
what happens if people's decisions to save should be inconsistent with other poeple's
decisions to invest and points out that the result would be indeterminate. He solves
this dilemma for himself by an appeal to the fact that buying and selling does go on.
The monumental confusion of the next paragraph (p. 65) indicates that he is not
happy with this solution.

employed it as the cornerstone of a theory. The propensity to consume dresses up in technical language what has long been held as
merely common sense by laymen and economists alike, including
many of Keynes' strongest critics. Price analysis likewise has developed on the supposition that income determines demands for commodities. It is taken for granted that how much a person has to
spend is the amount of his income. The theory is held by people
who think of themselves as Keynesians as well as by those who do
not. Treatment of income as the objective constraint in the theory
of demand for products is settled orthodoxy.[17]

The answers to the criticism that current income cannot determine current consumption expenditures may be described as
follows:

(1) Income determines consumption, provided a period of *sufficient
     length* is chosen (Lerner-Hansen).
(2) The consumption function holds continuously in the "schedule"
     sense (Samuelson-Klein).
(3) The consumption function holds under conditions of short-run
     perfect foresight (Fellner).

Each of these offers a possible defense for the theory that some part
of expenditures depends upon the income generated by those expenditures. Of these, (1) seems to be most widely held and can be
made consistent with (3), whereas (2) is inconsistent with both.

(1) Lerner, in an effort to meet the criticisms of the Keynesian
system by Haberler and others, restricts the operation of the propensity to consume to "short-period equilibrium."[18] Hansen makes
essentially the same observation, maintaining that the "normal"
consumption function is approached through time, and citing
Keynes' authority for this view.[19] Both Lerner and Hansen come
close to saying that consumption is not a function of simultaneous

[17] Cf. Hicks, *op. cit.*, pp. 26–41; K. E. Boulding, *Economic Analysis* (New York:
Harper, 1941), pp. 648–655, 665–676; George Stigler, *The Theory of Price* (New York:
Macmillan, 1953), pp. 74–75, 78–80, 82–95. Marshall is vague about this point, sometimes referring to the limitation on a person's expenditures as income, general purchasing power, money, or resources. Cf. *Principles of Economics*, Book I, chapter
ii, section 2, and Book III, chapter iii (London: Macmillan, 1930).

[18] See Friedrich A. Lutz, "The Outcome of the Saving-Investment Discussion,"
Quarterly Journal of Economics, LII (August, 1938): 588–614; A. P. Lerner, "Saving
and Investment: Definitions, Assumptions, Objectives," *Quarterly Journal of Economics*, LIII (1938–1939): 611–619; and Gottfried Haberler, "Mr. Keynes Theory of the
'Multiplier,'" *Zeitschrift für Nationalökonomie*, VII (1936): 299–305. All three articles
are reprinted in *Readings in Business Cycle Theory* (Philadelphia: Blakiston, 1944).

[19] Cf. Alvin H. Hansen, *Monetary Theory and Fiscal Policy* (New York: McGraw-
Hill, 1949), pp. 220–224.

income in the present period—the view here adopted. But they hold that if a sufficiently long period of time is allowed to elapse, consumption does depend upon simultaneous income.

This type of restatement of Keynesian income theory is shown graphically in figure 6. Consumption expenditure in dollars is measured along the vertical axis and income in dollars is measured along the horizontal axis. On the latter we also measure net invest-

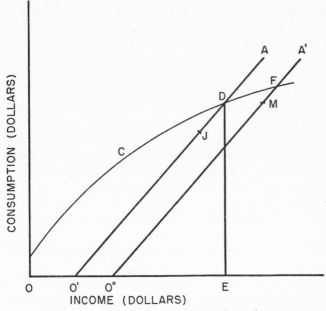

Fig. 6. Keynesian relation of consumption to income.

ment, treated as autonomous, by the distance OO'. The forty-five degree line $O'A$ states the necessary relation that if investment is zero, consumption expenditure equals income. Thus the line $OO'A$ is a geometrical representation of the equation $I + C = Y$.[20] Given the amount of investment, any actual solution must fall on this line since it expresses a necessary relation and is independent of any conceivable behavior. The line C is the Keynesian consumption function. The Keynesian solution in this case, with the amount of

[20] Government finance is left out of this representation, both because it is customary to do so in discussions of this sort and because no point of substance would be changed by including government expenditures and taxes. If government were included, government expenditures upon goods and services could be treated as autonomous, as is investment, and income relevant to consumption would be private personal income, that is, computed after deducting all taxes where persons are the legal taxpayers and not including all or some part of corporate undivided profits.

investment OO', is given by the point D with DE dollars of consumption expenditures and OE dollars of income. The aggregate multiplier $\dfrac{1}{1 - \dfrac{C}{y}}$ can be read off the graph as the number of times OE is greater than OO'. The solution as given by D is supposedly an equilibrium one in the sense that other solutions are possible, such as that indicated by point J. Neither Hansen, Lerner, nor Keynes would deny the possibility of such a result because no period has yet been specified to give people the necessary time to reach point D. But such is the magic of two intersecting lines in geometrical representations that such a solution seems almost axiomatic. It is customary in discussions of this sort to start at this point. Without conceding this procedure as admissible, let us start with D, and then suppose an increase in investment, namely $O'O''$ in the next period. We next ask: what will be the amount of consumption in that period? At this point non-Keynesians might want to know something about how the increased investment is financed before committing themselves to answering questions concerning the level of consumption. But in the Keynesian system this is irrelevant since the idea of financing investment does not even come into the picture.[21] To keep as close as possible to the spirit of the Keynesian system, we avoid this problem. The question can be stated in terms of how consumption gets from D, where it was in the period just past, to F—and how long it takes to get there. The Lerner-Hansen answer is that consumption stays unchanged, that is, at point M, at the moment of the increase in investment, and then moves up in an "orderly" fashion to F. For Lerner, point F is reached in a period labeled "short-period equilibrium" of undefined length. For Hansen, the point is reached when the "normal" consumption function has had time to exert its full tendencies—a period again of unspecified length.

Once it is admitted that income receivers require a period of time to adjust their spending habits to obtain the normal relation between income and consumption, the crucial question is: how long is the period? Strict logical consistency, within the Keynesian framework, requires that the period in question be of *infinite*

---

[21] Keynes comes close to saying that saving in his sense finances investment, which is really heretical to the spirit of the necessary equality between investment and saving (*op. cit.*, p. 187, n. 1, last line). To say that saving finances investment is equivalent to saying that the $1.50 my barber receives for giving me a haircut finances my payment of $1.50 to him.

length. This conclusion follows because the additional dollars obtained from the additional investment flow to certain groups as income, and some finite period is required for them to adjust to the new level of income. When they do adjust, it takes some time for the next group to adjust, and so on. Since it is assumed that each group spends a part of the increased income after a lag, there is a continuously diminishing series of incomes stretched throughout all time following the additional investment. According to this interpretation, the "equilibrium period" would arrive after we are all dead.

There is the further difficulty that investment must remain unchanged while all this supposed adjustment is going on. If, as is the case, investment varies from day to day, and if the hypothesis could be admitted that people tend to adjust their consumption in the direction of point F, they are continuously interrupted by finding their incomes changing because of fluctuations in investment. The most that should be said is that some tendency exists for people to adjust their consumption expenditures in the direction of point F, but they never actually do, because investment is not constant for a long enough period. Even this is an overstatement.

The basic difficulty with the consumption-function idea is the erroneous supposition that somehow or other event B, which is the result of event A, can nevertheless be contemporaneous with A. This premise creates the magical aura surrounding the "logical multiplier." It is an inherent contradiction which no appeal to evidence or reasoning can correct. *By the principle of contemporaneous independence, two contemporaneous events are causally independent of one another.*[22] Event A is an act of investment. Now there is no gap in time between an act of investment and the receiving of income by those providing investment items because these are by definition two ways of looking at the same activity. Event B is the act of consumption associated with the income from Event A. But Event A is viewed in the Keynesian system as a cause of Event B. One may test this proposition by attempting to explain the multiplier by starting with consumption instead of with investment.

The consumption function requires that some income be created in the present period which primes the system, so that people can decide how much to consume and how much to save. When investment is zero—a pure consumption economy—the system can-

[22] Cf. Alfred N. Whitehead, *Process and Reality* (Cambridge, England: Macmillan, 1930), pp. 95–96.

not conceivably get started. Everyone must wait around until some person decides to consume without regard to his income. But no one has any current income to guide him in his consumption decisions. If people strictly guided their conduct in the way the theory says they would, no one would commit himself concerning how much he is to spend for consumption since others must first commit themselves to provide him with income. Like a group of bathers at a cold mountain lake, everyone is poised for the dive but no one will take the plunge until someone else does. If the theory is that some group of bathers by taking the plunge induces other bathers to do likewise, one cannot also have it that all dive in simultaneously.

The facts are that consumption and investment expenditures go on simultaneously. Some investment is occurring right now and some consumption is occurring right now. They are mutually determined by factors in their past. Particular schedules of the demand for consumption items are interrelated with particular schedules of the demand for investment items. This type of interrelation or mutual causation concerns hypothetical possibilities, such as a person's decision that he will buy so many shares of General Motors stock if the price is $50 a share and if the price of housing service is no more than $75 a month. But we may not adopt the proposition that the money spent for rent can simultaneously finance the purchase of shares of General Motors stock.

Whitehead's principle of contemporaneous independence may not be violated in any sensible view of social or physical relations. Theories involving causal propositions must respect the principle that if A causes B, A must be in the past of B. The consumption function violates this principle. The same basic point has been stated correctly by Lerner in his attempt to prove that investment equals saving. He writes:

It is impossible for all income receipts "to be passed on" during any period, for the act of passing income on by one person is the act of receiving income by the other person, and whenever the gong goes to mark the end of our period, there must always be someone left with unspent income.[23]

This observation refutes his own contention in another context that some equilibrium period exists when everyone has adjusted.

(2) In contrast to the Hansen-Lerner interpretation of the con-

---

[23] A. P. Lerner, "Saving Equals Investment," *Quarterly Journal of Economics*, LII (February, 1938): 306.

sumption function, Samuelson and Klein have proposed that the consumption function and the saving function should be viewed as schedules.[24] Unlike other adherents to the Keynesian position, Samuelson and Klein claim that investment and saving defined in the simultaneous sense are necessarily equal only as observables but that they are not equal as schedules. In other words, there are hypothetical possibilities that the amounts that people are prepared to save are not equal to the amounts that other people are prepared to invest. This interpretation relies on the analogy to demand and supply schedules in the ordinary sense. At any actual price the quantities purchased equal the quantities sold. At unobserved prices these quantities are unequal. Samuelson and Klein rest their case upon the validity of this type of analogy. The relevant question is whether or not they are analogous.

Figure 7 portrays a saving schedule as visualized by Klein. Simultaneous income is measured along the horizontal axis; investment and saving are measured along the vertical axis. The equilibrium point Q supposedly illustrates the mutual determination of income from the given amount of investment OI and the propensity to save EF. In figure 8, ordinary competitive demand and supply schedules for a particular commodity are shown. The question at stake is whether the line EF (fig. 7) is a schedule in the same sense that DD' (fig. 8) is a schedule. Consider the point R on DD', the demand schedule for a commodity. Its meaning is that at the price RS people will actually buy OS. Suppose that by government decree the actual price is set at RS. Buyers wish to buy OS, and sellers wish to sell OT. However, these desires are incompatible; only the amount OS will be sold. Sellers of the commodity will be required to retain or not produce the quantity ST. Sellers are rationed out of the market by the overpricing of the item.

According to the Samuelson-Klein argument, point U in figure 7 can be viewed as analogous to point R in figure 8—but let us see if this is the case. Suppose that the government were to decree that people were not to save more than the amount UV (fig. 7) paralleling the assumption previously made of a decreed price for a commodity. We shall have to assume that people try to coöperate. At the same time, investment is assumed to be the amount OI. Would

---

[24] Samuelson's position on the point under discussion is briefly set forth in his paper, "The Simple Mathematics of Income Determination," *Income, Employment and Public Policy,* Essays in Honor of Alvin H. Hansen (New York: W. W. Norton, 1948), pp. 135–136. Klein provides a more elaborate discussion of the same idea in *The Keynesian Revolution* (New York: Macmillan, 1947), pp. 76, 91–93, 110–113.

110

Theory of Fiscal Economics

there be a result equivalent to that found in the case of overpricing of a commodity? The government decree regarding the amount to be saved could not conceivably be enforced if the amount of investment is *OI*. However hard people might try to save less than *QY*, they could not succeed. The amount of saving *QY* is inevitable because saving is defined to equal investment. This equality must hold regardless of any actual behavior. Unlike the point *R* on the demand schedule *DD'* (fig. 8), the point *U* does not indicate the

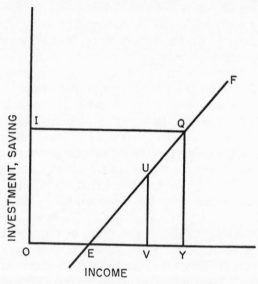

Fig. 7. Schedule concept of simultaneous saving.

amount that people would save independent of the amount that investors would invest. There can be no point, even hypothetically, at which investment is unequal to saving in the Keynesian sense.

A schedule concept is a series of "if-then" propositions, stating that if one condition is given a person or group will act in a certain way. Such a series of propositions may or may not accord with the evidence, and any schedule is subject to this test. In addition, a relation can be stated in the form of a schedule only when the "if" part of the proposition refers to something that could be ascertained by the behaving subject. A demand schedule passes this test because a price can be given to a particular buyer. When saving is defined in the simultaneous sense, a saving schedule cannot pass this test. As in the equilibrium-period interpretation, Samuelson and Klein assume that one event can cause another when both are supposed to be contemporaneous. Therefore their attempt to convert the concept of the propensity to save (or to consume) into a schedule relation must be a failure.[25]

(3) A further interpretation of the propensity-to-consume concept as a valid behavior proposition is provided by Fellner. His interpretation requires that people be regarded as having perfect foresight for short periods.[26] If people are assumed to know their income in the present period, they can make their consumption

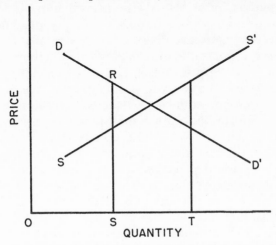

Fig. 8. Demand and supply schedules of a single commodity.

expenditures some fraction of this income.[27] This interpretation raises the question of the legitimacy of the use of perfect foresight assumptions in economic analysis. Fellner regards this procedure as proper, as evidenced by his extensive use of the propensity-to-consume concept in his analysis of business fluctuations.

We know that people do not possess perfect foresight, yet the

[25] If the Samuelson-Klein analogy were valid, there would not be any occasion for speaking as Hansen does of a "normal" relation between consumption and income achievable gradually through time; the relation could hold at each moment of time. The Hansen and Klein interpretations are contradictory. Hansen treats saving as identical with investment. The same graphical propositions are labeled both *I* and *S*, whereas Klein treats saving as opposed to investment in the sense that a demand schedule is opposed to a supply schedule.

[26] William Fellner, *Monetary Policies and Full Employment* (Berkeley: University of California Press, 1946), pp. 9–32. Fellner, it should be noted, is highly critical of Keynes' interest theory.

[27] Keynes explicitly assumes perfect foresight in this connection on a number of occasions (*op cit.*, pp. 122–125).

assumption has often been used in economics. Its legitimacy depends in part upon whether the assumption can be employed without internal contradiction. According to this test, the assumption does not appear permissible. Perfect foresight for one person with regard to income might be conceivable if the expenditures of all other persons can be assumed as given. In this event, a person can decide the relation between his income and his expenditures. But if the expenditures of others are not given, that is, if they are allowed freedom of choice to determine the amount of their expenditures, perfect foresight—which means definite knowledge of the size of his own income—is impossible for anyone. The assumption that everyone can have definite knowledge of the size of his income inherently contradicts the theory which Fellner adopts that expenditures must depend in each case upon income.

Fellner recognizes the fact that people do not have perfect foresight. In place of expected income, assumed to be equal to realized income, he substitutes the a priori most probable expected income to meet this difficulty.[28] Any connection between actual income and actual expenditure is indeed remote in this interpretation. To say that consumption depends on some a priori value of expected income is not the theory that Keynes suggested in the idea of the propensity to consume. Keynes holds that consumption depends upon current actual income.

Nevertheless, in his analysis of actual events, Fellner employs the consumption function in the Keynesian sense. The defense of this practice rests upon a belief in the usefulness of "equilibrium" analysis, and the consumption function in the Keynesian sense is regarded as equilibrium analysis. Each person is presumably in equilibrium when in fact he makes his consumption an amount which stands in the desired relation to what his income actually turns out to be. The equality of investment and saving, as defined by Robertson, is not used on the ground that such a relation is not a condition of equilibrium.[29]

The correspondence of expectations, including expected income, to realized magnitudes may be defined as equilibrium, although it may be difficult to tell what significance should be attached to

[28] *Ibid.,* p. 12. The reduction of many possible outcomes to a unique outcome by probability analysis might also be questioned.

[29] *Ibid.,* p. 9. This rejection appears correct. Robertson's equality between saving and investment is the condition of stability in expenditures over time—not equilibrium in the sense ordinarily employed in price and allocation theory. But this is not an objection to their pertinence in explaining change over time.

such a definition. Equilibrium theory in economics has developed along with the idea of mutual determination as incorporated in the concept of schedules. In this sense, equilibrium means outcomes which are consistent with some defined set of "if-then" relations. This concept does not require the assumption that what people expect to happen does actually happen. If one insists on using the term equilibrium to mean correspondence between expectations and results, that is, perfect foresight, the only changes over time which thereby are ruled out are unexpected changes. Such a concept of equilibrium is consistent with any conceivable fluctuations in expenditures over time. For the analysis of historical change, equilibrium defined in this way has little apparent application. What is even more serious is the implied theory that expenditures can be any amount that a person desires so long as he is sufficiently optimistic about his future income. There are no anchors to behavior; what happens depends only upon mental states.

None of the interpretations of the propensity-to-consume concept succeed in overcoming the basic difficulty that expenditures cannot depend upon the income to which they give rise because such a theory involves the impossible condition that contemporaneous events can cause one another. The Lerner-Hansen interpretation has a certain plausibility, but at the expense of undermining the basic idea. The Samuelson-Klein interpretation, in attempting to establish the idea of a consumption function holding good for any period, implies that saving does not equal investment when in fact they must always be equal. The Fellner interpretation becomes either a statement of an *ex ante–ex post* theory of consumption expenditures or, if viewed as meaning that expected income is always realized, impales itself on the logical self-contradictions inherent in assumptions of perfect foresight in this area.

The examination of areas of economic thinking which have employed income as an objective constraint has not suggested any need to qualify the theory that the value of assets inherited from the past is the constraint on the expenditures of a person and that the quantity of cash is the constraint on a closed group. An eclectic theory which employs both income and assets to determine consumption does not provide a proper answer.

SIMULTANEOUS SAVING AND TAXES

Saving has been defined in different ways for purposes of economic analysis. The implications of the simultaneous or Keynesian concept and the Robertsonian concept will now be examined with reference to fiscal activities.[30] Such an analysis will provide also an appraisal of the effects of taxes and subsidies upon private expenditures. Let us first consider the simultaneous concept of saving. In this sense saving means the difference between a person's income and the value of his consumption in the same period. For an economy as a whole, saving means the difference between aggregate income and consumption. The concept of consumption must, however, be amended when explicit account is taken of government activities. In the basic aggregate equation

$$E_g + I + C = Y_g + Y_P$$

E_g is defined as the value of current output and services taken by government, I is private net investment, C is private consumption expenditures, Y_g is government net income, and Y_P is private net income. E_g might be divided into the portion which is government investment and the portion which is not. To avoid unnecessary complications, this refinement is neglected. All government expenditures for current output are treated as if they were final.

Total saving by government and private groups together is therefore given by the equation

$$S = Y - (E_g + C)$$

It follows that total saving S necessarily equals private net investment I for a closed system. The following propositions emerge from these definitions.

(1) *The amount of saving for the entire community including government is independent of the size of tax yields.* This proposition follows from the fact that taxes are transfer incomes. The greater the yield of taxes, the greater is government income and the smaller is private income. A government decision to increase its tax yields is a decision to reduce private money incomes. The necessary equality of investment and saving implies in this context that any redistribution of income by tax measures or any other measures must leave the equality undisturbed. Taxes do not reduce aggregate saving.

(2) *Saving for the entire community including government is independent of the kind of tax devices (or subsidies) employed.* Since saving is unaffected by the amount of taxes (or subsidies), it

---

[30] The implications of the *ex ante* definition of saving will not be explored. Planned saving, being purely subjective as well as somewhat vague, does not lend itself to analysis.

must likewise be unaffected by the kinds of taxes or subsidies found. Again this is merely a reiteration of the necessary equality between investment and saving in a closed system.

(3) *Private saving is always decreased one dollar by an increase in taxes of one dollar, and private saving is always increased one dollar by a subsidy of one dollar.* This proposition follows from the equation

$$S = S_p + S_g$$

Since S is unaffected by the amount of taxes or subsidies, it follows that any dollar of taxes decreases private saving S_p by one dollar and increases government saving S_g by one dollar.

(4) *The amount of private saving is independent of the kinds of taxes or subsidies employed if net government revenue is held constant.* This proposition is of considerable significance because it is often implicitly denied in studies of this topic. The proposition follows from the same line of thought used in (3) above; some illustrations may help to clarify it. Consider for example a sales tax as compared with an estate tax of the same yield. Common sense might suggest that an estate tax should reduce private saving more than a sales tax. The argument is familiar. Sales taxes are regarded as falling upon lower income groups. They force these people to restrict their consumption expenditures. Estate taxes reduce the amount of wealth going to successors. Successors are believed to economize more on investment expenditures than on consumption expenditures because they are among the wealthier members of the community. It has even been supposed that an estate tax might eventually result in socialism because of the large amount of assets the government would acquire in this fashion. Such reasoning is not valid if private saving is defined in the simultaneous sense. Private saving equals private investment minus government saving. With any given amount of investment, total saving is given. Since the yield of the two taxes is taken as identical, government income is likewise identical in the two cases. Therefore the only difference which patterns of taxation directly make in private saving is to select who does the saving. Likewise, it is not true that a progressive income tax reduces private saving more than a proportional income tax of the same yield. Both must have precisely the same effect on the aggregate of private saving. If these results seem strange, the strangeness is attributable to the definition of saving. Observations concerning the effect of different types of taxes on private saving were made before economists became self-

conscious about the meaning of saving.[31] These observations have
been erroneously applied to a definition to which they are not
appropriate.[32]

The above propositions concerning the relation between taxes
and saving do not depend on any theory one may adopt with regard to people's behavior. They follow whether one is Keynesian
in sympathy or a strict quantity theorist. They have to do only
with the implications of definitions. If one chooses to define terms
in a certain way, it is necessary to live with the implications of
those definitions.

The objection may be offered, however, that the above propositions assume that people's consumption behavior is independent
of their incomes in contradistinction to the Keynesian premise that
consumption depends upon income. But this is not the case; if
the Keynesian premise is adopted, the propositions nevertheless
follow. No matter how much any particular tax or set of taxes is
believed to reduce consumption expenditures, aggregate income
must be reduced by the same amount. The equality of investment
and saving holds regardless of the absolute size of consumption
expenditures. Saving is the excess of income over consumption
looked at from the point of view of income recipients, and investment is the excess of income over consumption looked at from the
point of view of takers of products. The Keynesian system of
thought implies that taxes or subsidies result in a different relation
between consumption and income, but the system cannot validly
imply any proposition that denies the equality of investment and
saving. The above generalizations are merely different ways of
saying that investment necessarily equals saving in a closed system.
They are important only in guarding against self-contradiction.

ROBERTSONIAN SAVING AND TAXES

The Robertsonian concept of saving gives very different results.
To avoid confusion, we shall use the labels "lacking" or "thrifting"
to differentiate his concept from the simultaneous definition. Lacking in his sense means the difference between a person's consumption expenditures in the present period, 1, and his income in the
past period, 0. For a system as a whole, including government,
aggregate lacking (L) may be defined as

[31] Cf. Pigou, *A Study in Public Finance* (London: Macmillan, 1947) p. 59.
[32] Richard A. Musgrave and Mary S. Painter, "The Impact of Alternative Tax
Structures on Personal Consumption and Saving," *Quarterly Journal of Economics*,
LXII (August, 1948): 475–499.

$$L_1 = Y_0 - (C_1 + E_{g1})$$

where the numerical subscripts indicate the periods. We have the further definitional relation of *private* lacking (L_P)

$$L_{p1} = Y_{p0} - C_1$$

and of *government* lacking as (L_g)

$$L_{g1} = Y_{g0} - E_{g1}$$

Unlike the simultaneous definition of saving, lacking or thrifting defines a relationship which people can individually decide to make whatever amount they see fit. A person's income in the immediate past is given to him in the present. The assets resulting from that income are a part of his total asset holding as of the opening of the present period. Depending upon his choices with regard to consumption expenditures, a person or an organization can therefore engage in thrifting or its negative as he chooses. The same observation applies to government. The net revenue of government in the past period is incorporated in its present net asset position either in the form of cash or in the form of a decrease in its net outstanding debt position.

The greater the thrifting of private individuals, the lower must be their consumption expenditures. To say that a person consumes less means that he thrifts or lacks more. With the use of this concept, a number of general observations are possible about how tax yields and subsidy payments affect expenditure behavior over time.

(1) *The greater the size of tax yields in the past period, the smaller will be private consumption and investment expenditures in the present period.* Past taxes, by reducing people's present asset holdings, will *presumably* cause them to spend less for products in the present period. We have previously suggested that the expenditures of a person are objectively determined by the total value of his asset position inherited from the past. The greater last period's taxes, the smaller was his last period's income after taxes and hence the smaller his present asset position. For private groups as a whole, past taxes reduce their present cash holdings by the amount of the yield and therefore reduce their present expenditure power by the same amount. The generalization is a theory of behavior, not a necessary relation. People may, for example, choose to dishoard, if they can, in amounts which offset the decrease in their aggregate spending power occasioned by taxes. If we compare a tax yield in the immediate past of $10,000,000,000 with an alternative past

yield of $15,000,000,000, present private expenditures need not be smaller because of the higher tax yield. People may choose to dishoard by drawing upon their idle balances to pay the full amount of the extra $5,000,000,000 of tax liability and continue to spend at the same rate as they would have if taxes had been $10,000,000,000.

There is an important further qualification. Higher tax yields in the immediate past may also be offset by money creation by the banking system. With a sufficiently lenient monetary policy, taxpayers may borrow amounts equal to their increased tax liabilities and hand over to the government the new cash thus created. In this event higher taxes and lower interest rates may have a deflationary effect only to the extent that the increased assets held by banks reduce their potential lending power. If the central bank is prepared to offset the reduction in excess reserves, even this qualification is unnecessary. In practice, comparatively higher tax collections will reduce private expenditures by some amount. In a society where idle balances are virtually zero and a neutral banking policy is pursued, people will be forced to reduce their expenditures by the full amount of the increased tax collections.

Likewise if people insist on holding the same absolute sum of idle balances and the banking system pursues a neutral policy, private expenditures will be reduced dollar for dollar of tax liability. According to the principles of marginal analysis, people, confronted by higher tax obligations, may be expected to decrease both their holdings of idle balances and their expenditures for current output. There is no way of ascertaining on theoretical grounds alone what the actual reductions in private expenditures will be in any particular case. We need empirical evidence obtained by an examination of the behavior patterns of those people whose incomes are decreased because of the taxes employed. Theory provides guides for empirical observation, but it cannot be a substitute for evidence.

(2) *When saving is defined in the Robertsonian sense of thrifting, the common-sense observations about the relation between taxes and saving mentioned above regain their validity.* In the illustration of a sales tax and an estate tax of equivalent yield, an estate tax does reduce thrifting more than does a sales tax. Anticipating our analysis of the shifting of a cigarette tax, we may suppose that such a tax will reduce money incomes of a certain group in the community approximately proportionally. A part of this group consists of people with low incomes. They will be forced to curtail

their consumption expenditures in some cases and will choose to do so in others. An estate tax reduces the assets acquired by successors. Since they are often among the wealthier members of the society and the gain to them is a windfall on top of their regular income, their consumption expenditures will be affected slightly if at all. If a successor were to receive $150,000 in assets, he probably would not spend much more for consumption than he would if, after an estate tax, he received $120,000 instead. Thus a progressive estate tax can be expected to impinge on private thrifting more than will a sales tax.

It does not follow that total expenditures on output by private groups are smaller if an estate tax rather than a sales tax is employed. The liquidation of estates to meet tax liabilities may directly or indirectly reduce the amount of investment. This tax directly reduces the amount of investment so far as successors would have used the funds paid to the government to acquire new real assets. Because the groups involved are wealthy, and not because of the form of the tax, estate taxes tend to curtail investment expenditures. It does not follow that estate taxes should be regarded as inferior tax devices for this reason.

A progressive income tax reduces thrifting more than a proportional income tax of the same yield. The different distribution of income after taxes under the two types of taxes will induce the rich to curtail their consumption expenditures by small amounts, whereas middle and lower income groups will be forced to reduce their consumption expenditures substantially. Again it does not follow that the total demand for output is smaller under a progressive income tax than under a proportional one. Richer members of the society may economize on their investment expenditures. The total effect on expenditures may be positive or negative. Government measures leading to less inequality in income may be inflationary, but there is no inherent theoretical necessity that they should be.

THE "BURDEN" OF TAXES

If the monetary theory developed above is valid, we know that income in the present does not affect expenditures in the present. Taxes, viewed as present government revenue or income, are therefore also of no significance either to present private expenditures or to present government expenditures. This theory simplifies economic analysis. If correct, expenditures can be analyzed without having to be concerned with mutual causation between those expenditures and the income resulting from them.

The function of taxation viewed as a revenue device is therefore to reduce private money incomes and to increase government money income. The greater the yield of taxation, the smaller on this account is the ability of private groups to spend. Taxes are inevitably monetary devices; to the extent that they have a yield, they reduce private cash holdings. Taxes are monetary rather than "real" devices.

The concept of taxes as imposing a real burden is a myth which has plagued this subject from time immemorial. People may like to think that taxes "hurt" them; otherwise there would be no therapeutic value in the loud and bitter remarks about the tax load. But the idea that taxes must impose a real sacrifice and subsidies provide a real gain cannot be tolerated among those who like to keep their propaganda separate from their analysis.[33] If we regard the community as consisting of two parts, government and private groups, taxation does not make private groups "worse off" and subsidies do not make them "better off." In order to discuss this observation, we need to define such terms as "worse off," "better off," and "real burden" in connection with taxation. Investigators of welfare economics insist that such terms are dangerous because they imply ethical judgments which cannot be established on economic grounds alone. Without disagreeing with this position, we may nevertheless adopt the definition that a group is better off in situation A than in situation B if the quantity of "stuff," defined as output measured in constant dollars, in situation A is greater than in situation B regardless of what members of the group acquire it.[34] Distribution of stuff among members of the group is irrelevant in this definition. "Better off" means therefore more stuff and "worse off" means less stuff going to the group in question.[35]

---

[33] To pragmatists, such a statement must be meaningless since "truth" to them is in principle only definable with respect to purpose and purpose can be anything including deceit.

[34] Accurate measures of changes in output in different actual situations are not theoretically possible. The composition of output always changes somewhat. Such measures are so generally employed, even in theoretical work, that they may be used here also.

[35] This definition may seem cold-blooded; it is, however, an attempt to define what people mean when they speak of a change in a group's real income. No ethical implications should be drawn from our definition. On the contrary, an increase in real income in the above sense cannot be assumed to be ethically better unless it is assumed that "more" is per se better than "less." Hedonism has led to this conclusion because people are assumed to be happier if they acquire more output, and more

The quantity of stuff as defined depends upon the resources available to a community, apart from international considerations, and its efficiency in exploiting these resources. For private groups, the quantity of output depends in addition upon how much the government subtracts for its own purposes. What the government obtains depends directly upon government policy and, in a money-price system, upon the amounts which the government is prepared to spend for goods and services. With any given level of economic efficiency in resource utilization, the more the government takes, the less there is available for private use.

Taxes should not be viewed as equivalent to government expenditures. Rather, by reducing private money incomes, taxes reduce the spending power of private groups. If people spend less, the output available to them is not made smaller on this account; rather output can be rationed to them at lower prices than would otherwise be feasible. One function of taxation is to act as an anti-inflationary device. The alternative to taxation is more inflation or less deflation.

Taxes also redistribute money incomes among private groups. Taxes may increase or decrease the inequality of income distribution. They may be erratic in the sense of decreasing the incomes of some people in a given income group and leaving unchanged the incomes of others in that group.

Another function of taxation concerns incentives. Taxes must be tied to some base, and people may be induced to behave differently because of their relation to that base. In this aspect taxation is relevant to economic efficiency. A system of taxation can be imagined which could reduce an economy to chaos, such as an excess profits tax levied at marginal rates in excess of 100 per cent. Taxes can also be devised to induce people to be more efficient—

---

happiness is treated as better than less. This point of view ignores the distribution of happiness. In popular statements, the hedonistic ethic has been phrased as "the greatest good for the greatest number," but as Edgeworth points out, this attempt to include a distribution factor into the principle is not a success. "The popular, as compared with the exact, formula has only one disadvantage: that it is nonsense." (Francis Y. Edgeworth, *Papers Relating to Political Economy* [London: Macmillan, 1925] Vol. II, p. 155.) Yet the principle of greatest happiness could be used to justify predation if the predators are assumed to have a much greater capacity for happiness than those preyed upon. Such an ethical principle is subversive of democratic ideals. Respect for an individual as such, regardless of his capacity to add to the sum total of happiness, is a fundamental principle of democratic ethics. Therefore "better off" as defined in the text does not mean a better society although being better off in this special sense may be consistent with, and even necessary for, the achievement of a better society.

an observation at least as old as David Hume. The actual effects of taxes and subsidies depend on the kinds employed, people's attitudes, and the characteristics of the social order. Taxes and subsidies may be employed to reduce social waste. Or they can be a great deterrent to greater economic efficiency.

6

Excise Taxes and Subsidies:
Competitive Pricing

The doctrine that consumers can and do pay excise taxes has lived a long life; it is among the more ancient opinions held by both professional and lay groups about economic affairs. The theory has successfully survived revolutions which have torn other segments of economic thinking to tatters. So strongly is it entrenched that the few assaults made on it have been brushed aside, in fact scarcely noticed.

Yet the theory has highly vulnerable aspects of a rather obvious character. If excise taxes raise prices to consumers, what shall be done about monetary theories which hold that an increase in aggregate demand is a necessary condition for a rise in the general level of prices? Since in fact any tax which has a yield takes money out of private hands, a person unacquainted with accepted tax theories might conclude that such taxes, by reducing aggregate demand, should lower rather than raise prices. Yet we solemnly explain that excise taxes are deflationary because they raise prices, that is, because they are inflationary.[1] The absence of any satisfactory explanation as to why excise taxes reduce people's money expenditures has been a serious weakness in prevailing views.

The theory of excise taxation developed in this chapter is designed to provide an integrated theory applicable to any system of excise taxes, ranging from a tax on a single commodity at one extreme to a system of taxes levied on every commodity at a uniform ad valorem rate at the other. The theory differs in a number of respects from the usual explanations offered for the effects of excise taxes. The following are the main conclusions for the case of competitive pricing: (1) A system of completely general and

---

[1] Cf. E. Cary Brown, "Analysis of Consumption Taxes in Terms of the Theory of Income Determination," *American Economic Review*, XL (March, 1950): 74–89.

uniform taxes leaves the composition of output unchanged, does
not raise product prices, reduces the money incomes of resource
owners, and does so proportionately. (2) Any partial system of
excise taxes, including the case of a system restricted to a tax on
one commodity, alters the product-mix, raises the prices of heavily
taxed items, lowers the prices of lightly taxed and nontaxed items,
and reduces the money incomes of certain resource owners. Parallel
conclusions hold for partial excise subsidies. (3) All systems of
excise taxes are deflationary with respect to private demands for
products, not because they raise prices, but because they make
private money incomes lower than they would otherwise be.

H. G. Brown has demonstrated in a rigorous fashion that a general system of excises is not shifted to consumers, does not affect
the product-mix, but does reduce factor incomes.[2] For reasons not
easily discerned, Brown's argument has rarely even been thought
worth refuting.[3] Here, however, we are interested in constructing
a theory that can be applied to any system of excise taxes, including a system that happens to tax the output or sales of one commodity. The same theory is applied to excise subsidies.

ASSUMPTIONS AND CONCEPTS

The analysis is initially limited to an institutional setting of perfectly competitive pricing of all resource services, all products, all
real assets, and all claims. For present purposes, perfectly competitive pricing means that the actual prices are established so that the
market for each class of homogeneous items is continuously cleared
at a uniform price. Whether competitive prices are established by
government decree or automatically by atomistic economic organization is immaterial for our purposes. The application of the theory
to various types of monopolistic, oligopolistic, and arbitrary pricing
practices will be explored in the following chapter.

The main tools of our analysis are the two concepts, income
effects and price and reallocation effects of a tax or a set of
taxes. Income effect means literally the difference in a person's
money income occasioned by a tax. A tax is a transfer device which
reduces some people's money incomes as it increases the government's income. If any system of flat-sum taxes is levied on any

---

[2] Harry G. Brown, "The Incidence of a General Output or a General Sales Tax,"
Journal of Political Economy, XLVII (April, 1939): 254–262.

[3] John Due's studies are an exception. See, for example, his article, "A General
Sales Tax and the Level of Employment: A Reconsideration," *National Tax Journal*,
II (June, 1949): 123.

specified group, the income effect of the tax is the difference between the income of each person in the group considered before deducting and after deducting the tax. The concept relates literally to money income; its implications as to real income in any of the meanings of that term are left open.[4] Since the income effect of a tax is the private counterpart of the government's tax revenue, any tax which has a yield, by removing cash from private hands, leaves private groups with smaller balances in amounts just equal to the increase in the government's balance. Considered as a liability, any tax subtracts from a group's private money income what it adds to government revenue. Accordingly, a full reckoning of the source of the government's revenue from any set of taxes is possible without any unexplained shortages or leftovers. Whether this effect should be called "incidence" or not is to some extent a matter of taste, although, in view of the shortage of technical terms, a case could be made for this usage.

The concept of price and reallocation effects of a tax can best be defined by first recalling the concept of "announcement effects" developed by Pigou.[5] His announcement effects refer to any change which a tax makes in the alternatives confronting a person. Thus a lump-sum tax by definition has zero announcement effects because such a tax does not alter the "prices" on which alternatives may be chosen. By price and reallocation effects of a tax, we mean the change in the allocation of resources and any changes in the prices of resources and of products required by the new allocation that results from the announcement effects of the tax. Thus an income tax directly affects the cost of leisure and thus has an announcement effect in Pigou's sense. But if in fact a person cannot make a different choice between work and leisure, because of institutional arrangements or because he voluntarily offers the same

---

[4] The concept differs from Professor Hicks' concept by the same name employed in connection with his theory of consumer demand. (Cf. J. R. Hicks, *Value and Capital* [Oxford: Clarendon Press, 1939], pp. 27–38.) By "income effects," Hicks means the change in a consumer's financial means with given prices for products or the change in his financial means necessary to leave him on the same indifference schedule as the price of any commodity is varied. The identification of income with the financial means of consumers is, however, not generally valid. Expenditures can be financed from any current cash holding, however and whenever obtained, as explained in chapter 5. Hicks' concept might more properly be revised and described as the "expenditure-power effect" or some such neutral term, to avoid the implication that money income is necessarily identical with the objective limitation on consumer expenditures.

[5] Cf. A. C. Pigou, *A Study in Public Finance* (London: Macmillan, 1947), p. 55. Also see pp. 14–16 of this book.

amount of work as before, the announcement effect does not lead to a reallocation of resources or changes in product prices. It therefore has no price-reallocation effect.

Any tax or subsidy may thus be viewed as having two classes of possible effects: a negative or positive income effect and a price and reallocation effect. The reallocation effect arises from the fact that a tax or subsidy is nonneutral with respect to choices as to where or how to employ resources. These altered choices may change the composition of output available to the buying public and thereby occasion a different set of product prices to assure successful rationing of various products by price devices. The money income effect of a tax is the reduction in the money incomes of owners of resources, including human as well as nonhuman types, when the term "owners" is viewed as sufficiently broad to include those who obtain income by ownership of claims.

The income effect taken by itself has no direct product-price and resource-reallocation possibilities, when "direct" excludes the change in the financial position of various persons over time. A flat-sum tax cannot alter the terms on which alternatives are given to any person, but such a tax may change the relative pattern of money income distribution. Those lightly taxed gain at the expense of those heavily taxed, when "lightly" and "heavily" are measured with respect to the income distribution existing before deduction of the tax. In other words, the price and reallocation effects of a tax are to be viewed with respect to given tastes and to any given distribution of financial means among buyers, regardless of what factors, including taxation, may affect tastes or buying power over time.

GENERAL EXCISE TAXES

As a preliminary to the analysis of general excise taxation, let us first examine the standard economic argument used to reach the conclusion that excise taxes are shifted to consumers either completely or partly. It is as familiar as elementary price theory. An excise tax increases the marginal costs of each firm in the taxed industry. Sellers subject to competitive constraints are quantity but not price adjusters. They restrict output which, given the demand, simultaneously raises the price of the taxed item. Under "long-run" conditions, some firms move out altogether until a new equilibrium is reached, and eventually the money returns to factors in the taxed field become the same as those to competing resources in nontaxed fields. In an industry where unit costs are constant, the price is raised by the full amount of the tax; with declining unit costs, provided this case is thought possible, by more than the amount of the tax; and with increasing unit costs by less than the amount of the tax. The argument may be refined in any degree, but the basic conclusion remains—buyers pay a higher price because of the tax. This presumed consequence of the tax is interpreted to mean, and this is rarely an explicit step in the reasoning, that consumers of the taxed item "really pay" the tax in some meaningful sense whereas sellers are regarded as collecting the tax for the government from consumers.

Lay versions of the doctrine that consumers bear excise taxes usually rely on some "cost-plus" theory of pricing. A commodity tax is a cost, allegedly, and prices must cover costs. Hence, the higher an excise tax the higher is the price of the taxed item. Thus people are able to convince themselves that they pay a federal tax each time they buy a package of cigarettes.

Conventional economic theory of excise tax shifting reveals two basic points: (1) the output of the taxed item is reduced, and (2) the price of the taxed item is raised. These results go together. The price rises because the tax induces a restriction of output by those legally responsible for the tax liability.

Does the same type of argument hold for a completely general and uniform system of excise taxation? This case provides the logical extreme to a system of a single-commodity tax, and here we find the rather curious fact that there are few rigorous theoretical treatments of a general system of excise taxation in the literature. Many students have been disposed to generalize the conclusions reached for one commodity tax to any number. Yet it is easy to see that this procedure is not permissible. The twin facts established for a single-commodity tax—the reduction in output and increase in price—require assumptions which do not hold for a completely general system of excises.

In the case of a single-commodity tax, the adjustment process is visualized in terms of the initial reduction of income or profits of firms in the taxed field, the subsequent attempt to restore their position by curtailing output and possibly leaving the industry altogether, and the price increase following from these moves. A necessary condition for such adjustments is the presence of other fields where money returns are relatively more attractive. When all commodities are taxed, this condition is absent. There is no place for resources to go which is not subject to taxation. Thus, any particular seller of products or of resource services cannot escape his tax liability by entering tax-exempt fields. The shifting of excise taxes levied at uniform ad valorem rates on all commodities may not therefore be explained by generalizing the conclusions found when only one excise tax is under consideration.

A common method of reaching the conclusion that a system consisting of many excise taxes is shifted to buyers is by assumption. Sellers are assumed to increase prices by amounts corresponding to the increase in excise taxes.[6] Buyers are assumed to increase their money expenditures sufficiently to take the same output at the assumed higher price level.[7] But under competitive pricing conditions, it is impossible for sellers experimentally to charge higher prices merely because each is confronted with the legal requirement of an excise tax liability. Without this possibility, there are no apparent reasons for supposing that money demands rise.

This conclusion that a general system of excise taxes does not raise prices gives additional plausibility to the argument advanced

[6] Empirical studies of the distribution of tax burdens provide little aid in the solution of theoretical questions of tax shifting. These studies presuppose knowledge of the groups, identified by money income or other characteristics, who are forced to contribute to the government, and they can be no better than the theory of incidence on which they rest. This point is illustrated by the interesting and important recent empirical study of the distribution of tax burdens by Richard A. Musgrave, J. J. Carroll, L. D. Cook, and L. Frane, "Distribution of Tax Payments by Income Groups: A Case Study for 1948," *National Tax Journal*, IV (March, 1951): 1–53. The U-shaped pattern of tax burden they find is a direct consequence of assumptions that excises and parts of other taxes, including corporate net income, are shifted to consumers (*ibid.*, p. 38).

[7] This is a common assumption. A somewhat different and interesting line of reasoning is adopted by John Due in this connection (*op. cit.*, pp. 122–130). The basic steps in his reasoning are the following: (1) sellers arbitrarily raise prices by the amount of the tax, (2) consumers spend the same number of dollars and hence obtain less output, (3) as a consequence of (1) and (2), unemployment develops in the private sector of the economy, (4) the government steps into the breach and increases its expenditures by an amount sufficient to hire the released resources, (5) the banking system adopts a monetary policy to support the higher price level, (6) consumers, with some qualifications, pay the tax. The argument proves that on certain assumptions experiments by sellers of pushing up prices may succeed, or, in other words, if sellers have monopoly power and generally attempt to exercise it, they may increase their incomes before taxes when a coöperative monetary policy is assumed. But it would be a mistake to suppose that the shifting of excise taxes is being discussed. There is no explanation of who gives up how much money because of the tax. The selection of consumers as the ultimate taxpayers may appear plausible because it is assumed that the government takes a larger part of the output and hence reduces the real "take" of private groups. But on similar assumptions, it could be "proved" that a poll tax or indeed, any tax whatever, is shifted to consumers in the form of higher prices.

by H. G. Brown that excises are shifted from the taxed firms to owners of factors and not at all to consumers. His argument may be briefly restated. With any given set of resources and any given set of tastes, including the government's expenditure policies, and with any given initial distribution of financial means among private groups, a general and uniform system of excise taxes reduces the money earnings of each firm because the tax lowers the net prices of products sold by them. Each firm thus has an incentive to restrict output. This incentive means a proportional reduction in the demands for hired resources. Without the tax, the demand schedule of a firm for a resource service is a schedule of the values of its marginal product. With the tax, this demand schedule is the schedule of the net values of the marginal product of each type of hired resource when "net" means that the values are to be calculated from the actual price of the product as revealed by consumer payments minus the tax per unit of product. Thus a "wedge," to use Brown's term, is driven between actual price and producer's average and marginal costs equal to the amount of the tax per unit. With any given quantity of resources, the owners are forced to take a lower price for their use, and hence the money incomes of owners are proportionately reduced. Thus a person whose income is determined outside the price system, such as a government pensioner, is left in the same money and "real" position by a general system of excise taxes.[8]

According to the Brown theory, a general system of excise taxation leaves the composition of output and product prices absolutely and relatively unchanged as compared with a system of taxation of equal yield having zero announcement effects in Pigou's sense. Consequently, there can be no basis for the doctrine that consumers pay such taxes. Thus Brown has effectively exploded accepted theory if the latter is interpreted to hold that consumers do, in some sense, bear a completely general system of excise levies.

This explanation can be used to show the anti-inflationary effect of a general excise-tax system. In the interest of definiteness, we shall employ hypothetical figures for three periods, using the Robertsonian type of analysis. Let us suppose that at the outset the government's budget is underbalanced, since this state of affairs

---

[8] Frisch, in persuading Hotelling to abandon the equality condition for maximum welfare, comes close to H. G. Brown's conclusions. (Cf. Frisch, "The Dupuit Taxation Theorem," *Econometrica*, VII [April, 1939]: 145–150, and "A Further Note on the Dupuit Taxation Theorem," in the same issue, pp. 156–157.) The possible implications of welfare propositions for tax incidence were not under consideration in that controversy.

is typical of the times. Such a case avoids any implication that tax theory requires an assumption of a balanced budget. Congress decides, let us suppose, that the budget should be brought into balance, having been persuaded that a system of uniform excises of general coverage would help prevent price inflation.

THE MONETARY EFFECTS OF A GENERAL EXCISE TAX IN AN INFLATIONARY SETTING

Period 0

Consumption expenditures . . . 125 Private money income before
Private investment 25   tax 200
Government expenditures . . . . 50 Government income* 40
                                     Private money income after
                                        tax 160

Net value product. 200   Total income 200

Period 1

Consumption expenditures . . 134 Private money income before
Private investment 26   tax 210
Government expenditures . . . 50 Government income 50
                                     Private money income after
                                        tax 160

Net value product 210   Total income 210

Period 2

Consumption expenditures . . . 134 Private money income before
Private investment 26   tax 210
Government expenditures . . . . 50 Government income 50
                                     Private money income after
                                        tax 160

Net value product 210   Total income 210

* Government income is a net computation, government transfer payments to private groups being thought of as deducted from tax revenue.

In Period 0, the net value product is 200, employment is full, and hence any increase in expenditures occasions some price rises. The government's budget for this period is underbalanced by 10. At the opening of Period 1, a uniform excise tax is introduced applicable to all commodities currently produced. Prices rise in

Period 1 because private expenditures rise from 150 to 160, which in turn is a consequence of the underbalanced state of the budget in Period 0. The tax has no effect on the amount of private expenditures in Period 1. It necessarily takes time for the tax liability to come into being, and until it does there is no anti-inflationary effect from the tax. The deflationary effect of the tax reveals itself in Period 2 and in later periods. Instead of private expenditures on consumption and investment rising further in Period 2, as presumably they would have done in the absence of the higher tax yields in Period 1, the inflationary process is successfully brought to a halt.[9] In real terms, there is no change in the private take from the economy over the three periods, a conclusion which follows from the assumption that government expenditures remain unchanged and the supply of resources also remains constant.[10] This result follows independently of whether an additional tax is imposed or not. The tax keeps prices from rising as much as they would otherwise have risen, given the expenditure policy of the government. A similar conclusion would follow if another tax, such as an increase in the effective rates of the personal income tax, had been imposed instead of the general excise-tax levy of the same yield.[11]

In the inflationary illustration just employed, the added tax stops a price rise already in progress because of the initially underbalanced budget. If it were assumed that the government's budget was initially in balance in Period 0 and an additional excise tax yielding 10 in revenue was imposed at the opening of Period 1, aggregate private demands would fall in Period 2 because the tax would have reduced private money incomes in Period 1 below those of Period 0. In this case, the paradox that excise taxes lower rather than raise prices would be illustrated.

More generally, an additional tax, in this case a general and uniform system of excise levies, by reducing money incomes of private groups in the present period, *ceteris paribus*, reduces pri-

---

[9] The monetary theory used here is of course the stock-flow type as outlined in chapter 5.

[10] There are two qualifications to be made of this statement. Prices rise in Period 1 over those in Period 0, and with constant money expenditures the government would get somewhat reduced supplies. Hence private groups would slightly improve their real position in Period 1 over Period 0. In addition, there presumably would be some increase in potential output in each period because of the resources employed to produce more resources (investment) in the previous period.

[11] The treatment of one tax by conceptually varying the yield of another is discussed on pp. 141–142.

vate demands for products in future periods. Other factors such as increases in government expenditures, private dishoarding, or an expansionary banking policy may offset or more than offset this deflationary effect. During any period of time, the actual change in total expenditures and in prices may be in any direction. But excise taxes operate as deflationary influences for the same reasons as do income taxes; both act as negative influences on private demands for products as compared with less taxation. Thus we obtain an explicit reason for the deflationary effect of general excise levies.

A completely general system of excises, although it reduces the incomes of all owners of real resources, need not reduce the money incomes of every person in the society; it may apply only to those whose incomes are contractual residuals (e.g., business profits) or whose services are continuously priced. Holders of claims of various kinds, such as debt contracts, some types of stock, and pension rights, need take no immediate reduction in their incomes because of general excise taxation. Such persons are protected, for the period of their contracts, by custom or legislation from having to share in the reduction of private earnings, computed after tax, of owners of real resources. Debtors on the other hand must take a greater-than-proportionate reduction in their net incomes if all their gains computed before transfer payments arise from the employment of real resources. Their total gain before such transfers is reduced proportionately by excise levies whereas transfer payments made by them are left unchanged.

If the Brown theory is correct, as we believe it is, the theory that a single commodity tax is shifted to consumers becomes immediately suspect since the answer now depends upon the arbitrary choice of whether we think of a tax on a particular item without regard to taxes on other items or whether we view it as part of a general system of excise taxation. Theory cannot tolerate results that depend on such arbitrary choices concerning methods of investigation. Indeed, the final solution to be proposed requires abandoning the doctrine that even a single excise tax is shifted to consumers. We turn next to this more complex issue.

PARTIAL EXCISE TAXES

The following propositions are to be demonstrated. (1) A single excise tax or any partial system of excise taxes results in some reallocation of resources in favor of nontaxed fields. (2) The prices of taxed items rise and the prices of nontaxed items fall; the degree of absolute rise in the price of taxed items is smaller when the coverage of the excise tax system is larger. (3) Any system of excises, including one consisting of a single commodity tax, reduces money incomes of resource owners by an amount equal to the yield of the tax. Those whose incomes are reduced comprise the following groups: owners of resources located in the taxed field, owners of resources of the same physical (competitive) type located in other fields, and owners of resources producing products "complementary" on the demand side to the taxed item. (4) The deflationary effect of a partial system of excises arises from the income effect in a fashion similar to that found for a general system of excise taxation.

Consider first the simple case of an economy where only two commodities, X and Y, are produced and where all products and resources involved are perfectly divisible and all prices are set at competitive levels and all resources are fully employed. A tax is levied on X and not on Y. The question to be answered is what difference the tax makes in the prices of X and Y, the quantities produced of X and Y, and the money incomes of resources producing X and Y. Simple graphical representation may aid in making the argument definite. In figures 9 and 10, D_x and D_y are the demand schedules for X and Y. They are assumed to have an elasticity of unity at all points.[12] This assumption is made to eliminate any possible variation in national money income because of the character of people's tastes and to eliminate the need for redrawing the demand schedule of one product for a variation in the price of the other.

Without any tax, ON of X and OM of Y represent the equilibrium outputs in the sense that each type of resource earns equal marginal returns in either field. In figure 11, D_L is the derived demand for any particular kind of resource service used in both industries and OL represents full employment of this type of resource. We have the additional information that the national product of the economy (ignoring depreciation) is equal to the sum of the two areas $ORPN$ (fig. 9) and $OSPM$ (fig. 10). This total dollar sum also equals the total of money incomes in the economy, of which $OVZL$ (fig. 11) is the amount received by the owners of some particular type of hired resource, the precise ratio of $OVZL$ to $ORPN$ plus $OSPM$ having no significance in the case at hand.

---

[12] This assumption will later be relaxed. The demand schedules include government demands along with private demands.

Let an ad valorem tax at a given rate be levied on producers of
X and no tax on producers of Y. This fact may be represented by
the schedule T_x (fig. 9). It is computed by subtracting from each
demand price of X the amount of tax liability per unit of X. The
tax liability is found by applying the given tax rate to each price.
Thus T_x is a schedule revealing the net prices to sellers of X when
"net" means actual price charged minus tax.[13] The elasticity of the

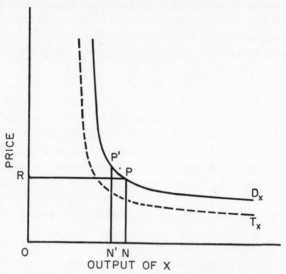

Fig. 9. Price-output effects on the taxed commodity.

net schedule is the same as that of the demand schedule for corresponding quantities.

Firms producing X have their alternatives changed by the tax.
This announcement effect takes the form of an incentive to reduce
the output of X because, with competitive pricing conditions, such
action reduces entrepreneurs' apparent tax liability. Marginal cost
for an unchanged output exceeds the net price of X, that is, actual
price minus tax. This desire to restrict the output of X means that
the firms in question stand ready to hire a smaller quantity of

---

[13] This method of representing an excise tax was suggested by Edgeworth *(Papers
Relating to Political Economy* [London: Macmillan, 1925], Vol. II, pp. 68–69). It has
marked advantages over the usual procedure. It avoids the assumption that a tax
is economically identical with costs. Since this assumption is controversial, the answer
should not be begged by the graphical method of representing the tax. On the purely
graphical level, cost curves are typically more numerous than demand curves and
hence fewer redrawings are necessary. The danger of the procedure is that the
unwary reader may confuse net price with actual price.

resources at any given set of prices for their services. If, for example, the demand for the hired service L by firms in the taxed field is W_1 without the tax (fig. 11), it becomes smaller, say W_2, with the tax. The condition for the output of X to remain unchanged in the presence of the tax is a reduction in the prices of services employed to produce X consistent with the reduced demand and the quantity of the resources in question. The implicit prices of nonhired resources employed by firms producing X fall automatically as earnings are reduced by the tax. They will continue to produce X only

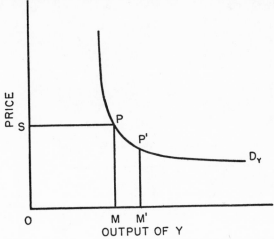

Fig. 10. Price-output effects on the nontaxed commodity.

if they cannot obtain a higher explicit price producing Y. Such reallocation of resources is easily managed if the same firms produce both X and Y, but will occur under competitive conditions even if this is not the case. Hired resources are usually thought of as more mobile than nonhired resources, but no difference in principle is involved.

Any actual reduction in the output of X requires that resources move from the production of X to the production of Y. Owners of resources need not take the reduction in their incomes, which is a condition for remaining in the taxed industry, provided their resources are capable of producing Y. Equalization of earnings at the margin is achieved by selling more services to industry Y. As resources move to Y, the output of Y increases and the price of Y decreases; the output of X decreases and price of X increases. The output of Y rises, say to OM', with the accompanying fall in price to $P'M'$ (fig. 10). Similarly, the output of X falls, say to ON', and is accompanied by a rise in price to $N'P'$ (fig. 9). This change in resource allocation, prices, and output occurs because the tax reduces earnings in X relative to those in Y.

If, instead of a tax, an equivalent shift in relative demands occurred in favor of Y, the same observations would apply with one important difference. In the case of a tax, there is an absolute reduction in the money earnings of resources. Within the framework of a given aggregate demand for the two commodities, the

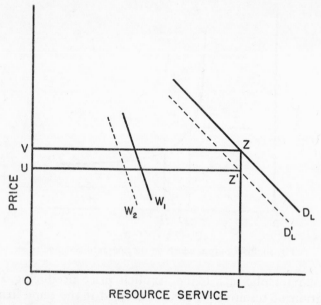

Fig. 11. Income effect on hired resources.

tax on X reduces the demand for resource services employed to produce X. Graphically, these facts are shown by the shift of the demand schedules for any typical hired service from W_1 to W_2 (fig. 11). The marginal value product of this type of resource has fallen because of the tax, when by value product we mean the price the employer realizes for a unit of the product, that is, the actual price minus tax. Here there is the same "wedge" driven between product prices and resources prices as that noted in connection with a general system of excise taxes. The aggregate demand for this type of resource service on the part of all firms must fall because one of its component parts, namely W_1, falls. Thus D_L (fig. 11) falls to

D'_L. A condition for full employment of hired resources is a fall in their prices. This condition is shown as a decline in the price of the hired resource to $Z'L$ (fig. 11). The income effect of the tax on the owners of the hired resource in question is shown by the area $UVZZ'$ (fig. 11). A shift in the demand for products, as compared with a tax, would result in a decline in the derived demand of the industry losing sales and a corresponding increase in the demand of the industry gaining sales. It would not imply any decrease in private money incomes in the aggregate.

The tax initially reduces profits in the taxed field by the full amount of the tax. Profits here mean the earnings of resources owned within the enterprise. This financial squeeze is relieved by a decline in money costs to the firm because of the fall in the prices of hired resources. The cost reduction is an indirect and unforeseen consequence of the action of taxed firms reducing their demands for hired resources. Profits in the industry remain lower absolutely and also relatively to those in Y unless the resources owned within the enterprise are also mobile with respect to product Y. If resources are specialized, they recover some of their initial reduction in money incomes by a lowering of costs, but that is all. If they are mobile, they can produce Y directly and thus directly compete for money income with owned resources located in industry Y. It follows that if all resources are completely mobile in the production of X and Y, if in other words the production-transformation relation between X and Y is a linear one, the tax reduces all resource earnings proportionately regardless of where the resources are located. In this case a "diffusion theory" of excise-tax shifting becomes approximately valid.

The generalization of this analysis to any number of products does not change the substance of our conclusions. Let us retain the assumption that the demand for each product has an elasticity of unity. In place of the product Y, assume any number of products. By the same line of reasoning, the tax forces resources out of X industry and into exempt fields. If these resources are demanded in every industry, they will distribute themselves among all, slightly increasing the output of each and thus slightly lowering the product price of each. If, as may be more typical, resources used in the taxed field are directly competitive with resources in only a few of the exempt industries, the output of these will be increased whereas others will be unaffected. A tax on the sale of new automobiles, for example, will release resources to the production of other manufactured items, but probably will not affect the output of milk in Idaho. The allocation, price, and income effects of the tax will be restricted to industries which compete for the use of the same type of resources.

The usual theory that a commodity tax has adverse financial effects only upon the taxed industry and its customers depends for its plausibility upon an oversight. With a large number of industries, a tax on one product changes the prices, outputs, and money incomes of resources located in outside fields only slightly. These effects can easily be overlooked. The methodological assumption commonly employed in partial equilibrium analysis that the prices of factors are unaffected under competitive conditions by the demand for them in one industry has accidentally lent added support to this oversight. Actually each industry must have some effect on aggregate demand for resource services since the latter is an aggregation of industry demands. A contrary assumption is fatal to an understanding of how and from whom a government is able to extract revenue by the employment of excise levies. The decline in the demand for services by taxed firms reduces money costs in all industries using these resources, and it is this fact which lowers the prices of nontaxed commodities. Partial equilibrium analysis in the ordinary sense cannot give a correct explanation of the effects of excise taxes.

The greater the coverage of a system of excise taxes, the smaller will be the rise in the price of any item taxed and the larger will be the decrease in the prices of exempt items. Greater tax coverage restricts the opportunities of resources to move out of the taxed field, and hence the outputs of taxed items are reduced less and the price rises are smaller. The smaller the area of tax exemption, the greater will be the incentive to invade that area to restore lost earnings, and hence the larger will be the output effect and the price decline in exempt fields. A system of excise taxation of, for example, 90 per cent coverage of sales would reveal itself more in declines in prices of exempt items than in increases in prices of taxed items. With complete coverage, there is no reallocation effect and hence no product-price effect—only a reduction in money earnings. For this case, H. G. Brown's observations hold.

The restricting assumption that the demand for each commodity has an elasticity of unity may now be removed. Very commonly, the government selects for excise taxation those items which are regarded as capable of yielding large amounts of revenue. These commodities have large sales and are often believed to have inelastic demands. The federal tax on tobacco products, particularly cigarettes, is a good illustration of such a case. It satisfies the political conditions of providing large revenues easily and without apparent deleterious effects on the industry. These conditions, combined with the peculiar human tendency to welcome outside punishment of one's vices and the fervor of the self-righteous to make other people's vices expensive, may explain why a democratic people tolerate heavy taxation of one of their favorite commodities. Since the doctrine that excise taxes are shifted to consumers seems especially plausible when the taxed commodity has a highly inelastic demand, it becomes a test case for our theory.

Let us return to the case of two commodities only, X and Y, but now the demand for X is assumed to be highly inelastic. For this condition to hold, the demand for Y must shift downward as the price of X rises. The substitution effect between X and Y is small and the Hicksian income effect operates mainly on Y. A rise in the price of X is equivalent to removing some cash from buyers since they have to spend more dollars to buy the same quantity of X, and this operates mainly to lower the demand for Y.[14] In terms of cross-elasticity concepts, our assumptions make X and Y complementary. It should be kept in mind, however, that these relations are not necessarily reversible.[15] Under competitive pricing conditions, the price of the taxed item is not automatically increased merely because of the inelasticity of the demand for it. A necessary condition is that the tax induces a curtailment of output of the taxed item. Once, however, sellers begin the process of restricting output in an effort to reduce their tax liability, the shifting occurs through both the demand and the supply of nontaxed items. With the reduction in the output of X, people spend more money for X and less for Y. The shift of resources to Y reduces the income of competing resources producing Y, and also the shift in consumer expenditures directly reduces the money income of resources *whatever their physical characteristics* used to produce Y.

Given any number of products, a government policy of selective taxation of those products whose demands are inelastic has the effect of reducing the demands and prices of other products and

[14] Cf. Hicks, *op. cit.*, pp. 48–52.
[15] Cf. George Stigler, *The Theory of Price* (New York: Macmillan, 1953), pp. 48–49. An analysis and evaluation of various theories of interrelated demands is given by Henry Schultz, *The Theory and Measurement of Demand* (Chicago: University of Chicago Press, 1938), pp. 569–654.

incomes of owners of resources producing those other products.[16] These are the commodities which buyers are prepared to forego. Heavy taxation on such items as liquor and tobacco may fall most heavily on producers of food items if it is true, as some maintain, that people prefer drinking and smoking to eating. Actually, of course, the choice turns out not to be such a hard one after all, because the reduction in the demand for the commodities people regard as less essential automatically reduces their prices and, what is more significant, leaves the output of them greater because the tax must reduce the quantity of resources used in the taxed field and thus make them available to nontaxed industries.

A final step necessary in our discussion of partial excise taxes levied in a competitive world concerns their deflationary or anti-inflationary effects. It was earlier argued that a completely general system of excise taxation reduces private demands for products through the income effect of the tax. In that case each owner of real resources is found to have a lower money income. The attempt has been made to identify these persons for a system of partial excises. They are the owners of real resources, including of course labor power, located in the taxed fields and the owners of all resources competitive with those in the taxed fields. This competition may be restricted to the supply side if the demands for taxed items have an elasticity of unity or more, but must also operate on the demand side if they have an elasticity of less than one.[17] When the competition operates from the demand side, the group whose income falls is larger although the reduction in income per unit of resource is smaller as compared to cases of elasticity of less than one.

The deflationary effect follows from the fact that these resource owners find their money incomes smaller because of the tax. Consequently they spend less money in subsequent periods than they would spend if their incomes had not been reduced, and therefore the general level of money prices, including taxed along with nontaxed items, is lower than it would be if no such tax had been imposed, or, if already in existence, had been repealed. Any tax makes the government's deficit smaller or its surplus larger, and hence the government's net income-generating effect, if debt operations are ignored, is made smaller.

---

[16] A policy of this type may give results closely similar to that of a completely general tax without the administrative inconvenience of a general levy.

[17] If the taxed product has an elasticity of unity or more, there *may* be negative repercussions with respect to the incomes of those producing other commodities. If the elasticity is less than unity, there *must* be such negative repercussions.

Some students of tax theory object to comparing a situation with a tax to one without a tax. Musgrave, for example, believes it improper to explain a tax in terms of a no-tax alternative. The following passage indicates his reasons: "But, if we wish to study the incidence of taxation as such, it must be recognized that this incidence cannot be thought of in absolute terms; an alternative means of finance must be substituted when the prevailing taxes are 'thought away,' and this means that the result will necessarily be in differential terms."[18] This view is needlessly restricting. If a tax of $10 per head is levied on people with red hair, to take a simple example, it is meaningful to say that any redheaded person pays a tax of $10 for the period in question and that the government collects in revenue an amount equal to $10 multiplied by the redheaded population. From this fact, we observe that the government's deficit is smaller or its surplus larger. The deflationary effect of the tax is explained by observing that redheaded persons have to economize in the future because their present expenditure power has been reduced. We may also note that in net income terms redheads lose relatively to other groups. All these matters presuppose knowledge of the *incidence* of the tax in the sense of knowing who parts with the money the government obtains. At some point, unless the effects of a tax can be assumed to be intuitively known, comparisons with a no-tax situation are unavoidable. Let us nevertheless compare a system of partial excise taxes with another system of taxation whose allocation and income effects are assumed to be known. A system of flat-sum taxes may be used for this purpose. Such a tax has no announcement effects and hence no price and reallocation effects. Let us further assume that the tax system in question happens, and this requires a stretch of the imagination, to be proportional to the money income of each person in the society. This assumption means that such a tax system is neutral with respect to the relative distribution of personal net income. Let us now suppose that a system of excises consisting of a levy on a single commodity is introduced, subject to the condition that the flat-sum tax is reduced in such a manner as to remain proportional to each person's money income and to leave government revenue unaffected in the aggregate.

The excise tax reduces immediately the profits of firms in the taxed field. As long as they do not take steps to shift the tax, their income is smaller, whereas everyone else's income, computed after

[18] Musgrave *et al., op. cit.,* p. 8.

deducting the flat-sum tax, is larger. But entrepreneurs in the taxed field have an incentive to restrict output; they thereby reduce the income of hired resources in their own industry and of similar resources in other industries. Both these groups now find their income falling by just the amount of the increase in the previously reduced profits of the taxed firms. If the elasticity of demand in the taxed field is unity or larger, the spreading of the tax burden proceeds in this fashion. Any competition by resources leaving the taxed field, to the extent it is successful, increases their earnings at the expense of others. This competition for income is to be viewed pragmatically; an owner who moves his resources out of the taxed field to increase his income as compared to what it would otherwise be may or may not succeed.

In the special cases where either all resources are completely mobile or the demands for all products except the taxed one are reduced in proportion, all resource owners are left with heavier taxes and only those persons whose incomes are determined outside the price system gain absolutely in money terms. They gain because their income before tax remains the same whereas the flat-sum tax on them is reduced. Unlike the no-tax comparison, there is no net deflationary effect on private demands for output. Those outside the price system now take the place, in part, of those within it at the counters for goods and services. They gain absolutely in money and in real terms. They may lose some part of this gain if they happen to prefer taxed items or they may gain even more if they happen to prefer nontaxed or lightly taxed items.

Thus the pattern of tax shifting and the effects on product prices do not depend in any fundamental way on whether we look upon any particular tax, in this case a partial system of excise taxes, as imposed in a setting where another tax is conceived as reduced, or whether we think of a tax as a net addition to the revenue, provided close attention is paid to the time dimension.

General Excise Subsidies

The analysis of the effects of excise subsidies must deal with issues similar to those found for excise taxes. What effects do excise subsidies have on the composition of output, the prices of subsidized and nonsubsidized products, money costs of production, private money incomes, and private money expenditures? Are excise subsidies shifted and if so, to what groups?

Excise subsidies are offers of a government to make money payments to producers of commodities when the amounts to be paid depend upon a rate or schedule of rates and the size of the commodity base per unit of time. Like excise taxes, excise subsidies may be of the ad valorem or of the specific type, depending upon whether the legislation defines the commodity base for computing the subsidy payment as a value sum or a physical quantity. Excise subsidies are negative excise taxes.

Excise subsidies may be general or partial. A general subsidy is an offer to pay producers of all commodities at a uniform and proportional ad valorem rate. This case, although never found in practice, provides a theoretical extreme. Subsidies may be partial in various degrees. The "most partial" system of subsidies is one limited to one product in the economy. Any actual system falls within these extremes. The procedure employed here is to examine the implications of these extreme cases under simplified conditions and then to generalize the results to any system of subsidies falling in between. Subject to the limitations of the assumptions employed, the conclusions should therefore be completely general for money-price economic systems.

Consider first a system of excise subsidies on all products levied at a uniform and proportional rate in a setting of competitive pricing of products and of resource services. An excise subsidy may be regarded as an addition to the market demand for a commodity. Suppose again for simplicity that only two commodities, X and Y, are produced. Both are assumed to be subsidized at the same ad valorem rate.

In figure 12, D_o is the market demand for commodity X as revealed by buyer preferences. D_s is the demand schedule plus the subsidy. Thus if the market price is PM, the total financial receipts of sellers per unit of product is P_sM. Given the subsidy per unit PP_s, firms have an incentive to expand output. Firms producing X have aggregate supply schedules passing through the point P and unless these supply schedules are vertical, they have an incentive to produce a greater output at the total remuneration per unit, P_sM. In terms of cost computations, the marginal cost to each firm at an unchanged output is less than the market price plus the subsidy. Profit maximization calls for an expansion of output by each firm to the point where marginal cost is equal to the market price plus subsidy.

For the same reasons, the subsidy also provides incentives for firms producing Y to expand output. These incentives become reflected in demands for resources. Firms in both industries, at given prices for resource services, increase the quantities demanded at those prices. But both industries cannot expand output. By assumption, the resources employed to produce the two commodities exhaust the resources available to the economy. With given demands for products, illustrated by D_0 in the case of X, the market price of X remains at PM and the output remains at OM. Similarly the price and output of Y remain unchanged. The effect of a gen-

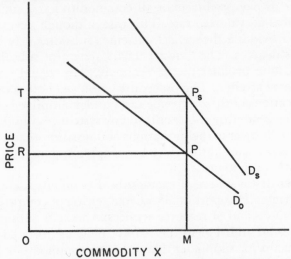

Fig. 12. Price-income effects of an excise subsidy.

eral and uniform system of subsidies is neutral on resource allocation. Each subsidy offsets the other.

The subsidy does have a positive income effect on all owners of resources by increasing the explicit and implicit prices of all resource services. The initial income effect of the subsidy is quantitatively equal to the amount paid by the government in the form of subsidies, that is, the area RTP_sP (fig. 12) in the case of X and an equivalent area in the case of Y. Before adjustment, the subsidy increases the implicit prices of resources attached to firms in each industry. With adjustment, a part of this increase in the profits of firms is shifted to owners of hired resources. The subsidy is partly shifted because firms increase their demands for resource services as a consequence of the subsidy, and with any given quantity and variety of resources, an increase in demands, if nonprice rationing of resource services is to be avoided, requires an upward adjustment in their prices. Thus marginal costs rise and exceed market prices by the amount of the subsidy per unit at unchanged outputs.

In terms of productivity analysis, the subsidy leaves the marginal physical product of any type of resource unchanged because resources stay where they are and the same output is produced, whereas the "value" of marginal products is everywhere raised proportionately, when by "value" is meant the financial payment to firms per unit of product. This financial payment is the sum of the market price and subsidy. In other words, in the ordinary sense of value, that is, market price, the value of the marginal product of each type of resource service remains unchanged whereas the prices of resource services are increased.

The above argument may be generalized to any number of products. If a subsidy is imposed on every product at a uniform ad valorem rate, each firm in every industry attempts to expand output. None can succeed; their efforts result only in bidding up the prices of hired resource services. Money costs of production are everywhere increased proportionately. If factor prices are equal to the prices of their marginal products without subsidy, they now exceed product prices by the amount of the subsidy.

Certain conclusions may be noted at this stage. A general and uniform system of subsidies is partly shifted from enterprise to the owners of hired resources in the sense that subsidies increase their private money incomes. No part of such a subsidy is shifted to consumers in the form of lower product prices. The composition of output (the product-mix) remains unchanged, and the prices of products are also left unchanged. These conclusions are consistent with the theory that equivalent excise taxes are not shifted to consumers.

PARTIAL EXCISE SUBSIDIES

We turn now to the effects of differential or partial subsidies. Suppose a subsidy is imposed on X and not on Y, where X and Y are again assumed to be the only commodities produced. If, as shown in figure 12, the subsidy equals the area RTP_sP before adjustment, producers of X have an incentive to expand output, since each firm's marginal cost at outputs aggregating OM is less than the price plus subsidy, or P_sM. The incentive to expand means an increase in the demand for resources to produce X. But in contrast to a system of uniform subsidies, producers of Y have no incentive to expand output. The Y industry cannot therefore retain the same quantity of resources as before because it is outbid by the greater competitive power of the subsidized industry. Thus the output of X increases as resources are pulled away from the Y industry. With any given demand, as the output of X rises, its market price falls. Likewise, as the output of Y falls, its market price rises.

In addition to these price and reallocation effects of the subsidy, there are positive money income effects as well. The income effect in the first instance is an addition to the profits of firms producing X. Because the subsidy increases the demand for resources by industry X, some of the subsidy goes to owners of hired resources. The aggregate demands for resources are derived from the demands for both products. The money demand for resource services to produce X increases whereas the demand to produce Y remains unchanged. The prices of resource services, with any given volume of resources, are therefore absolutely increased. In other words, the subsidy increases money costs of production in both fields and increases money incomes of some and possibly all resources employed in both fields.

The same line of reasoning may again be extended to any number of commodities. If only one commodity is subsidized, its output rises and its price falls, whereas the outputs of some, but not necessarily all, of the remaining products fall and their prices rise. Only those commodities which require resources that are competitive with those in the subsidized industry need have their outputs reduced; some commodities may be isolated from the subsidized industry in the sense that the resources used to produce them are specialized. Consumers get a different product-mix which contains more of the subsidized item and smaller amounts of some other commodities.

If several products are subsidized, their outputs increase and their market prices fall, whereas for the products not subsidized the reverse results occur. The larger the proportion of all output subsidized, the smaller become the price reallocation effects of subsidies because the smaller is the area from which resources may be obtained. In the extreme case of uniform and general excise subsidies, there are neither product-price nor resource-reallocation effects, as already shown.

The income effects of partial subsidies are similar to those already noted above for a two-commodity system. Prices of resource services are however raised only slightly when one commodity is subsidized, because any subsidy so imposed is almost certain to be small in relation to all incomes arising from production. Furthermore, the incomes of the owners of only some types of resources need be increased. The resource services whose explicit or imputed prices are pulled upward by the subsidy are those located in the subsidized industry or industries and those located elsewhere which compete with them for income. In the highly special case where all resources are perfectly mobile among all products, the subsidy becomes generally diffused throughout the economy. The diffusion of the subsidy is limited to those who obtain incomes by the management of real resources.

A general diffusion result may also emerge from a partial subsidy, even though there is resource specialization, provided the demands for the subsidized commodities are inelastic and buyers spend this extra money on all remaining products. In this event, the market demand for each commodity shifts to a higher level. The money incomes going to resource owners in all nonsubsidized fields are thereby also increased. This possible result is of course parallel to that found for excise taxes. A selective set of excises can reduce money incomes of resource owners generally even though resources are specialized.

7

Excise Taxes and Subsidies: Noncompetitive Pricing

In the last chapter, excise taxes were shown to reduce the money incomes of owners of resources by amounts equal to the yield of the tax. These taxes may also reallocate resources and, in so doing, increase the prices of some products and reduce the prices of others. A parallel theory was given for excise subsidies. These results were found for a system of economic organization characterized by continuous perfectly competitive pricing in all markets. Such a system is no longer assumed. An explanation of the effects of excise taxes and subsidies, to be general, must apply to the great variety of market structures found in actual systems.

There are various procedures which might be adopted for the purpose of learning the effects of excise taxes on prices, outputs, and incomes for a variety of market structures. The traditional, and still the dominant, method is the study of a tax in the light of the market structure of the industry producing the taxed commodity. Thus the tax on gasoline may be considered as it affects the price charged, the output of gasoline, the prices of crude oil, and closely related matters. This method has important advantages. It can give detailed information of the reactions of the business units to the tax in view of the institutional limitations surrounding the industry's operations. But this method has serious limitations also. It requires the assumption that the relevant effects of the tax are confined to the participants in the industry and its customers. A theory is thereby adopted implicitly and without critical consideration of alternatives. Given competitive pricing conditions, a tax does not simply affect the taxed industry; it has allocation and income effects on other groups. Such effects do not disappear in the absence of perfectly competitive pricing. Any system of economic organization is interrelated. A partial approach—the study

[148]

of one industry at a time—is highly revealing and pertinent, but it remains partial. Economic analysis must be concerned and traditionally has properly been concerned with the interrelations of the parts to the whole. An adequate tax theory can do no less.

The difficulty of the task of discovering the effects of excise taxes, once the world of perfect competition is left behind, may easily be pictured as insuperable. One needs to know the market structure surrounding the exchange of every commodity, the behavior pattern of each buyer and seller for each commodity in the system, and the precise way a tax "causes" these behavior patterns and institutional practices to alter. It may safely be said that no one has this amount of information. Students of price policies and business behavior have made various attempts to find guiding principles applicable to this welter of market structures. Thus various "cases" have been analyzed: simple monopoly, monopolistic competition and its variants, oligopoly, bilateral monopoly, and many others. In the area of the pricing of labor services, theory seems largely to have been banished in favor of a study of industrial relations or conflicting power tactics. Those intent on the larger view are thus confronted with virtually unlimited combinations of possible cases to consider. One is tempted to forego a theoretical solution of the effects of excise taxes applicable to any pricing circumstances and, instead, to hope to make progress by close study of the marketing and production practices in various taxed industries. Alternately one may insist that the only theory possible for general analysis is general competitive pricing throughout the economy—a view supported by Knight.[1]

In the following analysis, a compromise method is adopted. The case of simple monopoly pricing is first examined, to reveal the fundamental differences between a world of product competitors and a world of product monopolists. The case of overpricing is next examined, followed by a study of general underpricing. Excise taxes and subsidies are shown to have effects, different in some ways from those under competitive pricing, but yet similar with regard to fundamentals.

MONOPOLY PRICING OF PRODUCTS

Let us again assume, for simplicity, an economy with only two products. Each is controlled by a single seller. The sellers are cor-

---

[1] F. H. Knight, "Immutable Law in Economics: Its Reality and Limitations," *American Economic Review, Proceedings,* XXXVI (May, 1946): 103–106.

porations which own all resources used except labor service. Labor service is assumed, initially, to be bought and sold competitively. Each monopolist assumes that the demand for his product has an elasticity of more than one. (This assumption is necessary to keep the "case" from becoming nonsensical at the outset. If each seller assumes an elasticity of one or less, he has an incentive to restrict output to approximately zero, regardless of costs.)

The transformation relation between products is limited by movements of hired labor between the two industries. It is assumed that resources owned within the two industries are completely specialized. The actual prices of the products will depend upon the money demands for each, the costs of production, and the price policies of the monopolists. These may be studied by a comparison with competitive pricing. Simple graphical representations are employed to ascertain the effects of monopolistic in comparison with perfectly competitive pricing. In figures 13 and 14, the demands for the two products are shown as D_x and D_y. If monopolists of X and Y were to behave as though competitive conditions existed, the output of X would be OM at the price P_xM and the output of Y would be ON at the price P_yN (figs. 13 and 14). These prices would need to satisfy the following conditions: (1) each must be on the actual demand schedule for each commodity rather than merely on the sellers' "imagined" or projected demand schedule for his product; (2) each seller must maximize profits in the sense that, in his opinion, a change in price would reduce the earnings of the resources he owns; and (3) the money cost relations must be consistent with full employment of labor.[2] In income terms, the areas $ORSM$ (fig. 13) and $OUZN$ (fig. 14) constitute the wages of labor, which combined equal the area $OZWL$ (fig. 15). Profits (depreciation and taxes are assumed to be zero) equal the areas RQP_xS (fig. 13) and UTP_yZ (fig. 14).

Both monopolists attempt to maximize their profit position by experimentally increasing prices above the competitive level. As each does so, he decreases the demand for hired services. An incentive to restrict output means a decline in the money demand for the use of resources. D_L (fig. 15) shifts downward. The downward shifting ceases when each monopolist is content with his price policy.[3] Each is content when marginal revenue computed from his

[2] For simplicity, the demand for leisure by owners of labor will be treated as having an elasticity of zero.

[3] No monopsonistic action is assumed on the part of the monopolists. Each treats the going wage structure as given.

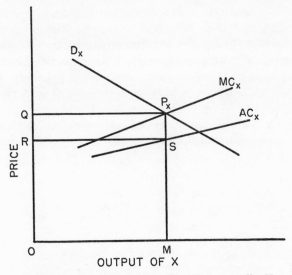

Fig. 13. Monopoly pricing effects on commodity X.

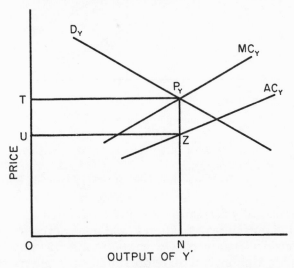

Fig. 14. Monopoly pricing effects on commodity Y.

"imagined" demand curve equals marginal cost in terms of the prices of hired services, and when the actual prices charged are on the actual demand schedules for each of the two commodities.

These results are shown as D'_L (fig. 15) which is the demand for hired resources by both monopolists when each has reached his best position. The exercise of monopoly power does not raise product prices in this case. The incentive to restrict output operates to lower costs to each monopolist. Although there may be some shift of labor from one product to the other, this result need not occur. Our conclusions, which are identical with those found by Lerner and Bain, are that product prices remain unchanged, and the prices of labor services are lower.[4] The exercise of monopoly power by sellers of products lowers the prices of hired services and increases the money income of monopolists. There may or may not be a

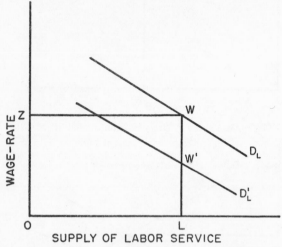

Fig. 15. Income effects of monopoly pricing on hired labor services.

change in the composition of output as compared with that resulting from competitive pricing.

This pattern of analysis may be applied to an economy with many products. Monopolistic power, by creating incentives to restrict output, automatically decreases the demand for hired services. The composition of output may be altered, and in any event the money income of outsiders is reduced. Owners of labor services are "taxed" by monopolists. Monopoly is therefore similar in its effects to excise taxes levied in a competitive setting. If the monopoly power of each product-seller is equal, there is no allocation effect—only a decline in the money incomes of owners of hired services. If monopoly power is unequal, there is an allocation effect as well as

[4] See A. P. Lerner, *Economics of Control* (New York: Macmillan, 1944), pp. 100–102, and Joe S. Bain, *Pricing, Distribution, and Employment* (New York: Henry Holt, 1948), pp. 168–172.

an income effect. The allocation effect shifts resources from industries with relatively more monopoly power to those with less. An important difference remains. Under excise taxation the income lost by resource owners accrues to the government whereas under monopolistic conditions, the income lost by some accrues to monopolists.

A system of excise taxation levied in a setting of monopolistic pricing has effects very similar to those just observed. With two products, each controlled by a monopolist, a proportional tax on the sales of each reduces the demand net of tax for each product. If therefore we substitute in the foregoing analysis the net-of-tax demand schedule for the market demand schedule, the same chain of reasoning may be employed. As compared with a no-tax situation, the incomes of the monopolists and of the owners of hired services are reduced proportionally by the tax. The demand for labor service shifts below D'_L (fig. 15) because the tax gives each monopolist an incentive to curtail output. Of the income generated by the collective resources under the control of monopolists, the government appropriates a proportional share. There is no allocation effect and no change in product prices, but there is a reduction in the explicitly priced services obtained from outsiders and a similar reduction in the implicitly priced services of resources owned within the organizations with monopoly power.

A tax levied on one product reallocates resources to the others as found under competitive conditions. If commodity X is taxed, the net demand for it is lowered by the amount of the tax per unit. An incentive exists to reduce its output. The demand for resource services falls, but the demand for hired resource services by the product-monopolist of Y remains unchanged. As the price of labor service falls, the Y monopolist buys more of it and his output increases.

The income effect of the tax on X is the reduction in the earnings of hired resources and the reduction in the earnings of the monopolistically controlled resources producing X. The pattern of results is virtually indistinguishable from that found for perfect competition. The same possible shifting through interrelations of the demands for products may also occur under conditions of monopolistic pricing.

The condition of full employment with monopoly and excise taxation is a lowering of the prices of hired services as compared with pretax levels. If the actual prices of labor service preclude "low" wage rates, the alternative is underemployment. Monopolistic power on the part of outsiders who sell to monopolists is not offsetting, in the sense of giving a solution closer to the competitive one than would occur in the absence of monopolistic power by either group. Thus if a floor exists under money wage rates, whether this floor is established by labor union tactics, by ideas of fair price on the part of employers, or by government decree, it is an accident if full employment results. In a setting in which these floors have already been established, excise taxes, by lowering the money demand for hired services (and this would also be true with competitive pricing of products but not of resource services), result in more underemployment of outsiders' resources. They are thus forced to take more "leisure" instead of working. This result holds even if the government has in effect a system of transfer payments which prevents underemployment from reducing the money incomes of labor groups.

In a social setting in which prices of resource services are rigid, any tax which, through its announcement effects, lowers the demand for labor service may be said to cause underemployment. Also, given any set of excise taxes, a social policy of setting effective floors under prices of hired services may be said to cause underemployment. Either statement is as correct as the other. Excise taxes require a reduction in the explicit prices of hired services. They automatically reduce the implicit prices of instrumental services of resources owned within enterprise. If social mores, private rules, or public law do not permit these adjustments by price, they occur in the quantities instead. In this event, the society adopts, unwittingly, a policy of forcing people to accept leisure instead of the commodities which they would like to consume or own.

Excise Taxes and Overpricing

In this section, the effects of excise taxes are studied on the assumption that sellers typically overprice their products. Overpricing may be initially defined as any product price in excess of the competitive price. A competitive price means simply that each participant in the market can sell all he wishes to sell at the single price prevailing. There is no exclusion from the market for reasons other than price. According to this definition, any exercise of monopoly power results in overpricing. When a monopolist attempts to exploit the higher reaches of a demand schedule by advancing the price, he would be willing to sell more at that higher price than he can. Yet as already observed in the preceding section, monopolistic pricing of products can give product-price results identical with those under perfect competition. Such results require a lower level of cost prices to induce sellers with price power to hire all the resources available to the economy. Overpricing as initially defined does not therefore necessarily imply gouging of the consumer; it may imply gouging of employees and possibly other suppliers. In a sense, therefore, overpricing of products occurs because owners of instrumental services are able, in one way or another, to charge prices which are too high for full employment.

A set of instrumental service prices may be defined as "too high" if suppliers of these services are willing to sell more of them at these prices. This is also our definition of underemployment. Employment is considered to be full when any owner of labor service can sell all the services he wishes to sell at the structure of wage rates confronting him. There are however difficulties with this definition which should not be concealed. One difficulty concerns the possibility of "disguised unemployment"—a concept suggested by Joan Robinson.[5] A person who has been fired from his regular job and now takes up the occupation of selling apples on street corners is underemployed in her sense even though he is free to sell apples for as many hours as he pleases. The concept of underemployment suggested by this illustration relates to the difference in the money rewards from different pursuits a person could follow if he had the opportunity. But such a concept of underemployment has the implication that full employment is never found in actual practice. A person is underemployed if he works full time in occupation A if his services could command a higher price in occupation B, provided that the person prefers occupation B to A at the prices being paid. By definition, he is partly underemployed because he could earn more than he does if he had the opportunity to enter the better-paying occupation. There is only a difference in degree between the situation of a person who, on common-sense grounds, is regarded as unemployed but who is able to earn some money by odd jobs and a person who is working full time in an occupation but who could earn more if he were allowed to compete for a position in another occupation. Full employment in the "ideal" sense means a situation in which each seller of labor service is content with his occupation in that (1) he may work at least as many hours

[5] Joan Robinson, "Disguised Unemployment," *Economic Journal*, XLVI (June, 1936): 225–237.

Theory of Fiscal Economics

as he pleases in that occupation, and (2) he would not change jobs if a position were offered him at prevailing rates of pay in another occupation for the quality of the labor service he has for sale. This definition of full employment is another way of stating the criterion for ideal allocation of resources from the point of view of owners of resources. Thus, disguised underemployment is found for some workers in virtually any period.[6]

Overpricing of products in a general equilibrium sense refers to any set of product prices which are inconsistent with full employment (no involuntary leisure on or off the job). But a set of product prices may be too high because instrumental services are overpriced, given the behavior patterns of sellers of products. If market structures surrounding the sale of products are such that a decrease in the prices of instrumental services would always be accompanied by a corresponding decrease in product prices, overpricing of products and underemployment could always be ascribed to overpricing of hired services. In the case of approximately perfectly competitive prices for products with monopoly elements in the labor market, underemployment is "caused" solely by overpricing of hired services. If, however, prices of products are invariant regardless of costs, overpricing occurs because of the price policies of sellers of products.

Overpricing seems to be the result of both a downward rigidity of product prices and cost-increasing policies of labor groups. Some reduction in costs is communicated to some product prices, but the many rigid elements in the price structure require large adjustments in cost prices to induce even small reductions in product prices.

For purposes of discovering the effects of excise taxes, let us first consider the extreme case of a perfectly rigid set of prices in a setting where there is general overpricing. The government introduces a general and uniform retail sales tax levied on sellers at uniform ad valorem rates. Further, it is assumed that sellers arbitrarily raise prices by the full amount of the tax. This practice may be called "tax-induced collusion." It is a kind of collusion because

---

[6] Mrs. Robinson (*loc. cit.*) relates her definition to a condition in which the demands for products have been falling. The definition is tied to the believed cause of the occupational change rather than to job alternatives at any given date. But disguised unemployment in the sense discussed above may be caused by many other factors—for instance, relative changes in the demands for products, monopolistic practices by sellers of products, restrictive policies by unions, conceptions of "fair" wage rates enforced by social mores, outright discrimination against some workers for reasons other than price, and many others.

sellers in competitive markets could not raise prices on their own initiative. Actually monopolists do not have an incentive to raise prices by the full amount of the tax. If it pays a monopolist to raise the price after the imposition of a tax, it would pay him to do so in the absence of the tax. The practice of sellers of gasoline or cigarettes to announce a price increase equal to a tax increase at the precise moment the added tax is imposed indicates explicit or implicit collusion among them.

Because prices are generally higher, more money is required to buy a given bill of goods. To maintain living standards, people would need to spend more money. To the extent that people possess extra cash holdings, they have the opportunity to protect themselves by increased expenditures. But larger cash holdings are needed to afford protection against contingencies—a circumstance which operates in the direction of reducing cash outlays. It seems appropriate, therefore, to assume initially that people spend the same amount of money.

A general increase in prices without any increase in private and public expenditures results in a reduction of output. Immediately after the tax is imposed, output and employment of resources decline in all fields. Some of this underemployment will take the form of idle equipment owned within enterprise. Some owners of hired services will become partly or wholly unemployed. Owners of hired resources which remain fully employed will not experience any change in their money income. It is assumed, of course, that money wage rates remain unchanged. The wage income of those dismissed from the working force falls to zero. Profits, computed after excise-tax liabilities, can typically be expected to decline because some profit is lost on the portion of output no longer produced and because some costs are fixed. But the pattern need not be the same throughout all industrial and marketing organizations.

The income, price, and quantity features of general tax-induced collusion may be illustrated by figure 16. *DD'* is assumed to be the public's demand for a representative unit of current output. Its elasticity is assumed to be unity consistent with the assumption that people spend an unchanged quantity of money. Since composition effects are of no immediate concern, the quantity axis may be thought of as a representative commodity. Before the price is raised, the income generated in production, apart from changes in the values of old assets, is equal to the areas numbered 1 and 2. As a result of the tax and the policy of sellers, the price level is

raised from OR to OV. The income from production is now equal
to the areas numbered 1 and 3, which by assumption equal the
areas 1 and 2. Area 3 measures the tax liability of sellers arising
from the government's imposition of general excise-tax levies. The
income after tax going to the owners of the resources producing
the now reduced output ON is represented by area 1. Given the
demand for products as shown and the new and lower volume of
employment, owners of resources receive smaller incomes after tax
by exactly the amount of the tax liability.

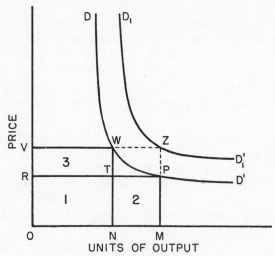

Fig. 16. Effects of tax-induced collusion.

The implications of the behavior patterns assumed to accompany the tax can be further studied by reference to a full-employment policy on the part of the government. The reduction in private money income in the first period after the tax has been imposed will reduce private demands for products in subsequent
periods. If there is no hoarding or dishoarding and the money supply is left unchanged, DD' will shift downward to pass through T.
Unless this deflationary effect is offset, there will be further unemployment of resources. Let us suppose that the government offsets
this latter effect by reducing by the same amount previously existing flat-sum taxes. There is as a result no downward shift of DD',
and further unemployment is prevented. Thus far the government
has left its tax revenue unchanged, but the initial unemployment
reflected by the decline in output from OM to ON remains. A full-

employment policy requires compensatory measures by the government or the banking system. To accomplish its full-employment policy the government must again reduce flat-sum taxes (or increase flat-sum subsidies) by an amount equal to the yield of the excise-tax levy. Compared to the situation before the imposition of the general excise tax, the government's *net* revenue instead of increasing has now declined by an amount equal to the yield of the excise taxes. If monopolists are content with the price policy as represented by MZ, the upward shift of demand for products to $D_1 D_1'$ will restore the initial level of employment.

If government policies are to be consistent with full-employment objectives, the imposition of a system of excise taxes accompanied by a general attempt of sellers to escape the tax by advancing product prices correspondingly requires that either additional subsidies be paid or other taxes be reduced. In the present instance, it requires that the government experience a net revenue loss. The reduction in other taxes or the increase in subsidies must be *twice* the yield of the system of excise taxes. This result follows because the tax has a yield and therefore makes private money incomes smaller and because the rise in prices requires that aggregate expenditures rise to keep the quantities demanded unchanged. If the assumptions made here fit the facts, excise taxes, apart from any "burden" considerations as such, are a fiscal nuisance. They are a nuisance because they lead directly to price inflation and underemployment.

Our assumption that sellers advance prices by the full amount of the tax does not always accord with the evidence. Not all sellers have the power to advance the price by the full amount of the tax. In addition, some oligopolists will think that it is not to their advantage to do this. The demand for their product in their own opinion may be so elastic as to make such a policy financially dangerous. It is more plausible to expect that tax-induced collusion will be complete in some cases and partial or absent in others. These patterns will depend upon the characteristics of the demand for the product and upon the market structures of the industries. An oligopoly such as the West Coast petroleum industry may increase the price of gasoline by the full amount of any excise tax imposed on that product. Even in this case it should be kept in mind that gasoline is the main outlet for crude oil, and any reduction in the amount demanded as a result of higher prices requires either that more crude oil be channeled into other products at prices sufficiently low to prevent surpluses or that crude oil supplies be backed up at the source. In any event, producers of crude oil take some reduction in their income as a consequence. The opposition of the petroleum industry to increased taxes on gasoline has an economic basis. The wine industry, by contrast, cannot readily push up its prices to accompany increases in excise levies without consequences that may be more adverse than "tax absorption." The competitive structure of the industry makes effective price collusion difficult. High taxes on wine reduce the demand for grapes and thus become reflected in lower yields to grape growers.

A general system of excise taxes, even if uniform, need not have a neutral effect on resource allocation. Sellers who belong to oligopolistic pricing groups and whose products have a low elasticity of demand may be expected to advance prices by amounts approximately equal to the tax. The reduction in output in such cases may be small. Sellers of products in more competitive industries are confronted by a double adjustment task. They cannot increase their prices much, if at all, to compensate for the excise tax imposed upon them. In addition, the demands for their products may fall because buyers economize on such products in order to maintain the same consumption level of other products now being offered at higher prices. With any given level of private expenditures, some additional underemployment of resources will occur in both oligopolistic and competitive industries. It is possible that owners of unemployed resources may make a place for themselves somewhere in the economy. If they do, they will have to be content with relatively low money incomes to make the adjustment. Their products will be in more abundant supply and will require correspondingly lower prices. The public obtains smaller quantities of some products and larger quantities of others. In this setting only a highly selective system of excise taxes could give a neutral effect on resource allocation.

The assumption that buyers respond to the higher product prices by spending an unchanged amount of money may also be relaxed. Buyers, confronted with higher prices, may choose to spend more or less money. Wealthier members of the community may refuse to allow their standards of consumption to fall. They may draw upon their idle balances, if any, or sell assets in amounts sufficient to finance the purchase of the same quantities of commodities. Unless these added expenditures are entirely at the expense of idle balances, some reduction of investment demands occurs. At the other end of the wealth scale, there will be many who will not be able to increase their consumption expenditures. These groups must buy smaller quantities of goods and services. Groups in between may be expected to increase their consumption expenditures somewhat at the expense of idle balances and asset holdings. Unless the banking system steps into the breach, some deflation of investment demands is highly probable. If, in addition, the sales of new assets are subject to excise levies, unemployment is likely to be especially heavy in the industries producing new resources.

If the demand elasticity for a composite commodity may be typically viewed as less than one but not zero, which appears to be plausible, the money value of national output rises by an amount which is smaller than the yield of the excise-tax levy. In this event employment falls as prices rise and output is curtailed. The unemployed may find employment in competitive industries, and there is more disguised unemployment. A general attempt by sellers to obtain higher prices will under the circumstances be financially successful. In fact, unless buyers discipline sellers by spending less money for products as prices advance, sellers with price power have a strong incentive to push up prices indefinitely. In a society of the kind visualized, substantial price inflation can occur even if government expenditures, subsidies, and taxes result in no additions to privately owned cash balances, and if the banking system does not permit any increase in the money supply.

Price stability in such a setting is likely only if sellers are restrained by fear of lack of coöperation by rivals or are socially minded in the sense of being content with less gain than their economic position permits them to take. Literal and cold-blooded pursuit of maximum gain in a setting in which large groups of sellers have unexploited price power might well result in government controls or in the breakdown of private management of enterprise. A system of excise levies may partly overcome any reluctance of sellers to advance prices. Public opinion sanctions price advances when they are accompanied by increases in excise taxes. This attitude, curiously enough, seems to be founded upon the theory that consumers pay excise taxes. In a social organization in which price policies are determined partly by public opinion and political factors, one might argue that any tax which removes some of these noneconomic restraints on business price policies is shifted to consumers. The rationale for the view that corporate income taxes are shifted to buyers appears to rest on some such theory. Such an approach implies that a close study of tax shifting requires an examination of social psychology.

These implications raise the question again of the meaning of tax causation. If tax causation refers to any changes in public attitude and business practices which can in some loose way be ascribed to the tax in question, the hope of obtaining a general theory of taxation might have to be abandoned. Statements made in the Senate Finance Committee, when an excise or other tax is under consideration, concerning what someone believes an industry should or might do if the legislation were adopted become relevant to the question of how the tax is shifted. Let us not assume that such talk is always irrelevant. The attitudes of business groups are not formed in a vacuum. Even the pronouncements of some college professor who is very sure that excise taxes or even corporate net income taxes are shifted in part to consumers may affect the behavior of some business groups. The very theories people hold about tax shifting may themselves affect price behavior. These opinions would be irrelevant in a competitive world where there is no such thing as price policies. Nor would they be relevant in the kind of monopolistic world visualized in the first section of this chapter. What then shall we conclude about the shifting of excise taxes in a society in which price policies are partly determined by the economic theories held by power groups?

The dilemma is serious but not, I think, insurmountable. In cases in which sellers have price power, it is not possible to discover how much the tax itself "causes" them to change prices of products. In practice any particular price policy is the outcome of innumerable influences, and the tax influence cannot be isolated in a precise way. We can say, however, that a system of excise taxes reduces the net demand for any particular product in the sense of the market price minus the tax per unit. Any group of sellers subject to excise taxes has its monopoly power reduced so far as monopoly power is measurable from the demand side of the market. However the over-all demands for products may change or be affected by the system of excise taxes, business and labor groups as a whole obtain lower money incomes net of tax liabilities by an amount equal to the tax liability. Economics, being a relativistic science, must study taxes in a relativistic manner. If monetary policies and actual price policies of private groups, however affected over time by tax devices, succeed in maintaining full employment, we know that the taxes have been absorbed by owners of resources in the form of reduced profits, wages, and other incomes determined currently in production, given the monetary demands for products. This knowledge follows from the rules of arithmetic and from the elementary fact that the taxes have a yield to the government. From this point of view, no matter what price policies are pursued by business and labor organizations—provided they are not inconsistent with full employment of resources—any set of excise-tax levies is borne by owners of resources. Full employment is roughly a competitive situation in the sense that, with given monetary demands for products, prices do clear the markets for resource services. It is not the competitive case in the sense that resource allocation is the same as it would be if no seller had effective price power.

If there is underemployment of resources, whatever its specific causes, including taxes, money incomes of resource owners taken as a group are reduced by the amount of the yield of the tax from what they otherwise would have been, given the demands for products. This conclusion likewise follows from the rules of arithmetic. Therefore we may say that any shifting of a set of excise taxes must be confined to groups of people who own resources which participate in production. It is difficult to trace the precise shifting of the tax within this group. If some power group succeeds in increasing its money income by the amount of an excise tax levied upon its output, other sellers find their money incomes lowered on this account; the tax liability has been partly shifted to them. However various power groups in the society may choose to compete among themselves for the dollars of consumers and investors, they can pass the tax liability back and forth among themselves, but they cannot get rid of it. The specific tax liability borne by each owner of resources is indeterminate to the extent that price policies are indeterminate. The pattern of income redistribution occasioned by any set of excise taxes, discovered by reference to a competitive system of price determination, provides the clues for ascertaining the specific income effects of the tax under other systems of pricing. Some shifting of such taxes to owners of hired resources is a virtual certainty regardless of the power of labor organizations. It is also virtually certain that business groups cannot shift all of the tax to owners of hired resources.

Excise Subsidies and Overpricing

With monopolistic pricing of products and of resource services, the effects of excise subsidies are with some exceptions the opposite of those noted above for excise taxes. If there is price collusion of the type discussed for excise taxes, sellers maintain unchanged prices and also accept the subsidy. Profits of business firms are increased by the amount of the subsidy payments. Unless the government offsets these subsidy payments by additional taxes, private expenditures will increase over time. In this aspect subsidies are inflationary devices with respect to the demand for products because they increase money incomes. Their effects in this regard are the reverse of those found for excise taxes for monopoly pricing. But there is no equivalent deflation of prices.

The announcement effects of the subsidies, by creating an incentive for producers to expand output, will lead to some lowering of prices in the competitive areas of the economy. Such industries increase the demand for hired resource services and, in a full employment setting, attract them away from monopolized industries. If perfectly competitive pricing throughout the system is taken as a norm for ideal allocation of resources, a general system of subsidies in a full employment setting appears likely to worsen the allocation. Competitive industries must allow the subsidy to reduce their prices and raise their output. They thereby pull resources away from monopoly industries. These changes are just the opposite of the adjustments needed for better allocation of resources.

In settings where considerable unemployment exists, excise subsidies are a corrective measure. They have a tendency to induce sellers to decrease prices of products. They also increase private money incomes. In addition, this income effect pushes up, in subsequent periods, private demands for products.

So far as monopolists and oligopolists gear their price policies closely to demand factors, subsidies of output tend to lower product prices. An excise subsidy increases the financial remuneration per unit of output. Marginal analysis, to the extent that it is relevant, suggests that a policy of maximizing profit results in greater output and lower market prices. If sellers with price power could be depended upon to behave in this fashion, excise subsidies limited to such industries would lead to a better allocation of resources.

To the extent that a system of excise subsidies induces some sellers of products to increase output and reduce prices, the money incomes of owners of hired resources will be increased. Under full employment conditions, money wage rates and prices of other hired services rise. Under underemployment conditions, incomes of the owners of resources previously unemployed will increase.

Like excise taxes, their subsidy counterparts are shifted among owners of various types of resources. With any given demands for products, and with a given employment level, subsidies increase money incomes without decreasing product prices. In addition, subsidies may change the composition of output in the fashion indicated.

EXCISE TAXES AND UNDERPRICING

Any particular price or set of prices may be higher or lower than a competitive or clearing price. Sellers, left to their own devices, have a tendency to set prices higher, and in many cases considerably higher, than competitive tests would dictate. On occasion, however, even in the absence of government action, underpricing practices are found. Even though the airlines may operate their planes at a fraction of capacity most of the year, they may find more customers than their equipment can handle at particular dates. Where, for institutional reasons, prices must be established well in advance of the dates when the services are to be provided, errors of this kind are always possible. Underpricing for a commodity means that sellers are willing to supply less at the established price than buyers are willing to buy at that price. Underpricing for all commodities means that sellers cannot supply commodities in amounts equal to those which buyers wish to buy.

Underpricing on a general scale is a theoretically possible result of private price fixing. In the first few years immediately following World War II, some major industries in the United States offered their products for sale at prices below competitive levels, for reasons associated with, but not fully explained by, the high level of private demands for products. When underpricing such as this occurs, the imposition of excise taxes will, in all likelihood, induce sellers to advance prices closer to competitive levels. The government obtains the income which otherwise is claimed by strategically placed groups such as retailers, "gray market" operators, or by the final customers themselves. Excise taxes in such special circumstances induce sellers to allow the price mechanism to function as a rationing device and forestall an increase in the incomes of strategically placed groups. If there is a general disposition by sellers to charge prices lower than competitive prices, excise taxes on their products do not burden private groups in any significant sense. Private sellers tax themselves, so to speak, by underpricing their products, and the government merely appropriates to itself the yield which these sellers have voluntarily foregone.

Voluntary underpricing is rare except for some government-supplied goods and services. By far the most important and persistent illustration of underpricing occurs in connection with suppressed inflation and government enforcement of maximum prices. In several European countries, price control was extensive and persistent during and after World War II. This extra-price rationing practice was often systematized by the use of coupons. In this fashion, ordinary money was supplemented or even effectively supplanted. We do not intend here to investigate in detail the complexities of multiple-money systems. For the purpose of learning the effects of excise taxes, it may be instructive to study a simple double-money system in which coupons are employed for general rationing purposes, and each good and service is priced both in ordinary money and in coupons. It is assumed that the government sets the prices in coupon money at levels which require no further nonmoney devices, such as being the first in line or especially friendly with suppliers. If coupon money is distributed equally per head or per family (with special weights for children), the government provides a flat-sum subsidy in coupon money to persons. Coupon money cannot, of course, be earned by work or by owning property. Firms are not allowed to spend coupons to finance employment of hired resources, although coupons may be used for interenterprise transactions. The effect of the use of coupon money is to reduce, on a very substantial scale, the inequality in the ability of different people to acquire goods and services. If prices in terms of regular money are maintained at very low levels so that any person can spend all his coupons, an equalitarian economy comes into being. The equivalent financial arrangement for a single-money system would entail a system of confiscatory taxes on the wealthy and flat-sum money subsidies to everyone.[7]

In a double-money system, excise taxes already in existence continue to divert money income from owners of resources and in this

---

[7] To reduce the spending power of wealthier groups in a single-money system to levels that can be achieved with a double-money system would require a highly progressive system of taxation. An income tax without a loophole, levied at highly progressive rates, would not be adequate. It would be necessary to levy taxes sufficiently high to take away all the income of the moderately wealthy groups and substantially more than this from the very wealthy. Theoretically a system of net worth taxation could be devised to have this effect. The technical difficulties, not to mention the political objections, of such heavy taxation make it easy to understand why governments prefer to adopt a second money in times of war. A double-money system is a technically simple and potent tax device. In peacetime, double-money systems have a strong appeal to political groups with strong equalitarian orientations. It is a mistake to look upon coupon rationing as merely an anti-inflationary weapon.

way reduce their money asset position. The effects of changes in excise taxes depend in part upon the actions of the government agencies in charge of the price control program. Any general observation concerning their price decisions in the light of changed excise taxes is dangerous because their decisions are commonly made with many considerations in mind. If they "hold the line" in the face of rises in excise taxes, the sellers subject to tax are financially squeezed and may be forced to absorb losses. Relief to them without subsidies requires a reduction in the prices they pay. Maintenance of the same relative price structure would, of course, require proportional reductions in cost prices. In this event, the excise becomes a proportional tax on those whose earnings depend upon the taxed industries.

If excise taxes are raised in a double-money system, and the price control agency allows prices in terms of ordinary money to advance by the full amount of the tax, the relevance of ordinary prices increases and that of coupon prices decreases. This effect, it should be observed, has nothing to do with excise taxes as such. Administrative decisions to increase prices for any or no reason reduce the spread between the amount that people would like to buy at those prices and the amount sellers can supply. If the administrative agency simply increases product prices and no new tax is imposed, the incomes of business organizations rise by the full amount of the per unit price increase. There will be no reduction in quantities sold as long as underpricing in terms of regular money continues. A rise in excise taxes accompanied by administrative decisions to increase prices differs from an equal increase in price without a change in tax rates because the government obtains the additional income. Excess demands are reduced both because prices, stated in ordinary money, are higher and because private cash balances are partly reduced. The additional tax has the effect of wiping up some of the idle balances of private groups and handing them over to the government. In this setting, excise taxes function as purely monetary devices. They are only a nominal burden on private groups. Similarly a reduction of excise taxes, under such conditions, does not reduce the tax burden on people in any significant sense.

The income of sellers in terms of coupons according to the rules usually employed in double-money systems is taxed at an effective rate of 100 per cent. The coupons they get are confiscated. As long as such a rule is adopted, other taxes in terms of coupon money are ruled out. The 100 per cent coupon tax rate also guarantees that coupon money cannot perform any function to induce people to manage resources. Ordinary money alone is left to do the job. The continued operation of such a system depends upon the willingness of people to manage resources for purely nominal gain. It is unlikely that people will do this during peacetime unless the acquisition of some products depends marginally upon money or unless they can look forward to times when coupon money will be eliminated from circulation and regular money will be of some use. A double-money system is equivalent to a heavy progressive tax system combined with flat-sum subsidies. The "tax" feature is dangerous to economic efficiency because it involves 100 per cent marginal rates. Equivalent taxes in a single-money system would not ordinarily be tolerated.

Excise Subsidies and Underpricing

Price control is often accompanied by direct subsidies in the form of ordinary money payments to keep sellers content or to permit them to be financially solvent. Although price control need not involve explicit money subsidies nor need subsidies involve price control, they are commonly tied together in practice. These subsidy payments are not always excises in the sense here employed. Nevertheless, it is convenient at this point to examine the effects of a system of price control where subsidies are paid to particular sellers because they sell particular commodities.

Government-enforced underpricing in terms of ordinary money can be viewed as a system of transfers in kind from sellers to buyers. If sellers are required to provide a commodity at a certain price, the difference between that price and a clearing price is the amount of the subsidy in kind to buyers. Thus tenants are subsidized by landlords to the extent that they pay less than a competitive market would dictate. If tenants can sublet at any price, the subsidy becomes directly measurable; tenants are presented with a gift of part ownership of the building. A general system of underpricing means that the value of output measured in market prices is understated. In a system of underpricing, the value of the subsidy in kind should be added to the incomes of buyers in a computation of incomes by groups.

Money subsidies financed by the government are necessary in such a system if in their absence the realized money incomes of sellers would be negative. Conceptions of fairness based on conventional markups or similar practices may require supplemental payments by the government to the sellers in question for political reasons. When sellers experience rising money costs, because of advancing prices of imports for example, subsidies become the alternative to relaxing the price-control policy.

These direct money subsidies paid to sellers, in such an arrangement, should not be regarded as consumer subsidies. Rather consumers (and investors) are subsidized by the underpricing as such. Sellers are "taxed" for the benefit of buyers by the forced sale of commodities at prices lower than clearing prices. This subsidy in kind and tax in kind exist because of price control; they exist whether any direct money subsidies are paid or not. The money subsidy offsets more or less the "tax" in kind levied on sellers in favor of buyers. If it fully offsets the "tax," that is, if the price allowed plus the subsidy equals what sellers could realize in an open market, only the consumer subsidy in kind remains. Money payments by the government are subsidies to sellers and offset sellers' subsidies in kind to buyers. The implication should not be drawn that such a system carries with it any "real" advantages in the sense that "real incomes" of people as consumers and investors are greater because of such subsidies. Even if the system is as efficient in the sense of inducing the same care in the management of resources and the same choices as between work and leisure, people do not as a group obtain more output from the system.[8] Output is limited by the resources under the command of the group and by the gains from trade with other groups. No system of finance can increase output beyond that given by the limitation of resources, although various systems of finance can and do make vast differences in efficiency. Subsidies in kind to consumers involve mainly distributional questions. Like a system of per capita money grants without price control, they are an income equalization device, but unlike such a system, they also involve a system of "taxes" in kind which would be difficult to defend by any presently accepted stand-

---

[8] If the double-money system is fairly general in the sense that any commodity one might like to have requires coupons, the marginal utility of money income, except for the psychological advantage of holding money, is zero. Money becomes meaningless and people have little or no inducement to work more unless they are paid in kind. In addition, subsidies in money or in kind permit people to enjoy some level of living without bothering to manage resources. In general, the income effect of such measures operates to induce those aided to demand more leisure, if anything, since they can afford more. In addition, the price of leisure is lowered by high marginal rates of income taxation. Countries which employ all these financial devices during long periods of time are apt to find themselves troubled with incentive problems. It is customary but not convincing to attribute the adverse incentive effects of these measures to taxation.

ards. In this, as well as in other respects, they are directly at variance with the ideal that redistributive measures should be systematic with respect to personal means and should not be discriminatory among persons otherwise similarly situated. Extension of such government rules undermines the relevance of money and prices as devices to ration products and manage resources. These devices, rather than "socialism," seem to be the main threat to systems called "capitalistic" in the contemporary scene.

GENERAL THEORY OF EXCISE TAX AND SUBSIDY SHIFTING

The theory of excise subsidies and taxes developed for competitive pricing conditions may be applied to overpricing and underpricing without fundamental alteration. Some precision is lost because of the vagueness of tax causation in a social setting in which sellers or government administrators have power to establish prices. A noncompetitive world is not determinate in the same sense as is a competitive world. Prices are the outcome of politics and group policies rather than of impersonal "forces." Although price policies are not purely arbitrary, significant differences in prices can exist for reasons which cannot be traced to objective considerations alone. We are driven back to an investigation of the implications of price policies actually adopted. Theories concerning the effects of taxes become less precise as power tactics are found to affect pricing arrangements.

Yet certain fundamental effects of taxes are clear. Even under conditions of arbitrary pricing, the belief that excise taxes are shifted to consumers has little basis. The function of prices, considered from the point of view of takers, is to ration available supplies among them. If prices do this task well, as they do if competitive pricing arrangements prevail, taxes matter to buyers only to the extent that they have a selective effect on the composition of output. Some products are made more expensive and others are made less so. If the system of taxes is neutral, people as buyers are not then affected by excise taxes.

Excise taxes may be accompanied by price changes which limit amounts of products demanded to the point of reducing employment opportunities. Whatever the "causes" of overpricing, it is overpricing of products and services which results in underemployment including disguised underemployment. If a society wishes to have full employment, it needs to avoid passing laws, including excise-tax measures, which induce further overpricing. If, nevertheless, excise taxes are employed, either the prices that are costs must adjust downward or else a monetary expansion must be engineered. Since monetary expansion can be managed merely by not taxing as heavily, excise taxes are a fiscal nuisance if it is proper to assume that sellers arbitrarily raise product prices by amounts roughly equal to tax increases. They are not a fiscal failure if the economy does adjust to them by allowing money costs of production to fall or by preventing them from rising. In this event, they do not require monetary inflation to offset their negative employment effects. If the usually held beliefs about the price implications of excise taxes are correct, they have an "excess burden" which is truly excess in the sense of creating avoidable social waste, and on this count they come off poorly indeed, even if they could be defended with respect to their distributional effects on money incomes. The classical indictment of excise taxes was buttressed by erroneous theories, but the judgment can be given a strong economic defense for societies in which substantial downward adjustments of prices of resources are effectively prohibited.

8

Import Duties:
Self-adjusting Exchanges

John Stuart Mill once wrote: "...a tax on imported commodities ... almost always falls in part upon the foreigners who consume our goods; ... this is a mode in which a nation may appropriate to itself, at the expense of foreigners, a larger share than would otherwise belong to it of the increase in the general productiveness of the labour and capital of the world, which results from the interchange of commodities among nations."[1] Thus Mill lays down the principle that a country by imposing import duties can force foreigners to bear taxes. By "foreigners," Mill does not mean foreign producers of products subject to duties when sold abroad. A case might be made for the view that duties are sometimes shifted "backward" to the producers of taxed items. It might be argued that duties imposed upon sugar imports lower the price of sugar paid to foreign sellers, and therefore they are bearing at least part of the burden. Discussions of the burden of import duties have often been conducted along these lines.[2] But Mill's views are quite different from these. He would deny that foreign producers might be forced to bear even a part of the burden of import duties of sugar-using countries and states positively: "It is the foreign consumer of our exported commodities, who is obliged to pay a higher price for them because we maintain duties on foreign goods."[3] If we adhere to Mill's theories, we must say that foreign buyers of United States exports are bearing part of the burden of United States import duties.

Mill developed his conclusions about the burden and effects of

[1] J. S. Mill, *Principles of Political Economy* (Ashley ed.; London: Longmans, Green, 1909), p. 854.

[2] Cf. Otto von Mering, *The Shifting and Incidence of Taxation* (Philadelphia: Blakiston, 1942), pp. 150–151, 182; cf. C. F. Bastable, *Public Finance* (3d ed.; London: Macmillan, 1903), pp. 551–573.

[3] Mill, *op. cit.*, p. 855.

import duties with the concept of reciprocal demand. This technique of analysis was taken over, improved, and made more definite by the neoclassical thinkers, including Bickerdike, Edgeworth, Marshall, and Pigou. They greatly refined the reciprocal demand technique without, however, reaching conclusions about the burden of import duties substantially different from those laid down by Mill. Edgeworth, who calls Mill's exposition of international trade theory "unsurpassed,"[4] examines the implications of the concept of reciprocal demand and Mill's doctrine that import duties are borne in part by foreigners, placing himself on the side of Mill in opposition to the critics who claim that import duties are borne by consumers of taxed imports.[5]

Marshall likewise endorses the Mill view of the incidence of import duties and is much concerned about the obstacles they interpose to international trade.[6] Pigou differs only slightly from Marshall in the analysis of import duties, but his remarks are nonetheless interesting from the point of view of tax theory because Pigou attempts to integrate the Mill theory of the burden of import duties with taxation theory generally. Pigou comes out unequivocally for the position that import duties ". . . will also always exact *some* contribution from foreigners."[7]

The achievements of the neoclassical writers in international trade in connection with the effects of import (and export) taxes are impressive. Not only is it argued that import duties fall in part upon foreign consumers, but the burden of import duties is shown to be symmetrical with export duties, if it is assumed that the tax is levied in export goods, or if levied in money, that the "proceeds" are spent upon export goods.[8] Unlike many other features of neoclassical economics, the theory of the incidence of import (and export) duties is couched in terms of general equilibrium analysis. It even takes account, as some students of public finance say it should, of how the government spends the tax proceeds.

---

[4] F. Y. Edgeworth, *Papers Relating to Political Economy* (London: Macmillan, 1925), Vol. II, p. 20.

[5] *Ibid.*, pp. 13–14.

[6] See Alfred Marshall, *Money Credit and Commerce* (London: Macmillan, 1923), Bk. III, chaps. 9, 10, and Appendix J.

[7] A. C. Pigou, *A Study in Public Finance* (London: Macmillan, 1928), p. 204. Italics are in the original.

[8] A. P. Lerner in his article "The Symmetry between Import and Export Taxes" (*Economica*, n.s., III [1936]: 306–313), attempts to refute Edgeworth's doubts to the contrary and also develops a formal technique for showing the burden of import and export taxes, no matter how the taxing government "spends the tax receipts." The symmetry argument is also presented by Marshall (*op. cit.*, p. 181, n. 1) and by Pigou (*op. cit.*, p. 203).

Yet with all due respect to the brilliance of Mill's arguments and the careful analytical support they have received at the hands of Edgeworth, Marshall, Pigou, and others, we may properly doubt the conclusion that foreign consumers of United States products bear part of the burden of United States import taxes. The neoclassical preoccupation with *real* matters, such as the terms of trade, to the exclusion of monetary mechanics makes it suspect. The lack of symmetry between their arguments concerning the incidence of internal taxes and of import duties also creates doubt as to the general validity of the theory.

In place of the neoclassical view, I shall propose first that the burden of import duties always rests upon a certain economic segment of the country levying the import duties and not upon foreigners, and second that this segment is not the consumers of taxed imports. It is, on the contrary, those who own resources, both human and nonhuman, in export industries and those who own resources competitive with resources located in export industries. These people bear the tax in the form of a reduction in their money incomes in a fashion analogous to a partial proportional income tax (with no exemptions) collected at the source. They must sacrifice money income equal to the yield of the tax to the Treasury. This position differs, therefore, not only from the neoclassical view of the burden of import duties, but also from the theory developed with the use of partial equilibrium technique concluding that domestic consumers of the country imposing import duties bear such taxes.[9]

NEOCLASSICAL THEORY OF IMPORT TAX SHIFTING

The essentials of the neoclassical argument concerning the incidence of import duties may be presented graphically by the use of reciprocal demand schedules (fig. 17). Suppose that two countries, the United States (A) and England (E), carry on their foreign trade in only two commodities and that there are no other international transactions: the balance of trade and the balance of payments are identical. E sells whisky to A, and A sells cotton to E. In figure 17, OA shows the amount of American cotton (measured along OX) which will be exported for various quantities of whisky imported (measured along OY) from England. Likewise, OE measures the export supply schedule of English whisky in

    [9] Cf. Lionel Robbins and G. L. Schwartz in William H. Beveridge and others, *Tariffs: The Case Examined* (London: Longmans, Green, 1932), p. 173. See also n. 2 above.

terms of cotton. The schedules may be visualized readily if it is supposed that traders in *A* buy cotton with dollars, export the cotton to *E*, sell it for pounds, buy whisky in *E* with all the pounds so obtained, and export the whisky to *A* where it is sold for dollars. If the traders' costs may be considered to be zero, and if perfect competition prevails among traders at every stage, traders will increase exports of cotton and imports of whisky to the "break-even" point, shown as *P* in figure 17.

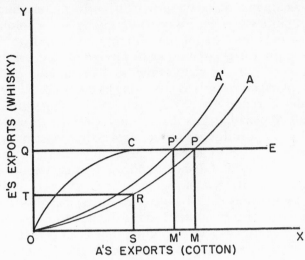

Fig. 17. Reciprocal demands: E's schedule elasticity unity.

As a limiting case, one which Marshall regards as an "Exceptional Demand" case, let it be assumed that *E*'s demand for *A*'s cotton has an elasticity of unity within the relevant range.[10] In figure 17, this case is illustrated by showing the relevant portion of *OE*, that is *CE*, as perpendicular to the *OY* axis. Still following the neoclassical argument, suppose now that *A* levies a duty upon whisky imports to be paid in exports.[11] With the imposition of the tax, the terms upon which the traders will now export cotton in exchange for whisky change, as indicated in the shift to the left from *OA* to *OA'*. If, as is assumed in figure 17, the English demand for cotton has an elasticity of unity within the relevant range, the tax leaves the volume of American imports of whisky unchanged

[10] Marshall, *op. cit.*, p. 355, fig. 22.

[11] Or, alternatively, we may assume, as do Marshall, Pigou, and Lerner, that the tax is levied and collected in money with the proceeds spent by the government to acquire cotton (or the resources producing cotton).

$(P'M' = PM)$ whereas the volume of A's exports of cotton falls (from OM to OM'). Thus Mill's conclusion appears to follow, namely, that in these circumstances, English consumers of cotton bear all the tax imposed by A upon whisky imports. English consumers of cotton must pay higher prices for cotton. On the other hand, A's consumers of whisky, their supply being unchanged, pay no more in dollars than before the imposition of the tax.

If, on the other hand, OE has a negative slope within the relevant range, a tax upon whisky imports will result in consumers in A getting absolutely more whisky while giving up absolutely less cotton; and thus the logic of the Mill argument leads to the conclusion that in these circumstances foreign consumers bear an amount greater than the yield of the tax.[12] Yet another possibility, one which Marshall regards as belonging to the "Normal Demand" class of cases, is found where OE has a positive slope throughout. In this case, Marshall argues that a country cannot shift all of the burden of its import duties onto foreigners, but must in part bear its own import duties. These cases he analyzes in some detail.[13]

What Mill, Marshall, Edgeworth, Pigou, Lerner, and others have demonstrated by this type of argument is that import duties (and their arguments apply equally to export duties) may shift the terms of trade in favor of the country levying the import duty. By thinking of import duties as levied in kind, they assume that changing the terms of trade favorably to the taxing country is identical with making foreign consumers of exports bear at least a part of the burden of the tax. Pigou goes so far as to define the foreign burden of import duties along these lines.[14]

But it is not true that import duties are levied in kind. Furthermore, it should not be assumed that the government "spends the money" upon exports or their equivalent. Import duties may be and indeed are levied without revenue considerations in mind, and the extra yield may merely mean that other taxes are not increased or the government deficit is smaller (or the surplus larger) than would otherwise be the case. In advanced economies, taxes are levied in money, and the explanation of the burden of import duties must be consistent with this fact. Fortunately we need not abandon the reciprocal demand technique even if we recognize that international trade is conducted in terms of money, that import taxes are paid in money, and that a market for foreign

[12] Marshall, *op. cit.*, fig. 16, p. 347, p. 348.
[13] *Ibid.*, pp. 344–345, figs. 13, 14.
[14] Pigou, *op. cit.*, p. 204.

exchange exists, provided we are willing to assume, as a simplifying case, a foreign exchange market which is automatically self-adjusting.[15]

If a freely fluctuating foreign exchange rate is postulated, the reciprocal demand technique can be applied directly as follows: Returning to figure 17, select any point R on schedule OA and extend perpendiculars to the axes OY and OX, giving points T and S. Thus OS measures the amount of cotton which cotton producers in A are willing to export provided that OT quantity of whisky is obtained in return. These producers are willing to export OS cotton for OT whisky because the quantity of whisky OT will sell for the number of dollars necessary to call forth the production and export of OS quantity of cotton. With a freely fluctuating foreign exchange rate, the dollars acquired by E's whisky exporters become the dollar income of A's cotton exporters. E's exporters acquire dollars by selling whisky in A. They then trade these dollars for pounds. Likewise, and for the same reasons, the pounds acquired by A's exporters of cotton become, through the exchange machinery, the pound income of exporters of whisky.

The position and shape of an export supply schedule of one country in terms of the imports from the other depends upon the local demand for the imported item and also the local demand and the local costs of producing the exported item. One of these may dominate and determine the shape of a reciprocal demand schedule. If, for example, the E demand for imports has an elasticity of unity in terms of pounds, E exporters of whisky, given their costs and the local demand for whisky, will export a certain quantity of whisky regardless of the quantity of cotton imported. There is, in such circumstances, only one quantity of whisky which they are willing to export for a given number of pounds. By the assumption that the English demand for cotton has an elasticity of unity, the quantity of pounds initially acquired by exporters of cotton in A becomes independent of the quantity exported. There is one quantity of whisky to be exported which, given the state of competition among British whisky producers, will maximize their income position. In such circumstances, E's reciprocal schedule for the exportation of whisky in terms of cotton can be shown as a line QE perpendicular to OY (fig. 17). If, on the other hand, the dollar

---

[15] If one is willing to make Marshall's assumption that "in the long run" international demands are independent of money (Marshall, *op. cit.*, p. 184, bottom), conclusions reached for fluctuating exchanges apply with equal force to fixed exchanges. No such assumption will be made here.

demand for English whisky has an elasticity of unity, the supply schedule of cotton exportation in terms of whisky may be shown as a line perpendicular to the OX axis (not shown in fig. 17).

With any given dollar demand for whisky, the greater the costs of producing cotton, the less will be the amount of cotton exported for any given amount of whisky. Thus any increase in the costs of producing cotton, resulting, for example, from the imposition of an export tax in dollars on cotton, will shift the schedule for cotton in terms of whisky to the left. For the same reason, any import tax upon whisky will, by reducing the number of dollars reaching the hands of A's exporters of cotton, shift the supply schedule of cotton in terms of whisky imports to the left. If A's production of cotton for export is independent of the dollar price of cotton, as it would be if resources were completely specialized to the production of cotton for export (perhaps only for a range), a tax upon either whisky imports or cotton exports will reduce only the money earnings of resources in cotton production and not affect the supply schedule in any way. Such a schedule is "nonshiftable" and has some importance in the following discussion.[16]

SHIFTING OF UNIFORM IMPORT DUTIES

We may now proceed to our main task of isolating the burden of import taxes. We suppose at this stage that the total demand for output is constant in both the United States and England or, in other words, that the national money income (gross and net) is constant. But we specifically do not assume that real income is constant. All products and all productive services are assumed to be competitively priced, which means that all markets are continuously cleared and that there is no rationing of buyers or sellers by methods other than price. This means further that we are assuming full employment in the sense that markets for the many varieties of labor services are cleared, as well as other markets.

Before any import tax is imposed by A upon whisky, let us

[16] The above labored exposition of the meaning of reciprocal schedules seems desirable because of the apparent confusion concerning their meaning even among close students of the subject. For example, R. W. Stevens writes: "A tariff would distort a country's offer curve ... because it would reduce the country's demand for imports." ("New Ideas in the Theory of International Trade," *American Economic Review*, XLI [June, 1951]: 371.) The reason given is incorrect. A tariff "distorts" trade because it reduces the relative financial rewards of exporters in the duty-levying country as compared to the financial rewards from using the same resources in other ways. Tariffs need not reduce a "country's demand for imports" in the schedule sense nor need they increase import prices and thus reduce the quantities demanded.

consider trade to be already under way and in equilibrium in the sense that the earnings of resources engaged in producing for export in both countries are equal to the earnings of resources employed in industries producing for domestic sale, to the extent that resources have alternative uses. The quantity of cotton exported (per unit of time) sells, let us say, for £1,000,000 in *E* and the quantity of whisky exported sells for $5,000,000 in *A*. All pounds are supposed to be traded for all dollars, giving an exchange rate

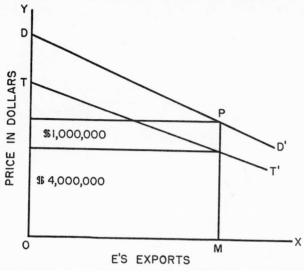

Fig. 18. A's import demand.

of $5 = £1. The trading is pictured graphically by the use of ordinary demand schedules in figures 18 and 19. Figure 18 shows the dollar demand for *E*'s whisky with *OM* the assumed equilibrium amount of whisky imports by *A* at the dollar price *PM*, giving a total of $5,000,000 obtained by English exporters of whisky. Figure 19 shows the pound demand for United States cotton with *ON* the assumed equilibrium amount of cotton exports at the pound price *RN*, giving a total of £1,000,000. *A*'s cotton producers realize $5,000,000 for the export of *ON* quantity of cotton, and *E*'s whisky producers realize £1,000,000.

Now let an import tax of 20 per cent be imposed by *A* on whisky. The line *TT'* (fig. 18) is the net demand schedule,[17] that is the

---

[17] This again follows Edgeworth's procedure of subtracting the tax from the demand schedule. The conventional method of adding taxes to costs is unduly clumsy for present purposes.

dollar price of whisky to *A*'s buyers minus the tax per unit of whisky. An ad valorem tax is assumed and therefore the net demand schedule *TT'* (fig. 18) has the same elasticity as the demand schedule *DD'* for identical quantities. With a tax of 20 per cent, the yield will be $1,000,000 (one-fifth of $5,000,000) for the same rate of importation of whisky. The volume of importation and the dollar price of whisky may of course change, but the initial task is to discover who has the incentive to change his operations because of the presence of the tax.

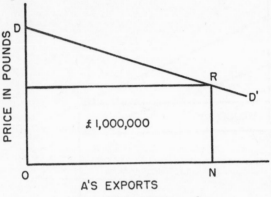

Fig. 19. E's import demand.

The analysis may be most readily set forth by a close examination of the following limiting cases: (1) a fixed supply of cotton for export; (2) a demand for cotton of an elasticity of unity; (3) a demand for cotton of an elasticity of less than one; (4) a demand for cotton of an elasticity of more than one.

Case 1. *A fixed supply of cotton for export*

If the supply of cotton is fixed in terms of whisky because the supply of cotton is fixed in terms of dollars, resources located in the cotton industry must be perfectly immobile. When the tax is imposed, it will reduce the dollar receipts of *E*'s exporters of whisky by $1,000,000. Sellers of whisky may anticipate this outcome and, in an effort to recoup, ship less and thereby obtain a higher dollar price. On the other hand, they may take an experimental attitude and continue to export unchanged amounts, in which case their optimism will be justified. Although immediately they find themselves with one million fewer dollars, this is a matter of little concern to them since they calculate their gains and losses in terms of pounds. When E's exporters trade $4,000,000 instead of $5,000,-000 for pounds ($1,000,000 having been paid to A's treasury in settlement of import taxes), A's exporters of cotton are clearly the losers. Upon selling pounds, exporters of cotton receive $4,000,000 instead of $5,000,000, and hence they lose $1,000,000 in income. As a consequence of the tax, the exchange rate moves from $5 = £1 to $4 = £1. Thus we find that the people who forego the money which A's treasury receives are A's producers of exported cotton.[18] If, as we have supposed, resources located in the cotton export industry are completely tied to this occupation, they lose precisely what the treasury gains, and they are not in a position to do anything about it.[19] All resources located in the cotton industry receive, as a result of the tax, smaller dollar incomes by the amount of the yield of the tax.

The terms of trade, under the conditions laid down, are unchanged. The quantity of cotton exported, by the nature of the assumptions, remains unchanged. E's exporters have no incentive because of the tax to change their behavior. They realize exactly the same price for whisky in terms of pounds as before the tax, and thus the quantity of whisky exported to A remains unchanged. The dollar price of whisky is unaffected, and therefore A's consumers of whisky are in no way injured by the presence of the tax. Thus the conclusion seems inescapable that A's exporters are bearing the full amount of the tax. Pigou's statement to the effect that the foreigner always makes some contribution to the treasury of the country levying import duties is shown already to be subject to at least this one correction.

Case 2. *Unitary demand by E for cotton*

In this and in the following cases, we make the more general assumption that resources located in A's export industry are mobile in some degree. From the analysis of Case 1, it seems apparent that, initially, the entire tax burden falls upon A's exporters of cotton, regardless of the elasticity of the demand for whisky in A or for cotton in E. Their earnings decline absolutely and therefore are relatively smaller than the earnings of resources in other fields.

---

[18] This conclusion is consistent with the neoclassical doctrine that import duties are symmetrical with export duties (Lerner, *loc. cit.*). If export taxes yielding $1,000,000 are supposed, the incidence is precisely the same as stated in the text. In either case, U. S. exporters sacrifice the money which the U. S. Treasury receives.

[19] Except, of course, they may resort to political action to get the tax removed. If the case were always as clear as this one, the political pressure on the U. S. Congress to keep down import duties might be much the same as it is for other excise taxes.

Thus an incentive exists to move out of the cotton export industry. As resources move away from the cotton industry, cotton production for export declines, simultaneously raising the pound price of cotton in E (and the dollar price in A). But since in the present case the pound demand for cotton is assumed to have an elasticity of one, the number of pounds obtained from the sale of the smaller volume of cotton remains unchanged—in our illustration £1,000,-000. The exchange of dollars for pounds results in whisky exporters' receiving the same pound price for whisky as before, and they have therefore no incentive to curtail their sales of whisky in A's market. It follows that exporters of whisky cannot be regarded as making any contribution to A's treasury. This conclusion holds regardless of the nature of the cost conditions surrounding the production of whisky in E. Even if resources are specialized to whisky production, and some are almost certain to be, E's exporters do not bear any of the tax. It cannot reasonably be argued that A's consumers of whisky bear any part of the tax. The volume of whisky imported remains unchanged and with any given demand for whisky, its dollar price also remains unchanged.[20]

The tax burden in fact falls entirely upon domestic resource owners. A's exporters find themselves initially bearing the tax. What would otherwise be a part of their dollar income through the exchange market becomes instead the Treasury's tax revenue. With mobility of resources, those located in the cotton industry need not, however, as in Case 1, bear the entire tax burden. They can place part (never all) of the burden upon others through the process of competition. The competition with other resources may merely mean that the existing firms produce more products for domestic consumption and fewer for export. In this event, the effect of the greater production of these domestic commodities will be to reduce their prices and thereby reduce the money income of all other resources engaged in producing these commodities. In addition, resources may shift to other industries in an effort to restore lost earning power and can, by increasing the output of these industries, reduce the prices and hence the earnings of resources in other fields. The extent to which the tax burden is spread depends upon the degree to which the resources located in the export industry can effectively compete for earnings with resources located elsewhere. In the special and very unlikely case of perfect mobility of all resources, the earnings and the money

---

[20] The neoclassical view would also, in this case, argue against the conception that domestic consumers bear the tax.

income of all resources, with any given total demand for all products, will fall by an amount which collectively equals the yield of the tax; each owner's distributive share will be proportionately reduced. Import taxes are diffused throughout the system.[21]

The proof of the proposition that an import tax is shifted in part sideways, that is, to other resource owners, can be presented in simple form if we suppose that resources producing cotton for export are capable of producing one other product, say, peanuts.

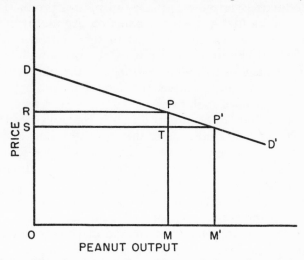

Fig. 20. Allocation-income effects of import duties on domestic industry.

Suppose a demand schedule for peanuts *DD'* (fig. 20) with a current rate of production of *OM* at the price *PM*, considered before resources in the cotton industry make any adjustment to the reduction in their money earnings experienced immediately after the imposition of the tax. For the sake of simplicity, we may suppose that firms in the peanut industry are self-sufficient in the sense that they do not buy current output from other firms. In this case, the area *ORPM* is both the gross and net value product of the peanut industry.[22] Each type of resource in the peanut industry receives the same income per unit of service as its counterpart in the cotton industry before the imposition of the import duty. The disparity of earnings created by the imposition of the import tax results in re-

[21] In a large country, where exports form a small proportion of total production, the imposition of import duties would reduce earnings per resource by a very small amount.

[22] This representation ignores depreciation of nonhuman resources.

sources moving from cotton production to peanut production, thus increasing the output and reducing the price of peanuts. At the output OM' (fig. 20), let us say, earnings in cotton and peanut production per unit of resources of each type are again made equal. Then the area $RPTS$ measures the loss of income to those resources previously entrenched in the peanut industry and therefore measures their share of the tax burden. The area $MTP'M'$ measures the net income obtained by resource owners previously located in cotton production and now employed in peanut production.

If resources located in cotton production are useful in still another industry, the resources located in that industry will share part of the burden, and each unit of resources will transfer a smaller percentage of its money earnings to the state in the form of tax yield. In the same manner, the argument can be generalized to cover all degrees of mobility.

As far as the burden of import duties is concerned, it therefore follows that the yield of the tax to the treasury is borne by owners of resources located in A's export industries and by resources with which they effectively compete. The tax is borne in the form of a reduction in their money earnings.[23]

For conditions corresponding to Case 2, the neoclassical argument leads to the conclusion that E's consumers bear the entire amount of the tax. In contending instead that A's resource owners are bearing the tax, we do not repudiate the neoclassical argument that, with the assumption of E's demand for cotton having an elasticity of one, the terms of trade will shift in favor of A. Imports of whisky remain unchanged, whereas exports of cotton decline. Thus it is clear that E's consumers, at least those who use cotton goods, are made worse off by the tax. They are worse off, but are they, in any meaningful sense, bearing the tax?

Mill, Marshall, and Pigou would, of course, answer this question affirmatively. For them, the fact that E's consumers of A's exports are made worse off is sufficient evidence to select them for the role of taxpayers. Neither Mill nor the neoclassicists give any argument to show how E's buyers of cotton manage, through some channel, to pay money to A's treasury. A theory of shifting which points to certain classes of people as ultimate taxpayers must be prepared

---

[23] The argument in the text does not assume a general deflation of income, either produced or received, in the taxing jurisdiction. It is based upon the assumption that the national net income produced (net value of all output) remains unchanged. The tax has the effect of diverting (not increasing or decreasing) money income from resource owners to the government or, in other words, the tax yield is transfer income.

to demonstrate how money given up by them eventually finds its way to the treasury as tax revenue. E's consumers of A's exports have no obvious medium in which to make payment, directly or indirectly, to A's treasury. The pounds that they pay for output become income for English concerns and their employees, and these people in turn make no payments which are of fiscal significance to A's treasury. E's consumers are indeed made worse off; they suffer from the fact that the economy which supplies them must, because of A's import duties, employ the same quantity of resources to produce exports while receiving a smaller volume of imports.

If the lack of a medium on the part of E's consumers to pay taxes to A's government is not sufficient reason to deny to them the role of taxpayers, there is the further and perhaps more important point that all the tax burden is accounted for domestically. A's export industries and owners of resources located in competing fields lose money income equal to the yield of the tax.[24] A definite medium does exist to get money from them because the treasury collects the tax at the source, which in the case of A's export industries is the dollar value of imports.

In real terms, if we look at both A's and E's consumers together, we find that, although E's consumers are worse off in real terms because of the tax, A's consumers are better off in real terms. A's consumers enjoy the same volume of imports as before the tax and yet obtain the additional products resulting from the employment of resources released from the cotton industry. The gain of A's consumers is offset by the loss of E's consumers.[25]

Case 3. *Inelastic demand by E for cotton*

In contrast with Case 2, it may now be assumed that E's demand for cotton has an elasticity of less than one within the relevant range. Such a case is represented graphically in figure 21. OA is A's supply of cotton exports in terms of whisky. OB is E's supply

[24] The equality holds because, with a tax yield of $1,000,000, the firms in the exporting industry together with their employees sacrifice an amount exactly equal to the tax yield before they make any adjustment. As they adjust by moving into the production of other products, what gains they realize must be at the expense of those with whom they compete, keeping in mind that we are holding constant the total of income produced and, hence, the total of incomes received.

[25] The present view also removes any need in import tax theory for the assumption that taxes are collected in kind. Even such a strong sympathizer with the neoclassical tradition as Taussig finds such an assumption repugnant. (Cf. F. W. Taussig, *International Trade* [New York: Macmillan, 1927], p. 142.)

of whisky exports in terms of cotton, based upon the assumption that, through its relevant range, the demand for cotton in terms of pounds has an elasticity of less than one. *OB* has a negative slope since, if greater quantities of cotton sell for fewer pounds, *E*'s producers, to cover their own costs, must export less whisky. A tax upon imports (whisky) shifts *A*'s schedule of cotton exports in terms of whisky imports from *OA* to *OA'*. The new equilibrium point *P'* shows absolutely larger imports of whisky as a result of

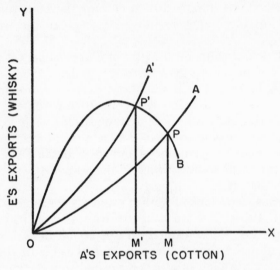

Fig. 21. Reciprocal demands: E's schedule elasticity less than unity.

the tax ($P'M' > PM$) whereas *A*'s exports decline by the amount *M'M*. If *E*'s demand for *A*'s products has an elasticity of less than one, a tax upon *A*'s imports not only improves the terms of trade for *A;* it results in absolutely more imports in return for fewer exports.

In money terms, a tax upon imports of whisky will reduce the earnings of *A*'s cotton industry because the dollars obtained by *A*'s exporters are now reduced by the duties paid to the *A* treasury. As in Case 2, with mobility of resources, production of cotton for export declines and its pound price rises, but in this case, the total number of pounds obtained from the sale of cotton rises. Through the foreign exchange market, English whisky exporters obtain more pounds for the same exports of whisky. The exchange rate moves first from $\$5 = £1$ to $\$4 = £1$; subsequently, because the supply of pounds increases, the dollar price of pounds declines still further. Thus the pound equivalent of the dollar price of whisky again rises. English whisky exporters now have an incentive to ship more whisky than before. As shipments increase, with a dollar demand for whisky of an elasticity of less than infinity, the dollar price of whisky falls. Thus we have the somewhat astonishing result that a tax upon whisky lowers the price of whisky. But this conclusion follows from the premises, and Marshall, although he regards the case as "exceptional," reaches the same conclusion concerning the *real* effects.[26] Marshall holds, however, in this case that some of the gain from trade resulting from the imposition of the tax is obtained by the government levying the tax.

The initial burden of the tax is thrown upon A's exporters in this case also because the tax removes dollars from importers. A's exporters have no way of throwing this burden upon foreign consumers. The best they can do is to force people who own resources similar (competitive) to theirs to share part of the burden. All the real gain accrues to A's consumers just as all the real loss accrues to foreign consumers. In terms of money, A's treasury gains at the expense of its exporters and resources located in industries which compete with the export industries. The rather spectacular change in the real gains from trade resulting in this case should not be allowed to detract attention from the monetary facts involved.

Case 4. *Elastic demand by E for cotton*

We now pass to the case in which it is supposed that E's pound demand for cotton has an elasticity of more than one. If A's demand for E's exports is also more than one, this case falls into Marshall's "normal" class of cases. The Mill-Marshall argument leads to the conclusion, in this case, that the tax will fall partly upon the foreign consumers of A's products and partly upon domestic consumers of taxed imports. This conclusion is also obtained by the use of reciprocal analysis. Let E's supply schedule of whisky exports in terms of cotton now have a positive slope throughout. Let OA (fig. 17) be A's supply schedule of cotton exports in terms of whisky before the tax is imposed and OA' the new schedule after the tax is imposed. It follows that both A's exports and imports will decline, but the terms of trade will shift by some amount in favor of A. This shift in the terms of trade is the basis for the neoclassical conclusion that foreign consumers bear the tax.

[26] Marshall, *op. cit.*, fig. 16, p. 347; p. 348 (top).

Translated into prices, the neoclassical doctrine means that the supply of *E*'s exports of whisky declines and the dollar price of whisky rises. Hence it is plausible to believe that *A*'s consumers of whisky bear a part of the tax. Likewise, since the supply of cotton exported to *E* also declines, the pound price of cotton rises, and hence it may be argued that *E*'s consumers of cotton are bearing a part of the tax. But without denying that both groups are made worse off, one can show that neither group is bearing the tax.

As noted in the discussion of Case 1, the tax initially deprives *E*'s exporters of dollars, and the smaller number of dollars sold in the foreign exchange market reduces the dollar income of *A*'s exporters. An ad valorem tax of 20 per cent, with $5,000,000 worth of whisky being currently imported, takes $1,000,000 from *A*'s exporters. This reduction in the supply of dollars not only reduces the exchange rate but leaves *A*'s cotton producers with $1,000,000 less than they would have received had the *A* government not intercepted this sum. With mobility of resources in cotton production, resources move to other fields, decreasing the output of cotton for export and increasing the output of other things. The prices of these other things fall, carrying down with them the incomes of resources previously employed in these industries. In Case 4, as the supply of cotton for export declines, fewer pounds are paid for less cotton (because the elasticity of the demand for cotton in *E* is assumed to be more than one).

The reduction in the supply of pounds, through the action of the exchange market, gives us, for the first time, an adjustment which injures *E*'s producers of whisky. The exchange of $4,000,000 for fewer pounds, say £800,000, again alters the exchange rate and worsens the position of *E*'s exporters in terms of pounds. They now have an incentive to reduce their exports of whisky, and if this incentive is accompanied by opportunity, that is, if resources producing whisky are mobile in *E*, whisky exports fall. If we assume that *A*'s demand for whisky is also elastic (more than unity), the number of dollars paid for whisky declines.[27]

A's exporters find themselves receiving smaller dollar incomes from exporting as a result of the tax. The tax initially worsens the money income position of *A*'s exporters, and their adjustment of

[27] If the U. S. demand for whisky has an elasticity of less than one, the reduction in whisky imports will increase the dollars acquired by English sellers and, after exchange for pounds, increase the dollars which cotton producers receive. This improvement acts as a brake upon the movement of resources away from cotton production. The reduction in trade will, therefore, be smaller than in the case discussed in the text.

curtailing cotton exports results in whisky exporters receiving fewer pounds. Whisky exporters therefore curtail whisky sales in *A;* this reduces the dollar value of *A*'s imports, inducing a further reduction of cotton exports; and this again sets in motion inter-actions making *A*'s exporters still worse off. Not only do *A*'s producers of cotton lose in dollars by the yield of the tax but in addition they lose by the amount of the decline in the number of dollars paid for the smaller volume of whisky imports. Shall we say, therefore, that they bear a financial burden greater than the tax?

If real investors and consumers in *A* are prepared to spend a given total amount of money for current output, when current output refers to that part of the output of *A* and of *E* which comes into the hands of *A*'s buyers, the expenditure of fewer dollars for whisky is accompanied by an increase in the demand for those items which are substitutes for *E*'s whisky, possibly domestic whisky or domestic fortified wines. The industries producing these sub-stitutes gain in money income by virtue of the protectionistic character of the duty. What these groups gain in income is equal to that part of the loss experienced by the industries engaged in exporting that is occasioned by the decline in the number of dol-lars spent upon *E*'s imports. The amount of income shifted away from *A*'s exporting industries to industries producing items which are substitutes for imports is the gain realized by pressure groups favoring protection on the theory that their products are com-petitive with imports.[28]

Where shall we say the burden of the tax rests in Case 4? From the point of view of those owners of resources located in the cotton industry and of the resources located in industries competing on the supply side with cotton production, their total loss of income is the yield of the tax plus the reduction in the number of dollars spent upon whisky. But the incidence of a tax cannot be greater than the yield of a tax. Part of the loss of these groups is offset by

[28] In my opinion, a duty should be classed as protective in the case of a uniform duty on all imports where the duty positively curtails imports, which in turn occurs only if the conditions set forth in Case 4 are satisfied. In Cases 1, 2, and 3, the duty does not curtail imports and therefore gives no protection. In Cases 1 and 2, domestic industries are exposed to the same amount of competition from abroad as in the case of no duty and in Case 3 because imports increase, they are exposed to more. Only in Case 4 is there any protection to domestic industries producing substitutes for import. Even in this case the neoclassical position supports import duties, judged on nationalistic grounds, in spite of rather than because of the protection given. The neoclassical argument rests upon the possibility of one country exploiting another in real terms, and the real gain decreases to the extent that a tariff restricts imports.

the gain of the producers of substitute for imports. The remaining part of their loss of income is offset by the yield of the tax to the A treasury. Only this part is the incidence of the tax.

Thus far, we have restricted our analysis to two countries trading in only two items. To obtain greater generality, we may now consider trade where there is any number of imports and exports. The conclusions already reached for two commodities apply, with a few qualifications, to any number of imports and exports.

With many imports and exports Case 1 offers no great difficulties. For the conditions of Case 1 to be satisfied, the resources employed to produce all A's exports must have no relevant alternative use other than the production of other exports. Immobility of resources need not now be assumed with respect to any one item exported. Mobility of resources as among classes of exports may be perfect. Case 1 requires only that mobility as between production of items for export and the production of items for domestic sale be zero.

If, as before, we suppose a 20 per cent ad valorem tax upon the value of all imports in a setting where, before the tax, the value of imports is $5,000,000 and the value of exports £1,000,000, the yield of the tax in the first instance is now $1,000,000 (one-fifth of $5,000,000) to A's treasury. By taxing imports, the Treasury takes $1,000,000 out of the hands of E's sellers, who therefore have $4,000,000 instead of $5,000,000 to sell in exchange for pounds. As before, A's exporters find themselves receiving $4,000,000 instead of $5,000,000, or, in other words, their money incomes from exporting fall by one-fifth. The dollar price of exports declines, likewise, by one-fifth and the exchange rate again moves from $5 = £1 to $4 = £1.

The answer to the question of who bears the tax is, therefore, clear. Owners of those resources located in A's export industries bear the tax in the form of a reduction in their money earnings. They sacrifice money income exactly equal to the yield of the tax to A's treasury, and because by assumption they are tied to the exporting industries, there is nothing they can do to shift even part of the burden to other groups. The tax leaves E's exporters where it found them, and they have no incentive because of the tax to alter the quantities or kinds of their exports. A's consumers of E's exports are likewise unaffected as indeed are E's consumers of A's exports. The allocation effect of the tax is zero, and the reduction in the money incomes of the export industries and the gain by the *A* treasury of tax yield are the only consequences of the tax.

There are greater difficulties, however, in generalizing the theory as applied to many imports and exports when we come to Cases 2, 3, and 4. These cases are classifications depending upon the elasticity of *E*'s demand for *A*'s exports. The main difficulty is the meaning to be given to the concept of a demand schedule and hence to its elasticity when referring to many items instead of to one item. What is the meaning of the proposition that *E*'s demand for *A*'s exports in general has, for example, an elasticity of unity?

If the relative quantities of *A*'s exports shipped abroad could be taken as constant, exports could be treated as units of a composite commodity, and elasticity of demand would then have the same meaning as in the case of one commodity. Such an assumption involves a recourse to Marshall's bales of exports and imports.[29] A bale may be regarded as a unit of a composite commodity, or it may be treated as a fixed dose of resources—land, labor, and capital. But the latter treatment has little to recommend it. It involves, among other things, the assumption of perfect mobility of resources, an assumption which even when restricted to "the long run" seriously limits the generality of conclusions based upon it.

A typical feature of economies is variability in the degree of mobility of various types of resources producing output, and we shall therefore develop the analysis upon this assumption at the beginning. The initial loss of income by *A*'s export industries, because of the tax, is almost certain to react differently upon each of the various commodities exported. In some lines of production perhaps no curtailment of exports at all will occur, because of a dogged persistence in producing and exporting certain types of products almost regardless of earnings—a situation which sometimes characterizes certain lines of agriculture. On the other hand, many products which are sold both abroad and at home are sensitive on that account alone to variation in the export price. In some fields, resources will move from the export industries altogether as a result of even small declines in earnings. Under the impact of a reduction in earnings of *A*'s export industries as a result of import duties, the composition of *A*'s exports is almost certain to change, and therefore a bale of exports will change in content.[30]

[29] Marshall, *op. cit.*, p. 157.
[30] Jacob Viner strongly defends Marshall's use of the concept of bales against the criticism that a bale changes in content and is therefore not a useful concept. He

It might be possible, by the use of detailed assumptions, to determine definitely the change in the composition of A's exports under the pressure of an initial reduction of the earnings of the resources producing them. It is a sufficient condition for present purposes that some, possibly all, exports will decline in such circumstances. The size of the reduction is governed by the pound demand elasticity for the particular product (in the sense that the less the elasticity, the less the reduction), by the elasticity of A's demand, if any, for exportable products, and, finally, by the degree of mobility of resources engaged in the production of the particular product.

Whatever the extent of the reduction of particular types of exports, we shall mean that E's demand for A's exports has an elasticity of unity (Case 2) if the number of pounds expended for the new and "smaller" volume of A's exports remains unchanged. In that event, the adjustment of A's export industries to a decline in their earnings will not change the number of pounds they obtain and, therefore, will not change the number of pounds received by E's exporters. The terms of trade, so far as this concept can be given meaning, change in favor of A, leaving E's consumers worse off and A's consumers better off. The burden of the tax is the same as that already discussed for Case 2 above; the proposition that the tax is borne domestically holds here as well as in the case of one import and one export.

Case 3 now means that as A's exports decline, E spends more pounds for the new and "smaller" volume of A's products. E's exporters now have an incentive to ship more goods than before, and the terms of trade turn absolutely in favor of A. Their incentive to ship more products will, to be sure, alter the composition of A's imports. The quantities of some imports are almost certain to increase more than others, especially those which have an elastic demand in E for home use, or an elastic demand in A, or whose production can be readily augmented because resources capable of producing them are highly mobile. With these qualifications, the conclusions reached for the simpler case apply here with equal force.

Case 4, of course, means that as A's exports decline, E spends

---

cites the parallel difficulty in the construction of index numbers, which we use although the composite commodity price either changes in content or if kept constant will almost never be typical for all periods compared. (Cf. Jacob Viner, *Studies in the Theory of International Trade* [New York: Harper, 1937], pp. 553–555.)

fewer pounds for the new and "smaller" volume of imports. In this event, trade will decline on both sides. *E*'s exports will change in composition for the same reasons and in the same way as *A*'s exports. There are no reasons therefore to change the conclusions reached with respect to the burden of import duties with only one import and one export.

SHIFTING OF PARTIAL IMPORT DUTIES

A tariff schedule of varying rates will in general have two classes of effects. Such a schedule reduces the profitability of the exporting industries of the country levying the duty just as in the case of uniform rates and for the same reasons. In addition, such schedules alter, possibly quite drastically, the *composition* of imports for any given volume of exports. Imports subject to high duties will decline, whereas imports subject to low or no duties will increase. Differential rates take foreign exchange from foreign producers of items subject to high rates and give an equal sum to the foreign producers of commodities subject to low duties. This change in earnings is accompanied by corresponding changes in the relative quantities of various products imported. This is the *composition* effect of differential rates upon imports.

The absolute curtailment of imports, to the extent that such a concept can be given meaning with changes in the composition of imports, will in turn depend initially upon what the export industries do when faced with a loss of earning power because of import taxes. If these industries do nothing, as in Case 1, the composition effect is the only effect, and the export industries are left bearing the taxes indefinitely. If exports fall, the tax burden is spread to competing resources. If the foreign demand for exports has an elasticity of unity (Case 2), the "volume" of imports remains unchanged, and the composition effect is again the only effect. If the foreign demand for export products has an elasticity of less than one (Case 3), the "volume" of imports increases accompanied by a change in the composition of imports. If the foreign demand has an elasticity of more than one (Case 4), trade will decline on both sides with a change in the composition of both imports and exports, the pattern of imports changing, however, more drastically than that of exports. In all cases, producers of exports and owners of resources in competing fields suffer a loss of income at least equal to the yield of the tax to the *A* treasury. In no case do either foreign consumers or producers bear the tax. Even with partial duties domestic consumers of taxed items do not bear the tax. Domestic resource owners bear the full yield of the tax.

The conclusions reached have been based on the assumption that the only transactions in foreign exchange arise out of trade. This assumption was made for purposes of simplicity and may be dropped without affecting the conclusions. If part of the dollars supplied in the foreign exchange market arise from the purchase of securities from foreigners or in settlement of interest or dividend payments to foreign owners of claims to property, it follows that the dollars appropriated by the *A* treasury from importers will reduce the earnings of resources in the export industries. Adjustments in trade start from this fact. The pattern of adjustment is not affected by the presence of nontrade transactions.

A CRITICISM CONSIDERED

To the foregoing theory as applied to differential duties upon imports, Kahn has offered an important objection. He poses the following case:

Assume, for example, that Britain exports two commodities to the United States, whiskey and woollens, receiving $5 million from each, that whiskey alone is subjected to a 20 per cent duty, and that the American demand for British whiskey is, within the relevant price range, completely inelastic. In this event, the price of whiskey can rise by the full amount of the tax, British dollar receipts need never fall, and the exchange rate never change. American consumers therefore enjoy no compensatory fall in the dollar price of British woollens, and American whiskey consumers pay the entire tax—the familiar conclusion of partial equilibrium analysis, under these assumptions.[31]

Theories are tested by exceptions. In the case in question, the partial duty appears to occasion an increase in the price of whisky and that is all. Exchange rates and both prices and quantities of American exports and of English exports appear to be unaffected. The case raises two issues: (1) the effects of the assumed partial levy and (2) the interpretation of these effects.

Cases of zero elasticity of demand give peculiar results in price and in excise-tax theory. In a partial system of excise taxes, a tax levied upon a product the demand for which has a zero elasticity produces complicated price and income effects. The price rises by not only the full amount of the tax; under competitive conditions

---

[31] Alfred E. Kahn, "The Burden of Import Duties: A Comment," *American Economic Review*, XXXVIII (December, 1948): 860, n. 8. An attempt is made to meet some of Kahn's objections in my "Rejoinder" in the same issue, pp. 867–869.

it rises to the top of the zero elasticity range. Any curtailment of output by any producer is sufficient to accomplish this result, and the tax does give incentive for such action. The full impact of the price rise falls upon the producers of those products upon which buyers economize in order to spend more for the taxed item. These producers do whatever adjusting is done. With some degree of mobility, resources move out of the industries which are hit by the economizing process into others, including the original taxed industry. Any entry, however slight, pushes down the price in the taxed industry to the bottom of the range of zero elasticity. An equilibrium solution in the sense of equal money returns in every field requires a *reduction* in the net price in the taxed field as compared to the original equilibrium market price solution. Needless to say, equilibrium under the conditions postulated is not easily attained.

Considerations of this kind cast some doubt on the real possibility, under competitive pricing conditions, of demands having a zero elasticity except for a limited range. Nevertheless, highly inelastic demands for some imports do raise the question of the correctness of treating imports as indirect devices for taxing exports—a problem to be discussed later.

If these complications may be temporarily ignored, is it convincing to believe that *A*'s buyers of imported whisky are the ones to whom the duty is shifted? There are other repercussions in *A*'s domestic economy to the price rise of imported whisky, and these need to be taken into account. Those whose tastes run to imported whisky are, by assumption, prepared to acquire the same quantities at the higher price. They are presumably prepared to forego the acquisition of other goods to maintain whisky consumption. As the price of imported whisky rises their demands for these other commodities fall. Under competitive pricing conditions, the prices of these other goods fall, and the income generated by these industries also falls. Owners of resources located in these areas experience a loss of income equal to the additional before-tax dollar receipts of whisky importers.

Teetotalers who have an unchanged money income benefit from the lower prices of commodities which whisky drinkers are prepared to forego. The prices of some of the goods they buy are now at lower levels. Thus we can distinguish four groups (they may partly overlap) whose positions have been altered by the tax: (1) buyers of imported whisky, (2) buyers of the other commodities,

(3) owners of resources producing the other commodities, and (4) A's government. Exporters in A and exporters in E obtain the same net prices as before the tax, and the exchange rate is unchanged.

How then shall we interpret the altered positions of these four groups? Two of these groups have changed money incomes; the incomes of owners of resources producing other things have fallen and the income of A's government has increased. To maintain everyone with the same *money* income, let A's government pay flat-sum subsidies to owners of resources producing other commodities. Now no group's money income has altered. Of the other two groups, whisky drinkers are now sacrificing some commodities and teetotalers are now obtaining more commodities. Anyone is privileged to maintain that the two groups taken together are worse or better off because of this change in the product-mix. Anyone may also insist that the drinkers are really bearing the tax, as Kahn and others do. But then, consistency demands that teetotalers be looked upon as being subsidized. They pay lower prices for some goods. These offsetting effects on drinkers and teetotalers do not add any revenue to A's government. But the loss of income by those producing other things does offset the income obtained by the government. Therefore the apparently self-evident inference that whisky drinkers in A are really bearing the tax is not truly self-evident, and the alternative inference that owners of resources employed to produce other commodities are bearing the tax does have some plausibility. It is they who will have to curtail their money expenditures, *whatever their tastes may be,* in subsequent periods because of the tax, and it is they who provide a deflationary effect upon private demands for products to allow room for an expansion of government demands without income and price inflation over time. These are effects commonly associated with the "bearing of a tax."

What is perhaps more serious is the implication of Kahn's case that the dollar value of imports cannot be taken as directly independent of the pattern of import duties. It will be recalled that the reciprocal theory of international trade as propounded by Mill and the neoclassical thinkers holds that it is a matter of indifference whether trade is taxed by duties on imports or on exports under conditions equivalent to self-adjusting exchanges. It is this doctrine which is the rationale for supposing, in geometrical representations, that a reciprocal schedule shifts to the left if a country imposes import taxes. This shifting representation makes sense provided that import duties can be shown to reduce the money returns of exporters located in the duty-levying country. This is the starting point of an analysis which employs the reciprocal demand technique. Marshall obtained such a result by visualizing the all-round merchant who both imports and exports. It is allegedly a matter of indifference to such a merchant whether his government taxes him on the imports or the exports.[32] This device is equivalent to the assumption of perfectly adjusting exchanges for a financial system with specialization among traders. Financially a system of import taxes is therefore treated as equivalent to export taxes of the same amount. The bale concept ignores the composition of trade and automatically makes any system of import taxes uniform on all imports. Kahn's case gives a very different result, however. A heavy tax is levied upon one import without any effect upon the composition of imports, upon the exchange rate, or upon the volume of exports. *It is not true in Kahn's case that import duties are symmetrical with export duties.* Edgeworth's doubts are vindicated. This means, in other words, that the reciprocal demand type of theory is inappropriate to the extent that Kahn's case is a real possibility. Therefore, the theory of tax shifting here proposed must be modified to avoid this limitation.

To develop a more general theory, let us think of imports as consisting of many items which have various elasticities of demand in *A*. Let us suppose that *A*'s exporters are obtaining, say, £1,000,000 from *E*. In the absence of any import duties, *A*'s consumers are spending $5,000,000 on *E*'s products. Now suppose that a system of nonuniform duties of any type is imposed. The supply of pounds is initially taken as given; therefore whatever adjustments initially occur, *E*'s exporters will end up with exactly £1,000,000. But British exporters of heavily taxed items restrict their sales in *A* because the tax forces down the net price to them in dollars. If the dollar demand for their products is inelastic but not of zero elasticity, the value of their products laid down in *A* rises. They realize a somewhat lower pound return for their sales in *A* because the price rise does not fully offset the tax rise. But other exporters in *E* find the demand for their products stated in pounds rising because they get a larger share of the supply of pounds. The reshuffling of *E*'s exports to *A* may be accompanied by a higher, lower, or unchanged dollar value of imports before tax in *A*. If this initial reshuffling is accompanied by a zero change in the dollar value of

---

[32] Marshall, *op. cit.*, pp. 180–182.

imports before tax, the conclusions reached in the section above headed, "The shifting of partial import duties," hold as stated. A's exporters are initially burdened by a loss of income equal to the tax yield. The reciprocal demand type of analysis then holds as set forth for the case of uniform levies, with the qualification that heavily taxed imports are reduced relatively to lightly taxed imports. If the reshuffling is accompanied by a reduced dollar value of imports in A, the exporters in A suffer a loss of income in dollars equal to the tax yield plus the decrease in the value of imports. The decrease in the value of imports is offset by the increase in the income of domestic producers competing with E's exporters in the A market. If the reshuffling is accompanied by an increased dollar value of imports, A's exporters lose by the algebraic sum of the tax yield and the increase in the dollar value of imports. The extreme case of this is a zero loss, which occurs when the demand for those imports which happen to be subject to tax have a zero elasticity (Kahn's case). The entire tax liability is initially thrown on those groups located in A who sell products which people are willing to forego rather than give up any of the imported commodity.

Thus there is no initial burden on A's exporters. There can be systems of import duties which are not equivalent to *any* system of export duties even with self-adjusting exchanges. A system of duties which results in increasing the dollar value of imports proportionately to the duty has the effect of "subsidizing" exports rather than of taxing them. Organizations devoted to supplying to the domestic market products which are competitive with imports subject to tax take the full brunt of the tax load. To the extent that resources are marginally mobile, they move into other industries including export industries. It is in this sense that a tax upon imports may operate as a "subsidy" to exports. To the extent that this type of case is found, the usual welfare argument that there exists some optimum tariff is invalid. Such theories rest upon the assumption that tariffs reduce exports of the country levying the tariff—an assumption which does not hold for the case in question.

The above adjustments in A in terms of the valuation of imports and of other commodities are not of course final. Except in the case where the adjustments of foreign sellers to partial import duties result in an absolute increase in the dollar value of imports equal to the duty, exporters in A have an incentive to curtail exports. The repercussions of these moves may then again be studied as suggested in the analysis of Cases 1 through 4 above.

The type of difficulty raised by Kahn reinforces the opinion of some students of international trade theory that the concept of a "bale" as applied to imports and exports is a dangerous theoretical tool. At best, the device should be viewed as a simplification for expository purposes rather than as a theory. Apart from the machinery of geometrical representation, the core of the Mill doctrine is the proposition that exporters are supplying the finance for importers and vice versa. The exploitive implications of the theory are wrong if they are taken to mean that foreigners actually contribute tax dollars to another country; they can be misleading if the composition aspects of nonuniform duties are ignored.[33]

---

[33] Frank Graham's lifelong attack on the Mill point of view in international trade theory is especially strong when directed against the "bale" concept. See *The Theory of International Values* (Princeton: Princeton University Press, 1948), pp. 3–26, 157–202.

9

Import Duties:
Fixed Exchange Rates

International trade is not usually conducted in the kind of setting visualized in the last chapter. When self-adjusting exchange rates are assumed, the differences in the monetary relations found in domestic trade and those found in international trade are clear and sharp. But fixed exchanges are the normal pattern. Exchange rates do not often vary every day, and commonly they are kept in a set pattern over considerable periods of time. Any general theory of the effects of import duties must therefore apply to settings in which the exchanges are fixed.

Many current ideas about import duties held both by economists and by laymen presuppose the presence of fixed exchanges. The theory that a tax upon one import is shifted partly to domestic buyers and partly to the foreign producer of the item involves the assumption that the rate of exchange can be treated as independent of the import levy. This type of approach provides support for the belief that increases in import duties automatically increase the domestic prices of imports. It is the same type of argument that has led to the common opinion that sales taxes raise prices. The tax is assumed to be imposed on top of the existing level of prices. The theory expounded below leads to the conclusion that import duties are not shifted either to domestic consumers or to foreign producers of the taxed import.

International trade theory under conditions of fixed exchanges involves the application of a monetary theory. The monetary theory employed in our analysis is of the stock-flow pattern. As such it dispenses with all propensities to import and foreign trade multiplier concepts. Such approaches are rejected for reasons identical with those which led us in chapter 5 to reject the concept of a propensity to consume and its kindred notion of the investment multiplier. A foreign trade multiplier involves the assumption that the income generated by sale of exports abroad is multiplied instantaneously at home. Such a theory violates the principle that contemporaneous events cannot be causal; it violates the first rule of monetary theory, namely, that a stock of money is a necessary condition for the expenditure of money. Unfortunately, however, international trade analysis in terms of a stock-flow type of monetary theory is more complicated than in Keynesian terms because specific attention must be paid to where the money goes as a result of trade. But there is the possible compensation that the results may be more definite and precise. In the analysis of any tax, including import levies, no exposition can pretend to have answered the relevant questions unless it is capable of showing at least the source of the government's tax yield. The elimination of vagueness is a major aim of theoretical analysis in this as in other areas.

Reciprocal Demands and Fixed Exchanges

Marshall, in his development of international trade theory with the use of the reciprocal demand concept, made the assumption that "in the long run" international demands are independent of money.[1] If a theory is confined to "long-run" adjustments alone, this assumption makes the particular type of foreign exchange rate pattern at any one time of no relevance. Fluctuating foreign exchange rates may provide a setting more conducive to the rapid attainment of full adjustments than do fixed exchanges accompanied by internal price and income movements, but the final results are presumably the same. The neoclassical assumption that international demands are independent of money, although proper in the initial stages of development of pure theory, unfortunately provides a theory of limited relevance. It cannot explain the burden and effects of import taxes where gold flows in the direction of one country and where other circumstances suggest a "disequilibrium" condition. During the 1930's, for example, the United States obtained substantial quantities of gold, and a point of view which rules out gold movements cannot hope to give a definitive explanation of the role played by import duties during such a period.

When the assumption that international demands are independent of money is not made, the task of explaining the effects of import duties becomes rather complicated. The simplifying device

---

[1] Alfred Marshall, *Money Credit and Commerce* (London: Macmillan, 1923), p. 184.

of reciprocal demand schedules may no longer be directly employed
to show how import taxes change a country's imports and exports.
The reason why they may not be so used follows from the
character of the schedules themselves. A point on the reciprocal
demand schedule of a country indicates the quantity of the country's exports which will be exchanged for a given quantity of imports. The entire schedule shows the amounts of exports which will
be exchanged for all quantities of imports. Such a functional relation between a country's exports and imports can properly be
postulated for self-adjusting exchanges, but not for fixed exchanges.
With fluctuating exchanges, the volume of a country's exports does
depend upon the quantity of imports for the reason that a particular quantity of imports will sell for a certain total amount in
terms of the domestic currency, the amount depending of course
upon the elasticity of the demand for imports. The quantity of
money so obtained from the sale of imports, when offered for sale
in the foreign exchange market, comes into the hands of the country's exporters. For the amount of money thus obtained, there is
presumably one optimum amount of commodities which exporters
are willing to produce and ship abroad in view of production costs
and the alternative prices to be obtained by selling the commodities at home.

With fixed exchanges, however, domestic exports sold abroad do
not *directly* depend upon imports; they depend rather upon the
demands of foreign buyers for exports at the given exchange rate.
There are several amounts of exports (instead of one) which will
be exchanged for a given quantity of imports, with gold (or other
international money) acting as a cushion to keep the exchange rate
fixed under these varying circumstances. Thus with fixed exchange
rates, a reciprocal demand schedule can be used only if it is assumed
that, at each moment, losses or gains of gold are immediately translated into changes in relative demands (in each country) for exports
and domestic products, or, in other words, that fixed exchanges
with gold flows give exactly the same adjustment as would be obtained with freely fluctuating exchange rates.[2]

For the purpose of our analysis of import duties with fixed ex-

[2] Jacob Viner, in defending the reciprocal demand concept against its critics, holds
that reciprocal demands by themselves directly determine trade. (Cf. Jacob Viner,
Studies in the Theory of International Trade [New York: Harper, 1937], p. 549.) His
position is correct, I believe, as long as foreign exchange rates are considered to be
self-adjusting. But with other types of exchange conditions, his view is valid only on
the assumption—Marshall's assumption—that the schedules are independent of
money.

changes, we shall first consider two countries only, the United States and England (A and E). The dollar value of E's products currently sold in A per unit of time is, say, $5,000,000. The pound value of A's products sold in E per unit of time is, say, £1,000,000. We disregard all changes in A's claims on E or E's claims on A and assume that there is no net transfer of income from one country to the other. This means we are assuming that in each country the value of current output (net) is equal to the total of accruing money incomes in each country. We shall assume that the price of gold in E is £7 per ounce and the corresponding price in A is $35 per ounce.[3] To give absolutely fixed exchanges, with gold acting as international money, we must assume either that there are no costs of shifting the ownership of gold between the two countries, a situation illustrated by the common practice of earmarking gold, or that if gold is shipped, the costs are borne by the government. For our purposes, it is convenient to assume that E, through its stabilization fund, always takes the initiative in selling gold for dollars and then selling dollars for pounds when the dollar price of pounds would otherwise fall, and A's government or central bank takes the initiative when the dollar price of the pound threatens to rise above the fixed rate.

In this setting, let us assume that A imposes without prior notice a general import tax at a flat rate of 20 per cent upon the value of all imports; the value is computed laid down in A and after the payment of duties.[4] E's exporters, it may be supposed, are caught for a short period with definite commitments to sell certain quantities of commodities through their agents who quote prices laid down, taxpaid in A. Until they have an opportunity to make new contracts, they become, literally, the *legal* taxpayers. They provide the tax dollars which the A treasury receives. As a result of the tax, E's sellers realize $4,000,000 instead of $5,000,000 per unit of time for their products sold in A's market after meeting the tax obliga-

[3] The argument could be developed equally well by assuming an international bank or other device which makes one currency freely convertible into the other.

[4] This method of computing import duties might be criticized as assuming that a tax is levied upon a tax in the sense that the value of an imported item is computed after the tax is known and after entry. There is no mechanical difficulty, however, in making this computation. It is the same as a gross receipts' tax where the base of the tax is the total of gross receipts and not, as retail sales taxes are calculated in most states, receipts computed separate from tax. Our method of computation makes the base of the tax larger than does the customary method. If our method were followed, import statistics might give a more accurate figure for the total value of imports. Even if these data contain no errors of estimation, they understate imports in value terms by the amount of taxes collected on imports.

tion; and they offer $4,000,000 instead of $5,000,000 to acquire pounds in the foreign exchange market. E's exporters therefore obtain £800,000 instead of £1,000,000 for sales of the same quantities of products.

This reduction in the pound gross income of E's exporters gives them a strong incentive to curtail their sales in A's market as promptly as contract terms permit. As rapidly as possible, therefore, they do curtail exports and raise the dollar prices of these products in A. A's buyers, as they find the prices of E's products rising, may spend a greater, smaller, or an unchanged number of dollars upon the reduced supplies of E's products, depending upon the elasticities of the demands for the various types of products imported. For the following argument, it makes no important difference which elasticity is assumed, but to avoid altering the illustrative figures just now employed, we shall assume that the weighted average elasticity of A's demands for E's products is unity. This assumption means that the number of dollars spent upon imports remains unchanged. As long as the value of A's imports stays constant, the base of the tax and the tax yield are constant. E's exporters continue to receive only $4,000,000 for products which they exchange for £800,000, but they receive this for a smaller volume of exports. The reduction in the pound income of E's exporters cannot of course be the only result of the tax. For the exchange rate to remain fixed, another $1,000,000 must be placed in the foreign exchange market to keep the supply and demand of foreign exchange equated at the fixed price. Under the assumptions initially made, E's government must sell £200,000 worth of gold to A's government for dollars and then sell the $1,000,000 so obtained in the foreign exchange market to insure that the exchange rate remains fixed.

Gold flows will have certain necessary effects in both A and E, and may lead to monetary deflation in E and inflation in A. Furthermore, there may be various degrees of adjustment in the total monetary demands in both A and E. The degree to which gold flows affect the internal monetary affairs of the countries depends upon the monetary policies of the respective governments and the power they have to make their policies effective.

It is convenient to divide the subsequent analysis into two general cases. We shall first consider the case where each country does not permit gold movements to affect its predetermined monetary policy. This is complete gold sterilization,[5] and may be called the

<hr>

[5] The concept of gold sterilization in economic usage has at least three distinguishable meanings. It may refer to the failure of a gold inflow or outflow to be accom-

case of *zero internal monetary adjustment*. In the second case, we shall treat partial and complete monetary adjustments together for the purpose of determining tax burden.

ZERO INTERNAL MONETARY ADJUSTMENT

The governments of E and A are assumed to have control over the supply of money in each country. Complete power over the supply of money requires that local banks may not alter the quantity of demand deposits by making or calling loans, or by buying or selling securities generally. In the case of zero adjustment, gold flows, likewise, must not alter either government's monetary policy. The aim of monetary policy in each country is, we shall assume, the maintenance of the demand for output at a given level or, in other words, a policy which keeps the money value of output constant. The level chosen is one which is supposed to give full employment. A policy of maintaining a constant demand for products may call for net inflationary, net deflationary, or neutral action by the government and its agencies, depending upon the monetary behavior of private real investors and consumers. If the desired level of gross national value product has already been achieved, deflationary inclinations on the part of real investors or consumers will call for a net inflationary policy by the government, and inflationary inclinations will call for the opposite. We shall suppose for simplicity that a neutral monetary policy is sufficient to maintain effective demand at a constant level. Private real investors and consumers are thus assumed to maintain constant idle balances. Each budgeting unit (other than the government) is assumed to maintain a constant relation between its inactive and total cash balance.[6]

---

panied by those adjustments normally expected of such movements, for example, the flow of gold to the United States during the interwar period. A second meaning is the more technical one that a gold flow is not permitted to alter bank reserve balances. In the case of a gold inflow, sterilization in the second sense calls for action by the U. S. Treasury, the Federal Reserve Banks, or both to offset the gain of reserves. The Treasury may reduce its balances with member banks without increasing its balance with the Reserve Banks by an exchange of gold certificates, or the Reserve Banks may decrease their earning assets dollar for dollar with an increase in their nonearning assets (gold certificates). A third meaning, and this is the one used in the text, is that a gold inflow (or outflow) is not permitted to increase the quantity of money in the hands of the public at all. This calls for an effective policy of offsetting the increase in the public's money supply resulting from a gold inflow, either by taxation, or, if possible, by the sale of securities.

[6] Followers of Keynes may restate the assumption in terms of a constant schedule of the marginal efficiency of capital, constant structure and level of interest rates, and a given marginal propensity to consume (and hence a given timeless multiplier).

The reduction in the amount of pounds received by E's sellers of exports, unless offset, means a reduction of the money supply in E. If E is to pursue a policy of immunizing its internal monetary affairs against unstabilizing acts of its neighbors, a number of mechanical adjustments are necessary to insure the success of its policy. These adjustments are perhaps more readily visualized and made definite by the employment of a "T" account for the E monetary system. Such an account is shown below.

"T" ACCOUNT OF E'S MONETARY SYSTEM, BANK OF E

A	B	a	b
Assets	Liabilities	Changes in assets	Changes in liabilities
(in billions of pounds)		(in thousands of pounds)	
Gold............ 3	Govt. deposits.. 5	(1) Gold..... −200	(1) Govt. deposits... −200
Nonearning assets 1	Private deposits. 20		(2) Private deposits ... −200
Earning assets....24	Currency....... 2		(3) Govt. deposits ...+200
Total assets.... 28	Total demand liabilities.....27		(4) Govt. deposits ... −200
			(5) Private deposits ...+200
	Capital and surplus......... 1	(6) Nonearning assets.. +200	(6) Govt. deposits ...+200

Column A shows the assumed assets and Column B the assumed liabilities. These constitute the assets and liabilities of the entire banking system which may be considered as consolidated into one bank. The demand liabilities of the bank constitute the sole means of payment internally in E. Columns a and b show the changes in assets and liabilities after imposition of the import tax by A. These changes should be considered as amounts per period, or, in other words, as flows—changes in stocks.

The sale of gold by E's government reduces that asset. The bank is paid for the gold by a reduction in the government's deposit, shown as (1) in Column a and (1) in Column b. The E government, however, sells the gold for dollars and then sells the dollars thus

---

In terms of Robertsonian analysis, the assumption means that saving (defined as the difference between income of the immediate past and present consumption expenditures) equals investment with a constant supply of money.

acquired for pounds to maintain the fixed exchange rate. It therefore acquires pounds in amount equal to the pound value of the dollars purchased by the gold, which in our illustration is £200,000. The government's bank balance declines pound for pound with the loss of gold but it increases pound for pound by the purchase of pounds.

This increase in the government's balance is offset by the loss of pounds by E's exporters. Before the tax, it will be recalled, E's exporters obtained £1,000,000 by the sale of products in A. Although they curtail their sales to A in an effort to minimize the unfavorable effects of the tax upon their earning power, whatever improvements they achieve are at the expense of other industries with which they are in competition in the home market. This reduction in the pounds acquired through the export market is a net reduction in private cash holdings. This is shown as (2) in Column b, the offsetting item being the increase in the government's deposit pursuant to its acquisition of pounds by the sale of dollars shown as (3) in Column b. Thus the net effect of the loss of gold is the maintenance by the government of its cash balance at the expense of a decrease in private cash balances at a rate of £200,000 per period. The imposition of A's tax on imports thus reduces the number of pounds obtained by E's exporters. E's buyers, on the other hand, continue to spend the same number of pounds for A's merchandise. The net difference between the value of its exports and imports (£200,000) is the rate of reduction per period in the supply of money in E. Unless some action is taken, this decrease in the cash position of private groups may lead them to curtail expenditures and the assumed full-employment policy is endangered.

The obvious remedy for this situation is action on the part of the E government to increase the supply of money in the hands of the public. It may increase its expenditures, decrease the yield of its own internal taxes, or both. We may assume that the policy adopted is to reduce the yield of the income tax by an amount equal to the reduction in private deposits. This step [see items (4) and (5) in Col. b] reduces the cash balance of the government once more and increases the cash balance of the income-tax-paying part of the population. The action prevents demands for products in E from falling. Those favored by the reduction in the income tax take the place, in part, of persons associated with the export industries and their competitors in demanding output. National income in E is maintained at the desired level and gold outflow is successfully sterilized. One last step remains, however. The E government's cash balance may easily not be large enough to stand an additional drain of £200,000 per period because of the reduction in the yield of its income tax. It may be necessary to exchange either earning or nonearning assets with the banking system—for present purposes, which one does not matter—to augment the government's cash balance [see (6) in Cols. a and b]. As a result of these adjustments, there is no change in the money supply; and if, as we have assumed, people keep the ratio of their idle to total cash balances constant, the gold outflow has no deflationary effects internally.

A similar "T" account is shown below for A. This represents the monetary situation pictured as the assets and liabilities of one bank with its demand liabilities being the supply of money. The changes in assets and liabilities shown in Columns a and b are simpler in this case than those found for E. Paradoxically, the acquisition of

"T" ACCOUNT OF A's MONETARY SYSTEM, BANK OF A

A	B	a	b
Assets	Liabilities	Assets	Liabilities
(in billions of dollars)		(in millions of dollars)	
Gold.......... 20 Nonearning assets........ 1 Earning assets...125 Total assets...146	Govt. deposits.. 15 Private de- posits.......110 F. R. notes..... 20 Total demand liabilities....145 Capital and sur- plus........ 1	(1) Gold.......+1	(1) Govt. deposits +1

gold in Column a (1) is accompanied by an equal *increase* in the A government's demand deposit in Column b (1), a point that requires explanation.

A payment for gold, like a payment for anything else, depletes the government's cash position. Anyone selling gold acquires additional cash, and this is a net addition to the monetary supply. In practice the government restores its balance, depleted by gold purchases, by exchanging nonearning assets (gold certificates) with the banking system for a deposit. It may be properly asked why this does not happen in the present case. The treasury, in purchasing gold, does pay dollars to someone; in the present case the E government. That government offers these dollars immediately for sale in the foreign exchange market in the interest of maintaining fixed exchanges. If we stopped the process just before this offering by the E government, we should have no change in the A government's account and have another dollar balance—the deposit of the E government with A banks—as the offset to the increase in gold stock. If we examine the situation immediately after E's government offers these dollars in the market, we find that these dollars go right back to the A treasury in the form of the yield of import duties. The dollar supply of the public is clearly in no way directly affected by the gold movement. A exporters are obtaining the same number of dollars out of the foreign exchange market as they obtained before the imposition of the tax. Therefore, there is no reduction in private deposits from this source. The balance of the A treasury increases dollar for dollar with its purchase of gold because its tax revenue increases by exactly the amount of the payment for gold. The A government provides dollars to the E government, which in turn places these dollars in the foreign exchange market, and then the A treasury takes these dollars as payment of import taxes.

Thus we have in this case the unusual circumstance which may be called *automatic gold sterilization*. The tax calls forth a gold flow and a revenue simultaneously, and thus the A treasury prevents the gold flow from increasing the supply of money in the hands of the public by taking away in tax yield the same dollars which it injects into the economy by the purchase of gold.

A necessary condition for continuous gold sterilization is a rigid policy of the government not to make more expenditures, reduce its other taxes, or retire debt because of its growing cash balance. Complete sterilization is ensured only if the A government permits its cash balance to grow at the rate of the yield of its import taxes. If it departs from this policy, gold is no longer completely sterilized, and there are instead partial or complete adjustments.

This rather lengthy presentation of the conditions for perfect sterilization leads to our next and main question: What are the effects of import duties under conditions of complete gold sterilization? Presumably E cannot continue indefinitely to lose its gold supply and maintain both its internal stabilization policy and its external policy of fixed exchanges. How long E can continue such a policy depends in part on how much gold it possesses and how large this drain is in relation to its stock. Although a policy of complete sterilization (zero adjustment) may have to be abandoned eventually, a close study of this case may have some value in explaining short-run developments.

Certain of the effects of the tax are fairly clear. A's consumers and real investors obtain fewer imports because the tax makes the sale of E's products in the A market less profitable. In real terms, the A public is worse off in the sense of obtaining less "stuff." The real terms of trade are made less favorable to A. E's consumers and real investors, on the other hand, are better off if the resources released from the E export industries are successfully employed to produce other things for the home market. These other things are a net addition to the E standard of living, provided of course that the loss of gold is not treated as a real loss. With constant money expenditures upon output in E, the additional supplies of commodities available for local sale may have the result of reducing prices somewhat, depending upon the degree of competition prevailing there. In A, the situation is reversed. The prices of imports rise absolutely and may carry up with them the prices of domestically produced items competing with imports.

Private money incomes in E, calculated after deducting local taxes, remain unchanged. There is some loss of income by those associated with the E export industries, but this loss is offset by an increase in other private net incomes because of the reduction in the rates of the E income tax. The increase in private money incomes in E by income tax reduction is made to ensure that the loss of gold does not sabotage the E government's internal stabilization policy.

The determination of the tax burden under these circumstances offers a number of important difficulties. In theory, there is a presumption that the results achieved from a study of fluctuating exchanges have some application to fixed exchanges. With automatically self-adjusting exchange rates, we found that the burden of the tax rests initially upon domestic producers for the export market by reducing their money incomes. Yet with fixed exchanges and zero adjustment, it is clear that domestic exporters cannot be regarded as bearing any part of the tax. Without the tax upon imports, they obtain $5,000,000 for products sold in E, and with the tax they continue to obtain the same income. They cannot, therefore, be properly regarded as contributing the dollars which become the A treasury's tax revenue.

E exporters may appear to be bearing the tax because of the unfavorable effect of the tax upon their income. Their immediate income loss is, however, offset in part by the restoration of money incomes resulting from the diversion of resources to the production of goods for the domestic market, and the remaining part is offset by the increase in the net income of other groups, computed after deducting taxes, occasioned by the reduction in the yield of the income tax. This suggests that E exporters are not bearing A taxes.

A's consumers may appear to bear part or all of the tax upon imports by paying higher prices for E products. Buyers of E's woolens, for example, may be expected, because of the tax, to pay higher prices for suits, and both the domestic wool lobby and domestic consumers of E's woolens may be convinced from this evidence alone that the latter group is bearing the tax. Yet, upon close examination, this view leaves much to be desired. A's buyers of E's products pay higher dollar prices for imports because the supply of these commodities in A is curtailed. Supplies fall because of the unwillingness of E's exporters to offer unchanging amounts of products for sale in the A market at lower net pound prices. As a result of the tax, the A treasury removes $1,000,000 from the foreign exchange market and yet, despite this fact, A's exporters continue to take away the same number of dollars from the foreign exchange market. It is possible, to be sure, that A's consumers have inelastic demands for E's products and pay absolutely more dollars for fewer goods. But the reverse may equally well be true. A's buyers may pay fewer dollars for imports in which case they subtract rather than add to the supply of dollars as compared with the pretax situation. It would be awkward to suppose that A's consumers bear the tax if their demand elasticity for imports is less than unity and that they do not bear the tax if their demand elasticity is more than unity. There is no inherent reason to suppose that A's consumers either add to or subtract from the supply of dollars in the foreign exchange market, and it may be better for purposes of developing a general theory to assume that their action is neutral in character, that is, that A's demands for imports have an elasticity of one. In these circumstances all the additional dollars must be supplied by the importation of gold.

In the case of complete gold sterilization, the A government should be viewed as paying its own tax. By levying duties, it removes dollars from the foreign exchange market. By purchasing gold, it adds to the supply of dollars in the foreign exchange market. The purchase of gold is the method by which dollars are provided to permit the maintenance of the exchange rate. What dollars the A government takes away by imposing import taxes, it gives back by buying gold. No private individuals or groups pay out the money which becomes the government's tax revenue. From this point of view, the worsened position of A consumers merely reflects the allocation of resources in E away from the production of exports in favor of production for domestic sale. The real loss of A consumers is reflected in the real gain of E consumers. In terms of money income, the decline in the income of E's exporters is offset by the increase in the net income of E's taxpayers. Private money incomes in A are not altered by the tax. Total incomes increase, to be sure, but all the increase accrues to the A treasury as tax revenue. Thus the treasury generates income by buying gold which accrues to itself in the form of tax revenue. Normally, it would accrue to private groups.

In stating that the A government pays its own tax, we do not mean that it is "injured" in any way. If a country wants to create money and, through a devious process, get it back again, we might raise the question of what sense this all makes as a policy. But tariff policy has rarely been sensible anyhow. Formally, in the situation here analyzed, A's government is deciding it is better to have more gold (or foreign exchange) than a higher level of living for its citizens.

Adjustment by Deflation in E

We turn next to the analysis of the effects of import duties when some internal monetary adjustments to gold flows occur. Internal adjustments may occur by deflation in E or by inflation in A or by both. It is convenient to develop the analysis initially on the assumption that only the E economy adapts its monetary affairs to the gold flow. E continues to lose gold as a result of A's import duties until such time as it corrects the adverse trade balance. E's monetary authorities may maintain either internal monetary stability or external stability of exchange rates, but not both unless their supply of gold is unlimited.[7] If they choose internal stability

---

[7] E's government can solve its problem by levying import duties equal in yield, computed at the assumed fixed exchange rate, to A's taxes. The loss of gold ceases under these circumstances. If both countries levy duties, export industries in both countries have an incentive to contract. This solution is stable if the demand for imports in each country has the same weighted elasticity for the smaller volume of imports. If E reacts by spending more pounds for fewer imports and A reacts by spending the same or a smaller number of dollars, E will continue to lose gold. If

and devalue the pound in terms of dollars, their problem is solved for the moment. But in this event, the burden of the tax is shifted immediately from the A treasury to A's exporters, and further repercussions must result from the adjustments of A's exporters to the reduction in their money earnings as analyzed in the previous chapter.

We shall assume that E's government chooses external stability and sacrifices internal stability. The deflation in E takes the form of restricting expenditures upon products of domestic origin and, of course, upon A's exports. Import demands need not, to be sure, decline in exactly the same proportion as demands in general. Whatever the particular relation may be, the deflation will have certain effects upon E's export industries, upon A's export industries, and upon the gold flow.

Each step in the deflation process in E improves the earning position of its export industries as compared with other parts of the economy. The export industries, their incomes being determined by A demands, are not injured by the deflation in E. On the contrary, as unemployment grows in E and prices fall, export industries are in a position to increase employment provided that money wage rates fall together with other prices. Unless E is to have unemployment indefinitely, either prices of resource services must decline of their own volition or official action must be taken to ensure that sufficient cost reductions are made. To the extent that resource services are cheapened in terms of pounds, the E export industries expand output and sales in the A market. This adjustment moves them in the direction of the position, relative to the other parts of the E productive system, that they enjoyed before the imposition of import duties in A. The elimination of unemployment altogether in E will find the E export industries producing about as much for the A market as they would in the absence of A duties. If, for example, the net value product of E export industries was 10 per cent of total income produced in E before the tax, and they employed a corresponding share of the labor

the opposite occurs, A will lose gold. If E counteracts the financial drain resulting from A's import duties entirely by adjusting its own import duties, instead of permitting monetary deflation at home, the results in both countries are virtually indistinguishable from those found for self-adjusting exchanges.

E's government may also meet the problem by limiting the dollars available to buyers of imports to the amount of dollars realized from its export sales, that is, by exchange control. In this event, the entire income effect of A's duties falls upon that segment of A's export industries which is cut off from E's market. They may and presumably will shift some of this burden to other groups by invading other markets.

force, the deflation in E may be expected to place export industries in the same relative position both in earning power and in employment power as before the imposition of A taxes. With the expansion of output in the E export industries, A imports rise in volume and their dollar prices fall to the pretax level.

The E deflation has immediate and severe results upon the earnings position of A's exporters. As E spends fewer pounds upon A's products, A's exporters find that the number of dollars they receive falls proportionately with the reduction in the number of pounds obtained. Hence resources in A's export industries now obtain absolutely lower dollar earnings. If A's treasury continues to pursue an effective policy of internal monetary stability, other A industries continue to enjoy the same earnings as before, and the money incomes of A's exporters are not merely reduced; they decline relatively to incomes of other producing groups. As the deflation proceeds in E, A's exporters become increasingly worse off, and when the deflation succeeds in correcting the trade balance and gold no longer moves to A, their losses of earning power per unit of time equal the yield of the tax.[8] If, under the impact of a reduction in earnings, A's export industries do not curtail output because, for example, resources so employed are specialized to the production of commodities for export, A's exports in terms of physical volume remain unchanged. In this event, complete adjustment finds the volume of both imports and exports unchanged, and the tax has not succeeded in giving any protection to domestic industries. A's consumers are in the same *real* position as before the tax since imports are increased to the old levels and no resources are released from A's export industries to produce any additional output. E consumers are in the same position provided that the E deflation does not leave resources in E permanently unemployed. They receive the same volume of imports and the same volume of domestically produced output.

The incidence of the tax under these conditions seems clear. When the deflation is in progress in E, but not completed, part of

---

[8] As the amount of gold purchased by the A treasury declines, the condition of automatic gold sterilization no longer applies. Gold is being "oversterilized." To satisfy the condition that the government adopt a neutral monetary policy, it must either increase its expenditures or reduce taxes (other than import taxes). Following the assumption used in connection with E, we may suppose that the government achieves a neutral policy by reducing the rate on the personal income tax so as not to overbalance its budget. This action will offset the possible deflationary effects of the decline in the cash and income position of the A export industries under the pressure of the deflation in E.

the tax is paid by the A government itself through the purchase of gold as found in the case of zero adjustment. The remaining part is paid by A's export industries. Their dollar income declines as the pound demand for their products declines, a reduction measured by the difference between the yield of the tax to the A treasury and the amount paid for gold by the treasury. When the deflation is complete in E or, in other words, when gold ceases to flow, the A treasury is no longer paying any part of its tax since it ceases to buy gold. The difference between the value of imports computed laid down, tax paid in A and the number of dollars offered for sale in the foreign exchange market is then offset by the decrease in the number of pounds obtained for the sale of A's products in E. A exporters have smaller gross incomes by the yield of the tax, and hence the earnings of resources in these fields are smaller by the yield of the tax. If they cannot move out of the export field, they take this loss of income indefinitely when adjustments to gold flows are complete. This is the equivalent under fixed exchanges of Case 1 under self-adjusting exchanges (see pp. 180 ff.).

We may next consider the circumstances where resources located in A's export industries are mobile and move out of the industry when they find their earnings lowered by the English adjustment to A's import duties. This movement of resources producing for export may have a number of repercussions, not only domestically, but upon the E economy as well. With some mobility of resources in the A export industries, the reduction in earnings occasioned by the tax and the adjustment in E will reallocate resources from export output to production for the A internal market. This reallocation of resources reduces the volume of exports and increases the output of the products of the industries to which resources move. The shift of resources into domestic fields reduces the prices in these fields and forces down the earnings of resources previously entrenched in the invaded industries. A reduction of earnings in those invaded fields occurs unless the demand for the products whose supplies are increased has an *actual* elasticity of infinity. Any reduction in prices will reduce the earnings of resources previously engaged exclusively in the production of these commodities. It makes no difference for the present argument whether the owners of invading resources combine to form new firms and compete for the public's dollars with old firms or whether they offer the services of their resources for hire to established enterprises. The competition of resources formerly in the export industries has the effect of forcing owners of resources in other fields to share some of the tax burden.

The competition of owners of resources from the export field with others for money income will not restore the former's earnings to levels prevailing before the imposition of the tax or to the level prevailing with zero adjustment. With the total demand for products in A remaining constant—which assumes that the government's monetary stabilization policy is successful—the dollar income per unit of resource employed both in exporting and in other fields will be permanently lowered by import taxes after E's adjustment. Exporters' incomes fall because of the deflation in E, and in their search for more adequate incomes, they can raise their own incomes through competition with other resources, but only by pulling down the incomes of other resource owners. The resources in exporting, those which move to other fields, and the resources previously located in these other fields together take a reduction in income which is offset by the yield of import taxes to the government.

There are certain effects, however, following from a reduction in A's exports. For one thing, E finds, even after the deflationary program is complete, that the prices of A's products rise and the volume of imports falls. E may in turn spend more pounds, equal pounds, or fewer pounds upon A's products accompanying the rise in their pound prices. Which of these actually happens makes some difference in the volume of trade and in international gold movements.

If E's consumers are prepared to spend the same number of pounds upon A's products (demand elasticity of unity) at the new and lower level of national income, the results are somewhat less complicated. For in this case, starting from the position where the value of their imports equals the value of their exports at the fixed exchange rate, the payment of an unchanging number of pounds for fewer imports does not upset the trade balance. No gold flows are necessary to preserve the fixed exchange rate. No further adjustments following from the reduction of A's exports are therefore necessary. In real terms, however, the tax worsens the terms of trade for E. Deflation in E has the effect, already noted, of increasing their exports to the volume prevailing before the imposition of the A import tax. On the other hand, E receives absolutely smaller quantities of A's products. To the extent that comparisons of real gains and losses are meaningful, it seems clear that the net result of the tax is to leave them worse off. Consumers in A, in contrast, are clearly better off. A's consumers and real investors receive the same volume of imports from E and give up in return a smaller quantity of exports. The net gain to A is the added production of the resources which move out of the export field to produce output for the domestic market.[9]

If E spends absolutely more pounds upon A's products as imports decline, the trade balance will be upset and further adjustments will be necessary on this account. An increase in the pound expenditures for A's products increases the supply of pounds in the foreign exchange market. To keep the exchange rate fixed, E must sell more gold to the A treasury, acquire dollars, and sell the dollars obtained to offset the increase in the supply of pounds. In a smaller way E's authorities are faced once more with the same problem they had immediately after the import taxes were imposed. If they continue their program of external stability, they must deflate still further. This deflation in E, by decreasing the demand for A's products, leaves A's export industries with yet smaller money earnings and leads to a still greater exodus from the industry and a greater reduction in A's exports.

At the same time, the deflation acts as a stimulant to E's export industries. It reduces the gross receipts of E firms producing for domestic sale, placing them in a less favorable position to compete for resources. The E export industries are placed in a relatively improved position and are able to expand exports above pretax levels. The increase in exports means, of course, an increase in A's imports. Accompanying this greater volume, with A demands for E's products less than infinitely elastic, the dollar prices of A imports fall still further. The original deflation in E lowers prices of E's products sold in A to the levels prevailing before the tax and therefore defeats any protectionistic intentions the supporters of import tax legislation may have had. With the E demand for A exports of an elasticity of less than one, the adjustments necessary to stop the loss of gold result in an increase of A's imports beyond the volumes prevailing with no taxes upon imports at all and lower their dollar prices below the levels prevailing before the tax. A buyers of E's woolens, in other words, pay lower prices for their suits than they would pay if import duties were not imposed.

The possibility that import taxes may have the effect of increasing (instead of decreasing) imports to the country levying them is of course ancient theory. What importance this possibility has in

[9] This is analogous to Case 2 for self-adjusting exchanges. (See pp. 181–185.)

any historical period is not easy to say, but it would be dangerous to dismiss it as inconsequential. Empirical studies of demands for imports and exports suggest that inelastic demands for imports are at least not unusual.[10] This case illustrates the pitfalls in the layman's belief that because the foreign price of an import item is much lower than its dollar price at the given exchange rate (when transport costs are taken into account) buyers must be bearing the import tax. Such a price spread will exist, to be sure, but in the present case, buyers in A are actually paying lower prices for E's goods than they would pay if A imposed no import taxes at all. Scarcely anyone would care to argue that A's consumers bear import taxes when they pay lower prices for imports because of the tax.

The third possibility is that consumers in E, as the pound prices of A's products rise, pay fewer pounds for imports. The demands for A's products may, in other words, have an elasticity of more than one. After the initial deflationary program, the E government finds in this event that it has gone too far. Because the supply of pounds arising from the purchase of A goods declines, it must be supplemented by imports of gold. If we continue to think of E as making all adjustments to gold flows, the proper corrective for the gold inflow is inflation in E. Such an inflation has the important effect of reducing E's exports. A general increase in the demand for products in E increases the income of those producing for domestic sale. E export industries, because their incomes are directly dependent upon the A market, fail to share in the inflationary rise in incomes. They are thus placed in a less favorable position to compete with other industries in E for resources. The shifting of resources to production for domestic sale reduces the volume of E exports.

When there is complete adjustment to gold flows, if the E demand for A products has an elasticity of more than one, trade will decline on both sides. As already noted, if E demands have an elasticity of one, E's exports remain unaffected by the tax. If their demands have an elasticity of less than one, E's exports expand as compared with pretax levels. In all cases, however, A's exports decline because the supply of dollars reaching A's exporters through the foreign exchange market is reduced. Only where the E demand elasticity for imports is greater than one do E's exports fall, and

---

[10] J. Hans Adler, "United States Import Demand During the Interwar Period," *American Economic Review*, XXXV (June, 1945): 418–430; The U. S. Department of Commerce, *The United States in the World Economy* (Washington, 1943), p. 15.

it follows that only in this case is a general and uniform tax upon imports functioning as a protectionistic measure, provided internal monetary adjustments are sufficient to stop gold flows.

Whatever the elasticity of the E demand for imports, A's export industry resource owners bear the tax in the form of a reduction in money incomes. They force the owners of those resources with which they effectively compete to share part of this burden with them. They have no means of shifting it to A's consumers. Nor can they in any way force this burden upon foreigners—producers or consumers. These resource owners are forced to assume that burden of the tax not borne by their government. Since the government pays all of its own tax only when gold flows equal the tax yield, it is clear that private resource owners will normally bear most of the tax.

ADJUSTMENT BY INFLATION IN A

The analysis thus far has been developed with the assumption that all the adjusting to gold flows is made in E. This assumption happens to be convenient to show in a definite way the workings of the tax upon the A economy. The analysis concerning tax burden and the changes which taxes make in the volume of imports and exports can be developed by assuming that the E economy is held stable and the A economy does all the adjusting to gold flows. To stop the gold inflow, the A government must initiate a monetary policy designed to achieve income inflation in A. If such a policy is successful, A's exporters are placed in the position of not sharing in the inflation. Since their gross value product is determined by E's demands at the fixed exchange rate, the increase in the demands for other domestically produced output leaves A's exporters with no greater dollar income in a setting of rising incomes. They bear the tax by failing to receive as large an increase in their money incomes as they would receive with inflation but without any tax upon imports. Their adjustment to this position, namely, reducing output for export in E and increasing output for sale in A, will force other income receivers with whom they compete to take a smaller increase in income as compared with what they would have received under income inflation in the absence of the tax.

The changes in trade volume are also similar. If resources in A's export industries are immobile, their owners have no economic power to share in the income inflation. In such a case, A's exports remain unchanged. E's exporters, on the other hand, although initially injured by the tax, find the A inflation a good thing. It increases the demand for their products, and they increase production levels prevailing before the tax. In this case, the tax alters neither the terms of trade nor the volume of trade.

If A's exporters shift away from exporting, A's exports decline and their pound prices rise. If E spends a constant number of pounds upon imports, the supply of pounds in the foreign exchange market from this source remains constant and the inflation in A, once it stops the gold inflow started by the tax, gives a stable result. English export industries will merely be pulled back into their original pretax status. A's imports will be the same in volume as before the tax, and A's exports will be smaller. If E spends more pounds upon A's products as their volume declines, the inflation in A must proceed still further before gold inflows are stopped. The inflation in A pulls more exports from E than before the tax, and the real gains from trade are substantially improved for A. If E spends fewer pounds for A products as A's exports decline, the inflation in A need proceed less far than in the other circumstances. In this event, an inflation in A will not succeed in restoring imports from E to the volume before the tax. Trade declines on both sides, and the duties have some protectionistic results.

Likewise, import taxes with fixed exchanges can be analyzed by supposing that each country does some adjusting to gold flows, the typical assumption of classical gold-flow analysis. With this assumption, the results are a combination of the cases already considered, and the effects of the tax upon the volume of trade and the incidence of the tax follow the same pattern.

MULTILATERAL TRADE WITH UNIFORM DUTIES

Thus far our analysis has been limited to two countries, an assumption which may now be dropped in order to reach conclusions which apply when any number of countries take part in international trade.

One of the characteristics of multilateral, as distinct from bilateral, trade is the lack of balance-on-payment account between pairs of countries. It is not necessary, for example, for England to obtain dollars by sales of goods or securities, or by receipt of income in the United States just equal to the pound receipts of Americans in England when there is multilateral trade. The English may obtain dollars indirectly by selling goods in Argentina or any other foreign country. For the purposes of determining the burden and effects of import duties, an extreme example of three-cornered trade is more revealing than any other. If our theory holds for three-cornered trade, it is reasonable to suppose that it holds for all degrees of lack of balance between pairs of countries.

Let us suppose the following conditions: United States (A) exports only to France (F), France exports only to England (E), and England exports only to the United States. Starting with a setting of fixed exchanges and no gold flows, A is assumed to levy a uniform tax upon all imports, which, in this illustration, consist only of E products. This curtails E's supply of dollars from trade since the tax takes some dollars away from the foreign exchange market. E may be expected to curtail exports and hence A's imports decline. The tax in no direct way affects A's sales in F or F's sales in E. E must, with fixed exchanges, ship gold to A to acquire dollars.

If neither A nor E adjusts to this situation, gold continues to flow to A and A's treasury pays its own tax by providing the dollars which become its tax revenue from import duties. F is not affected in this event by A's taxes at all, because it does not sell to A. Now if E adjusts internally by deflating, the international effect of this action is to reduce the supply of pounds which F's exporters obtain from the E market. They may, on this account, be expected to curtail their exports to E. F takes the place of E in shipping gold to A, provided that E deflates far enough to correct its adverse trade balance. If F does nothing and there is no inflation in A, gold continues to flow to A and A's treasury continues to pay its own tax by buying gold from F. But if F also deflates to stop its gold loss, this action will directly affect A's export industries because their income position depends directly upon F's demands. A's exporters therefore begin bearing the tax and bear it entirely if F reduces the volume of francs A's exporters obtain by an amount equal to the yield of the duties at the fixed exchange rate. If A's exporters simply take this loss of dollar income without reducing their sales abroad, possibly because F is still their best market and because resources employed in the export industries are immobile, the net effects of the duties, the E deflation, and the F deflation will be to restore trade to pretax levels. The E deflation, although it reduces F's imports, stimulates E's exports by placing E's export industries in a relatively better position to compete for resources in E. The F deflation offsets the decline in its exports to E (resulting from the E deflation) by improving the position of its export industries relative to other industries. The F deflation also reduces the demand for A's products, but if A's exporters simply take this reduction in their earnings, there is no change in A's exports. The character and volume of the three-cornered trade therefore remain unaffected by A's duties. This conclusion for three-way trade is the same as that found for two-way trade. Given full adjustment to gold flows, import duties have no effects if the exports of the country levying the duties do not decline.

It is likely, to be sure, that A's exporters will in fact curtail sales to F under the impact of a loss of earnings because of the tax yield to the A treasury. In this event F may spend less, more, or the same amount of francs upon A's products. If consumers in F spend the same amount, the adjustment in trade stops here. There is no need for F either to ship (or receive) gold or to change its exports to E. The reduction in F's imports from A leaves F, from the point of view of its foreign exchange relations, in the same position as in the case when A's exporters do not curtail sales in F. In real terms, to be sure, F's consumers are made worse off. Yet the real position of E's consumers is left unchanged by A's taxes. E continues to ship the same volume of products to A as before the tax and does not receive any fewer imports from F. F takes all the real loss arising from the impact of duties imposed by A.

One might analyze each possible case to show the effects of the import duties in A upon the trade among the three countries. Instead, the following compilation is presented which summarizes the results.

The compilation presupposes full adjustments in all countries. This means a situation where there is no net loss or gain of foreign exchange by any country. Partial adjustments, however, will give the same pattern of results, provided that each country does some of the adjusting. In all cases, A's exports to F decline. Unless this occurs, unless, in other words, A's duties actually divert resources from its export industries, there are no further adjustments provided that the import duties are uniform. Therefore, the elasticity of A's demand for imports is irrelevant. In this respect, our analysis basically follows Mill's.

A few observations concerning the implications of these summary results may be pertinent. As long as buyers in the country importing goods from the one that levies the duties are willing to spend the same amount of local money upon imports, the demand elasticity for imports in the other two countries is irrelevant. Although E exports to A, A's duties affect only F. Trade between

F and E and between E and A are unaffected (see Boxes *1, 2, 3*).

As far as gains from trade are concerned, duties levied by one country may affect the terms of trade between other countries. A clear case occurs under the elasticity conditions shown in Box *6* of the table. In this case, E gains absolutely from the presence of

THREE-CORNERED TRADE: FULL ADJUSTMENTS
ELASTICITY OF F's DEMAND FOR IMPORTS

	e = 1	e < 1	e > 1
e = 1	*1* *a* F's imports fall *b* F's exports—same *c* F's gain—negative *d* E's imports—same *e* E's exports—same *f* E's gain—none *g* A's gain—positive	*4* *a* F's imports fall *b* F's exports rise *c* F's gain—negative *d* E's imports rise *e* E's exports—same *f* E's gain—positive *g* A's gain—positive	*7* *a* F's imports fall *b* F's exports fall *c* F's gain ? *d* E's imports fall *e* E's exports—same *f* E's gain—negative *g* A's gain—positive
e < 1	*2* Same as *1*	*5* *a* F's imports fall *b* F's exports rise *c* F's gain—negative *d* E's imports rise *e* E's exports rise *f* E's gain ? *g* A's gain—positive	*8* *a* F's imports fall *b* F's exports fall *c* F's gain ? *d* E's imports fall *e* E's exports rise *f* E's gain—negative *g* A's gain—positive
e > 1	*3* Same as *1*	*6* *a* F's imports fall *b* F's exports rise *c* F's gain—negative *d* E's imports rise *e* E's exports fall *f* E's gain—positive *g* A's gain ?	*9* *a* F's imports fall *b* F's exports fall *c* F's gain ? *d* E's imports fall *e* E's exports fall *f* E's gain ? *g* A's gain ?

(Left margin label: ELASTICITY OF E's DEMAND FOR IMPORTS)

A's duties. This is of course contrary to prevailing opinion. We do not ordinarily think of people living in a country selling to us as benefiting from our import duties.

Box *9* shows the results for what has usually been regarded as the normal case for international trade. The demands for imports have an elasticity greater than unity in both F and E. In this case, trade declines between each pair of countries. The gains from trade are not explicitly stated. The question marks do not mean that gains are indeterminate; they mean only that the direction of change is not self-evident. Finer analysis might reveal the direction of the real gains or losses for each country, provided some sensitive objective test of real gains or losses could be found.

In all the cases considered, the tax burden is the same. The duties reduce the money earnings of resources located in the A export industries and in their competitors for money income. Our investigation of three-cornered trade reinforces the presumption that this theory holds for complicated as well as for highly simplified trade relations. Some difficult test cases for the theory might be discovered if an even more complicated set of trade relations were investigated.

Shifting of Nonuniform Duties

Nonuniform rates upon imports will, to the extent that the taxes yield a revenue, reduce the foreign exchange supply of local money of the country levying the tax and induce an inflow of gold (or other international money). In this respect, nonuniform tariff schedules act in the same manner as uniform schedules. But, in addition, a nonuniform schedule has a marked selective effect upon imports. In the absence of monetary adjustments to gold flows (complete gold sterilization), imports subject to high rates may be excluded altogether whereas imports on the free list are unaffected. Nonuniform rates, in other words, change the composition of imports.

The degree of change in the composition of imports depends, among other things, upon the extent to which the countries concerned adjust their monetary policies to the presence of import taxes. It is not difficult to see why items subject to high rates may not succeed in scaling the tariff wall. This fact is one of the main reasons for regarding duties as protective. But what has not always been noticed is how discriminating tariffs are apt to promote the importation of tax-exempt imports, provided that the duties levied upon the highly taxed imports are not so high as to exclude their entry. For example, if in bilateral trade certain classes of imports are taxed at high rates and the remainder are placed upon the free list, the immediate consequences will be to curtail only the importation of the highly taxed items and to leave the untaxed imports unaffected. But as long as the duties have a yield, gold must be imported to maintain fixed exchanges until such time as there is deflation in the gold-losing country or inflation in the country imposing the duties. If the gold-losing country adjusts by deflating, this action helps all of its export industries because they are then placed in a relatively better position to compete for resources with domestic industries. This adjustment improves the position of the producers of highly taxed items as compared with their status immediately after taxes are imposed, but it is unlikely to return them to the position they enjoyed before the duties. Exporters of items which are tax-free, however, lose nothing by the tax in the first instance, and the process of deflation creates a setting where they have an incentive to sell even more abroad than they did before. They are positively benefited by the fact that another country chooses to place taxes upon commodities other than those they sell. This financial gain arises mainly at the expense of the producers of heavily taxed products.

In the taxing country, the reduction in the supply of heavily taxed imports and the increase in the supply of lightly taxed or exempt imports is accompanied by a rise in the prices of the first group and a fall in the prices of the second. This occasions some redistribution of the real gain of economic activity in favor of the users of imports which are lightly taxed. In addition to this composition effect, nonuniform rates of duties may be accompanied by an expansion or contraction of imports as a whole, for the same reasons discussed for uniform rates.

The protective action of nonuniform schedules of import taxes is particularly marked in cases where tariff schedules provide heavy duties for classes of commodities which are deemed competitive with domestic production and low or zero duties upon raw materials. Roughly speaking, the present United States tariff rates are of this character. With full adjustments to gold flows, such a pattern of rates has a double-barreled action. Imports of manufactured items are curtailed, and this provides a more favorable domestic market for domestic producers of commodities which are substitutes for such imports and hence protects the domestic market. If domestic producers of such products use some imported raw materials, the low rates on such imports and the selective effect of the tariff lowers the domestic prices of these commodities. The profitability of the production of items using imported raw materials is increased. Thus protection is offered both by increasing the demand for products which are substitutes for imports and by reducing the costs of producing them. On the other hand, producers of those products which are substitutes for low taxed or tax-exempt imports are exposed to more competition from the protective tariff and are made worse off in terms of income than they would be with no tariff at all.

The incidence of import duties levied at varying rates is in general the same as that of duties at uniform rates. In either case, A duties remove dollars from the foreign exchange market, and this must be offset either by a purchase of gold by the A treasury or by a change in the trade balance itself. If the trade balance adjusts, A's exporters experience a reduced demand for their products abroad relative to the demands for the products of industries producing for the domestic market. If the exporters are in a position to protect themselves, they move out of the export field, increase the production of commodities for domestic sale, reduce the prices of these commodities, and thereby force resources engaged in the production of such commodities to accept lower money earnings. Producers for export and owners of the resources with whom they compete for money income are always found to bear import taxes (to the extent that their government does not), regardless of the character of the rate schedule employed to tax imports.

In view of the complexity of actual tariff schedules employed by governments, the temptation is strong, when "realistic" results are desired, to study each class of imports by itself and reach conclusions concerning the incidence of import taxes on this basis. This approach is almost certain to suggest that import taxes are borne (partly or wholly) by domestic buyers of taxed imports or by foreign producers of products subject to import duties. Although detailed information about particular imports is highly desirable, it is a mistake to assume that this approach can give a proper explanation of the effects of import taxes. Partial analysis in the field of import taxes does not give merely partial, that is, incomplete, answers—it is likely to give wrong answers. The determination of what groups bear import taxes and the allocation effects of import duties can be discovered only by an analysis of the economy as a whole. The impact of import taxes upon the constituents of the balance of payments must be the point of departure for the determination of the incidence and effects of such taxes.

IO

Taxes and the Incentive to Work

In the previous discussion of the shifting of taxes, the supply of resources to the exchange economy has been taken as given at any moment in the history of a society. No actual system is characterized by complete participation of all resources in exchange. Here we shall investigate how taxes, mainly income taxes, may affect the amount of work that people offer. A tax may affect the allocation of resources between the production of exchangeable products and "leisure" pursuits. Like so many other aspects of fiscal economics, this topic is controversial. The discussion will also consider the possibility of the shifting of income taxes from legal taxpayers to others, because of the effects of the tax upon the supply of work. For some time, students of this topic have recognized that income taxes do not necessarily have neutral effects on choice; income taxes are not the same as flat-sum taxes.

Studies of the relation between work and leisure have not established a consensus as to the direction of change in the supply of work resulting from any set of tax devices. By far the most frequently employed line of reasoning gives the conclusion that an income tax may either increase or decrease the supply of work. An income tax is regarded as having a substitution effect and an income effect, operating in opposite directions. The substitution effect of the tax induces people to take more leisure because an income tax reduces the "price" of leisure. But the tax also reduces the net income of the taxpayer, and this operates in such a way as to make him economize on leisure and work more.[1]

The usual analysis has a serious defect: it is partial analysis. A particular person is considered to be taxed in a setting of given prices for products and for the services he sells. Any tax imposed on him is then assumed to reduce the amount of his possible taking

[1] See Duncan Black, *The Incidence of Income Taxes* (London: Macmillan, 1939), pp. 157–167.

of goods and services from the economy. In other words, the tax is viewed as imposing a real burden on him. Any positive and negative redistributive aspects of the tax device are ignored. Effects arising through these repercussions are left out of the analysis. Pigou, however, did not so limit himself in his study of this subject. Yet, although his work has been available for many years, his contribution seems to have had little influence. We shall begin our analysis with a reëxamination of Pigou's argument.

Pigou's Theory

Pigou holds that a tax which is "used up" by the government, provided the tax device in question has a zero marginal rate, induces people to work more to the extent that they have a choice in the matter. By a "used up" tax, Pigou means one that finances the government's acquisition of current output. If, however, the tax is a redistributive device—that is, accompanied by a government transfer payment of opposite sign—people will work the same amount as before.[2] The conclusion that people will work more if a flat-sum tax is levied on them is justified as follows: "For with a poll-tax, if they only do the same amount of work, the marginal utility of the income left to them will be larger than the disutility of the work done in producing the marginal unit of it."[3] It follows that to obtain a better combination of work and leisure, a person subject to such a tax will want to work more. Pigou's conclusion that people will offer the same amount of work if the flat-sum tax is accompanied by a transfer payment, such as interest on government debt, is demonstrated by the use of the "representative man" concept. If the government removes a sum of money from such a person by a tax and at the same time returns to him an equal sum by a transfer payment, his income remains unchanged. Since the tax and the compensating transfer do not change the marginal cost of leisure, there is no inducement on this account for a person to alter his work habits, even if he can. Thus, according to Pigou, flat-sum taxes which are used up induce people to work more, and flat-sum taxes offset by transfers induce people to work the same amount.

Pigou's analysis has arbitrary features which it is desirable to avoid. The distinction between taxes which are used up and

---

[2] A. C. Pigou, *A Study in Public Finance* (London: Macmillan, 1947), pp. 64–65. Pigou maintains that a tax of zero marginal rate is a sufficient, not a necessary, condition for these results.

[3] *Ibid.,* p. 64.

those which are offset by transfer payments is not satisfactory. In practice, it would not be possible to tell whether a tax falls into one classification or the other. Tax receipts go into the common pool of government cash, and there is no nonarbitrary way of designating the subsequent use of particular tax receipts. There is the further difficulty that the classification is not exhaustive. Government funds are used for purposes other than to acquire goods and services and to effectuate transfers. Tax yields today may be used in future periods to finance the repayment of debt, to acquire land and other old real assets, or to assist in the reconstruction of war-torn countries.

Pigou's representative man concept restricts the analysis of the tax and transfer device to the case in which the distribution of income is left unchanged. Obviously taxes and transfer payments do not ordinarily have this effect; some people collect from the government more than they pay, and others pay more than they collect. It is therefore proposed here to treat all taxes as transfer payments by private groups to government and to abandon any attempt to distinguish taxes on the basis of what they finance, as Pigou does. This procedure requires a somewhat roundabout method of analysis to do proper justice to Pigou's findings.

CHANGES IN PRIVATE WEALTH AND THE INDUCEMENT TO WORK

Let us for the moment neglect government finance altogether and ask how the choices between work and leisure are altered by an increase in wealth. It is initially assumed that each person and family shares in the increase in wealth. More "wealth" is here used in the same sense as we earlier defined "better off" in chapter 5. A society is regarded as becoming more wealthy over time if at later dates all the output of each kind produced at earlier dates continues to be produced plus something more. For a two-commodity system, an increase in wealth means that the compound-production or transformation curve is higher at later dates than at earlier dates. For a many-commodity system, it means that the equivalent multi-dimensional relation has similarly shifted upward.

To isolate the effects on the work-leisure choice attributable solely to an increase in wealth or productive capacity, one must visualize a setting in which all other relations are held constant. Money wage rates must not change in relation to the prices of products. If they do change, the price of leisure changes, and people may make a different choice on this account. But how may a society grow in productive capacity without any change in relative wage rates? Commonly, money wage rates rise relatively to product prices in a progressive economy. This need not happen, in a full employment setting, if the new productive capacity is perfectly competitive with each type of labor service. In this event, the marginal physical productivity of labor in terms of any product can remain constant while over-all productive capacity is growing.

A monetary policy is assumed which succeeds in holding the level of product prices unchanged over time. As productive capacity grows through new net investment, the money demands for products also grow at a rate which just offsets the deflationary price effects of expanding output. However, instead of this extra money being introduced by the banking system's acquiring the securities of business organizations, as is commonly the practice, it is assumed that the government makes flat-sum subsidies financed by the central bank to each person in the society. In each period, a somewhat larger grant of money must be made so that, in the following period, the additional expenditures of private groups finance the purchase of the additional output at constant prices. Money wage rates do not rise in this setting because the additional productive capacity competes with each type of labor service. The rentals paid for the services of the new equipment are equivalent to the unchanged money wage rates paid for labor services. The growth in the demands for resource services by business enterprise, derived from the growth in the demands for their products, operates to pull the new productive capacity into employment without inducing any change in the demand for existing amounts of labor service. Thus the setting visualized assures no change in the relative level of wage rates and hence the price of leisure is unchanged. There is no announcement effect from the increase in productive capacity.

As people become more wealthy, which in monetary terms is reflected by the size of the flat-sum subsidies paid to them, they may be expected to increase their demands for consumption items of many kinds. People have their shoes shined more often, visit their dentists more frequently, and acquire more expensive television sets. The demands for personal services supplied by others will also grow. It is possible that personal services will be regarded as "inferior" commodities, but experience suggests that they do not fall into this class. On the contrary, wealthier societies exhibit, if anything, relatively greater demands for personal services as compared with other things. Therefore, as people become wealthier, the demands for personal service will rise at least in proportion to the increase in the demands for other items.

There will also be an increase in the demand for one's own services for nonexchange purposes. Some kinds of personal services obtainable from others can be supplied by oneself. A person may hire painters to redecorate the living room or get out the paint equipment and do it himself. If, typically, people wish to live with cleaner walls as they find themselves becoming wealthier, the demand for painting services, whether supplied by others or themselves, increases on this account. If the wage rate of a person in his regular occupation is equal to or less than the wage rate obtained by professional painters, he may do his own redecorating and, given the added income, do so more often. Furthermore, many kinds of activities require the employment of a person's own services for enjoyment, such as playing golf or fishing. Therefore some increase in the demand for leisure may be expected as a result of the increase in productive capacity.

Whether a person's tastes take the form of increasing his demands for the personal services of others or for his own services, the supply of labor services to the remainder of the economy is reduced. There is no difference in principle between hiring more servants and reducing the amount of service that the person himself supplies to the rest of the economy. If housewives take in one another's washing, there is no change on this account in the supply of effective work. Some people prefer activities which require that they work fewer hours for others. Such people are prone to take longer vacations and to retire from work at earlier ages as they find their wealth position increasing. Others prefer to work fixed hours regardless of their wealth position. They prefer commodities and assets to increased leisure. Given the fact of a variety of personal tastes, people may be expected to demand more personal services from others and more leisure for themselves as their wealth position grows. *The "wealth" effect on the demand for leisure is therefore positive.*

Institutional arrangements may preclude certain people from reducing the number of hours worked. If a person must make an all-or-none job decision because the labor contract prohibits a choice of working less than a stipulated workweek or workyear, he may not work less as he gets wealthier even if he prefers leisure to other things. This qualification is well known and need not detain us. All-or-none choices preclude fine adjustments.

In a setting of full employment and growing wealth, people may tend to shun jobs which require such all-or-none choices. A wealthier society can be a more pleasant society simply because people can afford to take jobs with more flexible working arrangements instead of higher paid jobs with fixed hours of work. Employers may be under pressure to provide more flexibility in employment opportunities as people become more interested in taking time off from work for self-employment.[4]

Institutional rules and customs may also make marginal calculations irrelevant in another, and perhaps more important, way. Rules may prevent a person from engaging in his regular occupation as many hours a week as he would prefer. The five-day week, for example, forces some people into partial involuntary unemployment. A worker takes more leisure and less of other things than he prefers. Growing wealth reduces this disparity unless it is accompanied by a change in the rules setting maximum periods of work. It is true, to be sure, that no set of rules can be expected to fit the interests of every person. The actual institutional practices on this score might be regarded as reflecting, more or less, the average interests of the occupational groups concerned. Although this may sometimes be true, it is unlikely that the rules found in practice reflect average choice. Labor union decrees in this connection appear to be determined more by economic theories held by trade unionists than by average group preference between work and leisure. Forced reduction of the workweek in an occupation is closely related to various other restrictive practices designed to increase money wage rates, spread the work, or maintain union membership. Thus actual practice may not be indicative of the representative choice of union members between paid work and leisure.

If people generally prefer to work more hours at their occupations than regulations permit, the process of becoming wealthier reduces the difference between the utility of the income from an hour of work and the utility of an hour of leisure for persons who like leisure. But no more leisure may be taken. Marginal considerations may never actually enter into the calculations of many persons, not because people are irrational, but merely because they do not have the opportunity to make a relevant choice. I would

---

[4] The large number of men to be found almost any pleasant day on golf courses suggests that the rigidity of working schedules may be overemphasized. Fixed workdays do not of course prevent adjustments in average hours worked; people commonly take off entire days for leisurely pursuits.

hazard the opinion that private and government rules restricting the length of the workday and workweek for money-making pursuits are quantitatively more important in determining the supply of work in industrial occupations than all public finance considerations put together.

Pigou's observation that taxes which are used up result in people's offering to work more is consistent with the above analysis. If the government decreases the productive capacity available to supply private wants, people may be expected to work more. Procurement activities of the government designed to promote government ends reduce the output available to private groups. Such activities may absorb only a part of the growing productive capacity, but even in this case there is a decline in supplies available to private groups. The relevant comparison is not the absolute change over time; rather it is the potential amount of output available to private groups at a given date and the potential amount available if government use of resources were on a smaller scale. Any increase in the amount of output taken by government for its own ends reduces the amount remaining for private groups and, in this sense, private groups are worse off.[5]

As before, government monetary policy is assumed to be directed toward the goal of stable prices of products over time. As government expenditures expand to implement its procurement program, private money incomes also expand. To prevent an undue increase in private expenditures, the flat-sum subsidies may be reduced or some flat-sum taxes increased. In monetary terms, the decrease in the rate of increase in private wealth or the actual decline is revealed in the reduction in the subsidy or the increase in the tax. Thus people are induced to spend less money for current output, and product prices are kept from rising. Provided money wage rates remain unchanged, people may be expected, if anything, to work more hours than they otherwise would. Since they must economize (and one way to do so is to work more) it would be strange indeed for any different result to emerge. Some of this economy will also take the form of a reduction in personal services hired from others. The formerly wealthy members of the community release labor services to others. The observed fact that people work

---

[5] It is important to avoid the implication that the community as a whole is worse off because of an expansion of government use of resources. Greater military power in a discordant world may be better than the products sacrificed, and a diversion of resources to this objective presumably means that the community as a whole obtains a preferred composition of output.

longer hours on the average during wartime is consistent with these theoretical results. However, the breakdown of prejudice against women workers and other groups in many occupations, the relaxation of rules establishing ceilings on the workweek, and the disruption of family life occasioned by military conscription are no doubt more important factors in this connection.

The above analysis accords with Pigou's analysis of a used-up tax, with the exception that I attribute the increase in the supply of work offered to the government's procurement program rather than to tax policies. In such a setting, the practical alternative to taxation is inflation, a situation also in which many people would find it impossible to maintain former living levels and hence would tend to offer more work. The tax device employed in the analysis merely permits a stable monetary setting. Instead of thinking of a particular tax as used up, I view the added tax or the decrease in the subsidy as a monetary device to prevent prices from rising. But on the point of substance, the conclusion is the same as Pigou's—lowered real income induces people, if anything, to work more themselves and to lower their demands for the labor services of others.

DISTRIBUTIONAL EFFECTS

Pigou, it will be recalled, holds that a flat-sum tax offset by a subsidy has no effect on the supply of work. This conclusion was reached by the representative man concept. The same person is taxed and subsidized in equal amount. Pigou's position could be viewed as implying that a redistribution of income does not alter the supply of work. His position may be correct, but it requires further analysis. A set of flat-sum taxes which redistribute income may conceivably increase or decrease the supply of work.

In contemporary fiscal systems of democratic countries, the attempt is made, not too successfully perhaps, to redistribute income in favor of poorer groups. A system of taxation with or without subsidies which is progressive in effect, that is, one which reduces income inequality,[6] may therefore be studied. At this stage, however, the effects of marginal rates of tax continue to be ignored. But it is difficult to find a tax which systematically reduces income inequality and yet has zero marginal rates. A net-worth tax is here used as an approximation of this case. Such a tax makes use of an

---

[6] This is one definition of tax progression proposed by R. A. Musgrave and Tun Thin, "Income Tax Progression, 1929–48," *Journal of Political Economy*, LVI (December, 1948): 510–511.

index of income-getting capacity.[7] The base of the tax is the present value of all resources under the control of a person plus the value of all claims against others minus the value of all claims of others against him. The base of the tax in question must also include the unencumbered part of the present value of a person's future earning power. Although there are grave theoretical as well as practical difficulties in ascertaining such a figure, we assume that a reasonably accurate appraisal could be made.

The base of a net-worth tax is a multiple of the base of an income tax with no loopholes other than the gains from leisure use of time. To obtain the same yield as that of an income tax, therefore, the government needs to impose the tax at much lower rates. If, for example, the effective rate of an income tax on a $10,000 family income is 10 per cent, and if the capital value of that income-obtaining power is $100,000, a net-worth tax rate of only 1 per cent would obtain the same yield. Such low marginal rates may be treated as negligible in their effect on the choice between work and leisure.

The redistributional effects of a progressive system of net-worth taxes may be studied by reference to a distributionally neutral system. A proportional net-worth tax levied on each person is such a system. It performs the sole function of acting as an anti-inflationary device. Presumably it is the ideal tax from the point of view of taxing for "revenue purposes" alone. It has no effects on the work-leisure choice or on the allocation of resources.

A progressive system of net-worth levies will, by comparison, redistribute income from wealthy to poorer groups. Wealthier groups, on this account, may be expected to demand smaller quantities of personal services from others and also to offer, on the average, more work themselves. Since wealthier groups usually take more leisure and also use greater amounts of the labor services of others, there may be considerable room for economy in this area. As far as institutional arrangements permit, many people in this group may therefore be expected to work more. In a society in which substantial numbers of the wealthier classes do not work, heavy taxes on them will, as a practical matter, force them to work. Thus we see, in Britain and in other countries, a movement of the leisure classes into paid employment as a result of their impoverishment.

[7] See Alexander Henderson, "The Case for Indirect Taxation," *Economic Journal,* LVIII (December, 1948): 545.

On theoretical grounds, a progressive system of net-worth taxation should have the opposite effect on the poorer groups who gain as a result of the redistribution. (Pigou's use of the representative-man concept suggests that he regards these effects as offsetting.) Although these people can now afford more leisure as well as more of other things, the argument may be misleading if applied to poverty groups in an industrial society.[8] It is well known that poverty tends to be self-perpetuating. People at this economic level often do not have the financial means to raise themselves into better-paying occupations because movement requires some initial investment. Nor may they be able to afford the investment in training, if the opportunity is present, to permit their children to move up the economic ladder. A progressive system of taxation serves indirectly to provide such means. Given time, the "quality" of service offered by such groups would improve, and in this sense, a progressive system of taxation would increase the amount of work offered as compared to a proportional system of the same yield. Strictly speaking, the favorable redistributional effect of the tax on such groups does not "induce" them to work more. The added work is more closely associated with the return from investment in human earning power than with the work-leisure choice. Taxes may indirectly affect the supply of the kind of work relevant in an industrial society. Since, given time, human beings are adaptable, the alleviation of poverty of the lowest-income groups would be likely to increase the supply of work demanded in industry. When this sociological consideration is taken into account, a policy of heavy taxation of the wealthier groups increases the amount of work supplied as compared with a proportional tax of the same yield.

Announcement Effects

The foregoing analysis is based on the assumption that the marginal rates of the tax are zero or approximately so. We now consider the relevance of positive or negative marginal rates of tax upon the inducement to supply work to others. Our main proposition may be stated as follows: *Any tax with a positive marginal rate on money gains from work, if it has any effect at all, reduces the supply of labor services to others and any tax with a negative*

---

[8] It is not easy to define poverty in any absolute sense. Roughly it describes people whose financial means are insufficient to maintain health and continued working capacity without outside assistance. Many of the low-income groups in the United States are in this class.

marginal rate (subsidy) *increases the supply of work to others.* This proposition is distinct from any redistributive effects of taxes and subsidies. It may be examined initially by comparison with a distributionally neutral system of taxation with zero marginal rates. A net-worth tax levied at proportional rates is again taken to be such a neutral system.

A personal net income tax, for example, has a distortion effect on the choice between work and leisure because the gains from leisure are excluded from the tax base. If it were administratively possible to design an income tax law in such a fashion that a person would be taxed the same amount whether he worked as much as he could or spent his time in leisure pursuits, a positive marginal rate of tax would not induce him to change his working hours as compared with a flat-sum tax of equivalent yield. Incentive questions in the work-leisure choice arise because of loopholes in the tax law. Some types of activities are given favorable tax treatment, and on this account they may be preferred by the legal taxpayers.

It may seem plausible to conclude that an income tax with no loopholes has no announcement effects and is equivalent to a flat-sum levy. However, there are theoretical difficulties in the conception of a personal income tax without loopholes. It might be possible to design an income tax which includes the gains from leisure use of work time in cases where there are accepted standards in an occupation of what constitutes working full time. Thus a doctor or a lawyer who takes a second month's vacation a year might be required to include in his income-tax base his usual monthly income for any vacation period in excess of one month. The income of factory workers might be treated for tax purposes as if they were working when they take off a day of the regular workweek. It would be dangerous, however, to push the application of this principle very far. Some people give up substantial money incomes in favor of occupations which they prefer on other grounds. For a government to tax a person on the maximum amount he could earn violates beliefs in personal freedom as ordinarily conceived in democratic countries. A tax base which includes such potential gains would force people to accept high-paying occupations regardless of personal tastes.[9] Different occupations are also accompanied

---

[9] The legal system sometimes forces persons to remain in higher-paying occupations against their will. A man whose earning power is indentured to his former spouse may be prevented by court action from moving from a higher- to a lower-paying job. When a person falls behind in the payment of his tax liability, a government may also in effect force him to remain in a more remunerative employment until he is clear of debt.

by features other than the remuneration, which are agreeable to some people and disagreeable to others. There appears to be no theoretically precise way of reducing these "by-products" of work to the common denominator of money income. The money calculus cannot be applied to every feature of working life without absurd results.[10] The conception of an income tax without a loophole breaks down for lack of any theoretically precise way of defining such a tax in a social setting in which considerations other than explicit money earnings are relevant to people in their choice of work.

The proposition that an income tax which "exempts" leisure reduces the supply of work may be demonstrated by graphical analysis. In figure 22, OR is the maximum time a person can work per day if he is perfectly free to determine his working habits. This period is presumably less than twenty-four hours a day since a person must ordinarily eat and sleep to maintain productive capacity. If a person has no other income and is not subject to any tax or other obligation, such as interest or alimony payments, the maximum income he can obtain per day is measured by RB, and the line OB shows, at the assumed given wage rate, the amount of income he can obtain for each number of hours worked. The slope of the line OB is proportional to the wage rate and is the reciprocal of the wage rate. If a flat-sum tax, in amount equal to OS, is imposed on him, the line SA now represents his possible income for each number of hours worked. He now has to work OT hours to bring his net income up to zero. Alternatively, if he receives a subsidy or an income from assets other than his own earning power in amount equal to OM, the line MC shows his possible income.

The indifference schedules I_1 through I_4 show his relevant choices between work and leisure. These schedules are constructed on the following assumptions: (1) The marginal utility of work is negative. (2) The marginal utility of income is positive. (3) The utility of work and income are independent. These three assumptions assure that the indifference curves are concave to R. (4) The marginal utility of income decreases with increasing income. This means that points F, H, and J fall on a negatively sloped line. (If the marginal utility of income were constant, the points F, H, and J would fall on a line parallel to the horizontal axis.) If these as-

---

[10] See Henry C. Simons, *Personal Income Taxation* (Chicago: University of Chicago Press, 1938), pp. 52–55; and William Vickrey, *Agenda for Progressive Taxation* (New York: Ronald Press, 1947), pp. 44–52.

sumptions are generally true, a person will work the same or fewer hours as his wealth position increases.

Because the validity of these assumptions is crucial, they may be further examined. The assumption that the marginal utility of work is negative may be challenged on the ground that some people like their work. Our assumption is not necessarily contradictory to this observation. If a person likes his work so much that he works the maximum number of hours he physically can each day, varia-

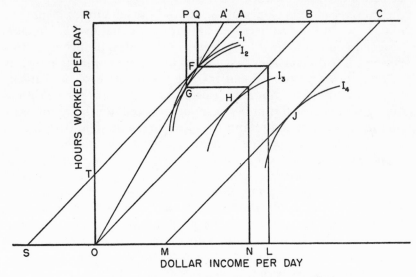

Fig. 22. Announcement effects on work-income choice.

tions in his income position will not affect the supply of work he offers.[11] It may also be claimed that the marginal utility of income may be negative for some people. This means that a person would refuse to take income which he could obtain without cost to himself. Although once in a while cases of such behavior are reported, they may be treated as of negligible importance.

---

[11] A person may enjoy his work to the point of sacrificing some money gains in order to work longer hours. Such a sacrifice is involved in cases in which a person deliberately works to the point where his marginal productivity is negative. This means he could increase his total earnings per day by working fewer hours. The greater the outside income of such a person is, the more he can afford to indulge his desire for work, and conceivably such a person might work longer hours as his income from other sources increases. Such behavior should not be treated as an increase in the amount of work supplied to others. If he works beyond the point of maximum productivity, he is reducing the supply of effective work.

A person might conceivably work less at lower levels of income. This would mean that a person treated all commodities obtained through exchange as technically inferior goods. The poorer he became, the more leisure he would take and the less he would work. Although there is no method of proving that such choice patterns may not exist, it is prima facie implausible for a large group of commodities to be treated by consumers as inferior to leisure.[12]

We are now in a position to ascertain the effects of an income tax on the supply of work. Returning to figure 22, point F shows the number of hours a person works and the amount of income he obtains when he is subject to a flat-sum tax equal to OS. He takes leisure in amount equal to QF, earns OL dollars of income before tax and RQ dollars after tax. Let us now assume that the government imposes a proportional income tax in place of the flat-sum levy. The line OA' shows the various amounts of a person's after-tax income for each number of hours worked, on the assumption that the government attempts to collect the same yield from him as under the flat-sum tax if he continues to work the same hours. Now a person who has a choice and who need not take income and leisure in fixed proportions works less and takes more leisure ($PG > QF$). G is the point of tangency of OA' on the superior indifference curve I_2. By the same token, other workers take more leisure. Thus the attempt of the government to collect the same tax revenue by the income tax reduces the supply of work and also reduces the tax liability if all prices are kept constant except the price of leisure. Whether other prices can remain unchanged will be examined shortly.

If, in contrast, the government imposes a system of income subsidies at a positive marginal rate, the effect of the rate alone is to increase the price of leisure. If a person earns $1.00 per hour and the income subsidy is 20 per cent, the marginal cost of leisure becomes $1.20 per hour. On this account people, to the extent that they have freedom of choice in their hours of work, may be expected to offer more labor service to others. If the absolute amount of the subsidy is offset by a flat-sum tax, the absolute amount of goods and services which a person can buy from others is unchanged. Again the positive marginal rate of the subsidy taken alone operates solely in the direction of increasing the supply of labor service.

---

[12] See J. R. Hicks, *Value and Capital* (Oxford: Clarendon Press, 1939), pp. 34–35.

DISTRIBUTIONAL AND ANNOUNCEMENT EFFECTS

The price-of-leisure effect of an income tax may now be combined with its possible distributional effects to ascertain the over-all results of a system of income taxation. If a system of personal income taxation is proportional, people who have freedom of choice in their working hours offer either less or the same amount of work because the price of leisure is reduced. The higher the marginal rate of tax becomes, the greater, presumably, will be the amount of time taken for leisurely pursuits. At 100 per cent or higher rates the marginal cost of leisure is zero or negative, and in this case a money-price system of ordering economic affairs breaks down. Some other incentive system must be found to get work done.[13] A proportional system of income taxation discriminates in favor of people with strong preferences for leisure and against people who prefer goods and services which can be bought for money. Consequently people who like to work will pay heavier taxes than similarly situated persons who have a strong preference for leisure. This point may be stated more generally: Any system of income taxes which exempts some "gains" from the tax base, whether these gains are of a nonmonetary or monetary type, allocates resources in the direction of activities which are tax-exempt. In a two-commodity system, a proportional income tax on the gain of persons engaged in the production of X moves resources into the production of Y. The price of X rises, and the price of Y falls. In the leisure case, this adjustment is automatic since the tax directly reduces the price of leisure relative to the prices of other things. Whether this constitutes a form of tax shifting will be examined in the section headed "Leisure and income tax shifting."

If a system of income taxation is levied at progressive rates, the over-all effects on the supply of work can be found by combining the negative effect of the marginal rate itself and the positive and negative redistributional effects. As previously argued, a system of wealth taxes which redistributes wealth in favor of poorer groups at the expense of wealthier groups results in the poorer members of the society offering to work less, if anything, and the wealthier members to work more. If this redistributional effect is accom-

---

[13] Although legislators are usually aware of the danger of marginal rates of tax in the neighborhood of 100 per cent, there is less awareness of the "disincentive" results of high marginal rates of subsidy. For example, when eligibility for relief payments is determined by need, and the relevant wage rate is low, a person is sometimes financially penalized for working.

plished by progressive income taxes, the wealthier groups, being subject to high marginal rates, will on this account work less—which may or may not be offset by their need to economize on goods and services, including self-service. The very low income groups, not being subject to the tax at all, are not affected by the rate of tax. Since, however, their spending power is increased absolutely through reduction in the spending power of wealthier groups, they may on this account alone work less. But, as already pointed out, this theoretical consideration is probably irrelevant for people in the lowest economic strata because their income-earning power is closely dependent upon their wealth position.

ALTERNATIVE VIEWS

The conclusions set forth above differ in certain respects from the findings of other students of this topic. Robbins has explicitly taken issue with Pigou's position, which he treats as similar to the analysis of Knight.[14] Robbins holds that the effect of a change in real wage rates or of a tax upon earnings depends upon the elasticity of the demand for income in terms of effort. In the presence of a tax, if this elasticity is greater than unity, less work is done, and if less than unity, more work is done. He also holds that theoretical analysis gives no unequivocal indication of which elasticity is likely to be found in fact. His elasticity concepts, being classification devices, indicate that people will in fact work either more or less if they are subject to a tax.

Robbins interprets Pigou as maintaining that an income tax will induce people to work more, when in fact Pigou held that a flat-sum tax which is used up induces people to work more.[15] Thus Robbins' main criticism which assumes that the tax device in question reduces the price of leisure is misdirected if applied to the strongest feature of Pigou's statement. A flat-sum tax does not alter the price of leisure at all. Granted that a tax which is used up will induce people to work more—on the theory that people will economize in all directions including leisure—it follows that there can be a positive rate of tax which will also induce people to work more. The positive rate might have to be very low.[16] Robbins

---

[14] See Lionel Robbins, "On the Elasticity of Demand for Income in Terms of Effort," *Economica*, n.s., X (June, 1930): 123–129. Reprinted in *Readings in the Theory of Income Distribution* (Philadelphia: Blakiston, 1946), pp. 237–244.

[15] *Ibid., Readings*, pp. 242–244.

[16] Robbins' apparent misinterpretation of Pigou's position may be ascribed in part to the obscurity of Pigou's exposition on some occasions.

also assumes that any tax makes people worse off in the sense that they are forced to give up goods and services. But this implicitly assumes that taxes are always used up—a position that is empirically false, as Pigou has pointed out. If, instead, one views a system of flat-sum taxes as the background against which to discover the effects of taxes with positive marginal rates, as I have attempted in the foregoing analysis, the income effect of a tax does not imply that people must be worse off in real terms.

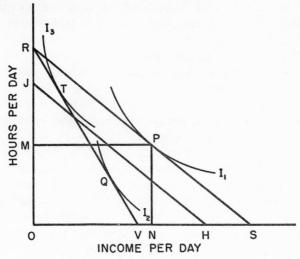

Fig. 23. Leisure-income choice.

Another type of analysis of the relation between taxes and the work-leisure choice is presented by Black and Wald.[17] Black maintains, like Robbins, that the effect of an income tax on the supply of work is indeterminate. His argument may be discussed by reference to the type of graphical analysis that he uses.

In figure 23, OR is the maximum number of hours a person can work per day if he has free choice, and therefore it is apparently the maximum number of hours of leisure he can take. At the assumed hourly rate of pay, he can earn a maximum of OS dollars.

[17] Black, *op. cit.*, and Haskell P. Wald, "The Classical Indictment of Indirect Taxation," *Quarterly Journal of Economics*, LIX (August, 1945): 577–596. Wald is mainly concerned with showing that income taxes have an "excess burden" and in this respect are like excise taxes. This feature of the argument seems formally correct in the sense that an income tax is not a flat-sum levy and therefore has an announcement effect. It involves, however, the implicit assumption that resource allocation is necessarily ideal for each person in the absence of taxes—a theory that appears to be correct only if the initial pretax allocation is the best possible one.

RS shows the various amounts of income he can earn per day. The indifference curve I_1 portrays the person's relative tastes for leisure and income, so that he works *MR* hours, obtains *OM* hours of leisure, and receives *ON* dollars of income per day. Now let a proportional income tax be imposed on him, equal to *VS* if he works the maximum amount he can. The explicit wage rate is assumed to remain unchanged. *VR* shows the amounts of income net of tax he can receive per day. If the highest indifference curve he can achieve is I_2, he will work more hours than before, earning more dollars before tax, but fewer dollars after tax. If, however, the relevant indifference curve is I_3, he will work fewer hours and earn fewer dollars, both before and after deducting the tax. Thus Black concludes that no definite statement concerning the effect of a proportional tax can be made on theoretical grounds alone. A person may work more or less when confronted with a proportional tax on his earnings. The argument is not changed in substance if the tax is levied at progressive rates.

There are objections to Black's analysis. The first is his assumption that the real income of a person must be reduced by a tax. The line *RV* gives possible combinations of leisure and income which are inferior to those shown by *RS*. If the tax is distributionally neutral, there can be a reduction in real income only if it is assumed that people are better off by experiencing inflation than by being taxed. A reduction in the real position of groups presupposes that the tax is not distributionally neutral, and Black's analysis therefore applies only to those groups who are taxed more heavily than the average. For low-income groups, the reverse holds. They can increase their income and leisure as compared to their opportunities under a distributionally neutral system of taxation. Thus the income effect of a set of tax devices is either zero for the group as a whole or it is negative for some and positive for others—an implication of Pigou's analysis.

The second objection concerns the theory of the choice between work and leisure assumed by Black as illustrated by I_3 (fig. 23). The choice there exhibited implies that a person will work less if he is made poorer by a flat-sum tax. But actually such a tax must be greater relative to his income than are flat-sum taxes levied on others. The line *JH*, for example, shows the position of a person who is subject to a flat-sum tax of *HS* amount. Black's argument implies that the person regards income as an "inferior good," that is, a person would want relatively less income if some money were removed from him. For reasons previously mentioned, it is not plausible to believe that there are many—if any—people who treat goods and services obtainable through exchange as inferior commodities.[18]

These opposing views furnish no arguments that necessitate modification of the theory that a positive marginal rate of tax always operates in the direction of reducing the incentive to work. If it is social policy to maximize the amount of work offered, any tax that strikes at marginal earnings is, on this score, inferior to one which does not. Thus from this point of view a system of net-worth taxation would be better than a progressive income tax. Work incentives are increased by taxing leisure and subsidizing work rather than the reverse. A progressive subsidy to earnings from work would give such a result.

Under socialism, the government might provide additional incentives to work by a general policy of paying "high" money wage rates in relation to product prices, thereby making leisure more expensive. Such a policy carried to extremes would entail the operation of industry generally at a loss. The difficulty of such a policy even under socialism is the practical one of devising tax measures which would have sufficient yield to offset the policy of paying excessive wages and salaries. Otherwise, either nonprice rationing would need to be employed, and this has a disincentive effect through lessening the significance of money income of any kind, or price inflation and its accompanying difficulties would have to be tolerated. Fiscal systems do not often permit the luxury of subsidizing work. There are few practical tax devices of a neutral sort to offset the inflationary effects of the subsidies.

The disincentive effects of income taxes provide a reason for the consideration of other taxes, such as net-worth levies, to achieve the desired change in the pattern of income distribution and yet not

---

[18] The graphical device shown in figure 23, used by Black and others, has important limitations for the analysis of the work-leisure choice. The point R is invariant because it is assumed there are only a certain number of hours of work possible in a day. Thus there is no way of showing the choice of a person whose income from other sources is positive, unless the vertical axis is taken to mean leisure use of a person's time and "leisure" use of other people's time. If this interpretation were placed on the construction, it would then be possible to use it to handle variations in wealth position. Yet there is something artificial about treating hired "leisure" as equivalent to one's own time. It means that services hired are always perfect substitutes for one's own services. To avoid this special assumption, we use the less familiar construction presented in figure 22. It does not imply that any tax or subsidy must change the slope of the price line of work and leisure.

encourage people to work less. Income taxation should not be regarded as the last word in equitable taxation.

LEISURE AND INCOME-TAX SHIFTING

Income taxes have been regarded by some students as equivalent to flat-sum levies. Seligman appears to hold this view.[19] The basis for this opinion is the idea of income maximization. A management policy which maximizes profits before tax, for example, maximizes profits after tax. Unless the tax exempts some types of profits, therefore, the tax has a neutral effect on behavior.

One weakness of the maximization theory as applied to an income tax is the neglect of leisure—a weakness which critics of the doctrine that general income taxes are not shiftable have been quick to point out.[20] There is also the possibility that an income tax may be regarded as partly shifted through its effects on investment decisions. This matter will be considered in the following chapters. We shall here concentrate on the question of whether or not an income tax may be shifted because of its possible effects on the choice between work and leisure.

If people are not sensitive to the price of leisure, or, in other words, if they work the same amount and select the same occupations, there is no possibility of the shifting of an income tax because of leisure effects. There are none in such a case. Although people may not in fact be sensitive to the price of leisure, it is nevertheless instructive to investigate shifting possibilities on the assumption that people are sensitive to taxation in the work-leisure choice.

The complexity of the subject makes it advisable to use simplifying assumptions; otherwise, it may be impossible to reach any definitive results. On the aggregate level, let us assume that the demand for products is kept unchanged, in the sense that people are prepared to spend the same number of dollars on current output other than leisure, whatever the level of prices. The over-all

---

[19] See E. R. A. Seligman, *Incidence of Taxation* (2d ed.; London: Macmillan, 1902), pp. 295–298, 307–309. Seligman, although claiming that a tax on net profits cannot be shifted, holds that a tax on wages may be shifted, depending upon the relative strength of labor unions and unspecified other conditions. His analysis of an income tax proceeds according to the income-share approach—the traditional but now largely obsolete procedure.

[20] See Black, *op. cit.*, p. 10, and Richard Goode, "The Income Tax and the Supply of Labor," *Journal of Political Economy*, LVII (October, 1949): 428–437. The following passage appears to summarize Goode's position on the shiftability of the income tax: "Thus the tax forces consumers of some goods to pay higher prices and enables consumers of other goods to pay lower prices. We do not know how much of the tax is shifted in this way..." (*ibid.*, pp. 436–437).

demand for labor service of each type is also assumed to have an elasticity of unity. Initially each member of the working group is viewed as having the same tastes for money income and leisure. As before, let us again also assume that there exists a set of flat-sum taxes which is distributionally neutral. These two conditions mean that the marginal cost of leisure must be equal to the marginal money wage rate and that the existing tax system does not change relative wealth status. Further, this tax system may be regarded as adequate in yield to offset government expenditures and to main-

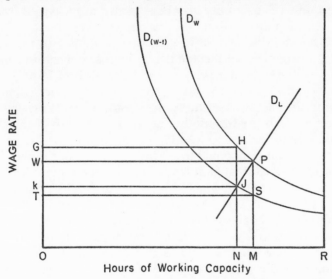

Fig. 24. Shifting of a personal income tax.

tain private demands for products at a given level without positive or negative debt operations. In this setting, we propose to isolate the possibilities of the shifting of income taxes by the legal tax-payers to others and to identify the latter group.

Let D_w in figure 24 be the demand schedule for a representative type of labor service, the schedule being drawn with reference to the left-hand vertical axis, and let D_L be the demand schedule for leisure, this schedule being drawn with reference to the right-hand vertical axis. The distance OR measures the maximum working capacity of the group. The maximum working capacity of any one worker may be defined as the average length of the work day or work week that results in the maximum output of effective work. This period is not twenty-four or even twelve hours per day; when account is taken of the need for week-end rest and for annual vacations, it may be as much as eight hours per day in some occupations and as little as four hours per day in others on the average. Given the market demand D_w for labor service and the workers' demand for their own time, D_L, the money wage rate is PM with OM units of labor service being hired for monetary remuneration and MR units being taken in the form of leisure. The total wage bill is measured by the area OWPM. In the absence of outside income and of taxes, it is the aggregate net income of this group. The initially assumed flat-sum tax may be regarded as measured by the area TWPS, keeping in mind that this tax has a zero marginal rate and therefore the distance PS is without significance in this case.

Now let a proportional income tax be imposed, when income is defined to exclude nonmonetary gains in the form of leisure, subject to the condition that the total yield of the revenue system remains constant. Each worker finds, before adjustment, that he has traded one tax liability for another of equal size. This change can make only one difference to him. The marginal cost of leisure is now lower by an amount equal to the marginal rate of the tax. This reduction in the marginal gain from work is shown graphically in figure 24 by the line D_{w-t}, which, like D_w, is drawn by reference to the left-hand vertical axis. D_{w-t} shows the market price of work minus the marginal rate of tax on the gain from work, and it is drawn parallel to D_w because D_w is a rectangular hyperbola and the tax is a proportional one. Thus at the wage PM, the price of work realized by the seller, that is, the net price, becomes SM. The tax liability under the income tax is now equal to the area TWPS, which is, of course, equal to the revenue from the displaced set of flat-sum taxes.

If the demand for leisure depends at all upon the price of leisure, workers will take more leisure. The tax rate induces workers, therefore, to offer less work. But as they offer to work less, the price of labor service adjusts by rising, and this rise in the price of labor service increases the net marginal cost of taking leisure. The mutual adjustment of these variables leads to the wage rate HN and to the net wage rate of JN.

The condition that the total revenue shall remain unchanged continues to be satisfied. Even though the money wage rate has risen, the total wage bill remains constant because it is assumed that the demand for labor service has an elasticity of unity. But the prices of products bought with money will rise because of the reduction in the supply of labor resources devoted to such purposes. Let us think of the increase in product prices as approximately measured by WG, the rise in the wage rate, with the qualification that the increase will vary from commodity to commodity depending upon a variety of circumstances. Each owner of labor service finds his situation altered as a result of the presence of a proportional income tax instead of a flat-sum tax in the following ways: the quantity of leisure he takes is larger, the quantities of various commodities he takes is smaller, the price of leisure to him is lower, and the prices of commodities are higher. His tax liability measured in money terms as well as his income before tax remains unchanged.

At least two positions may be adopted about the incidence of an income tax under the conditions set forth. One is that the workers have not shifted the tax at all. This is the view here adopted. Another is that the workers have shifted a part of the tax from themselves to consumers. Such a position is supported by the rise in the prices of output. Is there any rational way of choosing between these positions?

There is the indisputable fact that all the tax liability continues to be accounted for among the members of the working group in question. They have not shifted the tax in the sense that they have managed to increase their income computed after taxes. This evidence may be regarded as sufficient to establish that the income tax has not been shifted at all. But it may be contended that something has happened to consumers. They are paying higher prices for output and therefore should be regarded as having a real burden thrust upon them. This point may be examined more closely.

Whether people looked upon as consumers are made worse off by a tax upon earnings requires weighing the loss in the form of reduced output and the gain in the form of increased leisure. This comparison applies to those who both work and consume. Although they find the prices of output somewhat higher, they also find the price of leisure lower. People are taking more of their productive capacity in the form of leisure and less in the form of marketable goods and services. It is possible to show that people are worse off provided that the initial allocation of resources between work and leisure happens to be ideal. In that event, any tax or subsidy on work must make the allocation less than ideal. If, on the other hand, the initial allocation is not ideal, which, of course, will typically be the case in practice, the new allocation may be a superior or an inferior one depending upon whether a movement in the direction of more leisure happens to place each worker on a higher or a lower indifference schedule. The initial allocation may be deficient because it induces people to take too much leisure. The demand schedule for labor service may reflect the presence of excise taxes upon sellers; in this event, the income tax makes matters worse. But the income tax may improve the allocation if workers have been induced to take too little leisure, because, for example, the demand for labor service reflects subsidies in the production of products or because the groups concerned overestimate the average number of hours per day or per week that would maximize the amount of work accomplished. This latter possibility should not be lightly dismissed. Such overestimates appear to have been the rule in industrial occupations from the early days of mass production until recent decades. Because a tax may induce people to work less, it may not be immediately inferred that the public is impoverished. It is true, to be sure, that deflated money incomes must fall if the deflating index is constructed from observations of prices of output, but it is not necessarily true that deflated money incomes must fall if the deflating index includes the price of leisure. For some or all workers, income in this latter sense may even rise because of a tax imposed upon the gains from work.[21] Consequently one cannot hold that an income tax is partly shifted to consumers unless he is prepared to accept the possible outcome that the tax system makes consumers better off. It is a peculiar doctrine that leads to the conclusion that a tax is shifted to persons who are made better off by the tax in question. Just such inconsistent results must

---

[21] This analysis is a repudiation of the excess-burden doctrine as applied to individual income taxes. The excess-burden doctrine, stated generally and without the implication that any tax must have a burden, is the proposition that a tax with announcement effects inflicts a real burden on the public as compared with a flat-sum tax of equal yield. Reasons for rejecting this view and replacing it with the proposition that a set of taxes with announcement effects may inflict a real burden or occasion a real gain are set forth in an article by George F. Break and myself, "The Welfare Aspects of Excise Taxes," *Journal of Political Economy*, LVII (February, 1949): 46–54. Essentially the same proof and conclusions are developed by Milton Friedman in his article, "The 'Welfare' Effects of an Income Tax and an Excise Tax," in the same journal, *ibid.*, LX (February, 1952): 25–33. Some recent articles, though apparently endorsing the conclusions found in the two articles cited above, presuppose that excise taxes are shifted to consumers. On this assumption, excise taxes must inflict a real burden on the public and can never result in a real gain because the incidence theory adopted already presupposes that the shifting reduces the supplies of commodities to consumers. In this connection, for example, see R. K. Davidson, "The Alleged Excess Burden of an Excise Tax in the Case of an Individual Consumer," *Review of Economic Studies*, XX (1952–53): 209–215.

emerge, however, if only the evidence about tax-induced price changes is examined to identify those upon whom a tax rests.

Let us now relax the assumption that people's tastes for work and leisure are identical. Some people work less when subject to a tax on earned income; some work the same amount as before. If, in the aggregate, the reduction in the supply of labor service is equal to MN, wage rates will move to HN as before (fig. 24). The total money earnings of workers remain unchanged, but those who work full time earn more and are subject to a greater tax liability as compared to the initial flat-sum levy, whereas some, but not all, of those who work less are subject to a smaller tax liability. Some members of this latter group reduce the number of hours worked below the amount necessary to maintain the same pretax earnings. Their tax liability falls in absolute terms. A proportional income tax which exempts leisure does not necessarily remain proportional to money-earning capacity. People whose demands for leisure are sensitive to its price computed after tax reduce their tax liabilities relatively to those who work unchanged hours.

The facts in this case are clear, but again their interpretation raises some difficulties. Those who continue to work the same amount obtain higher money incomes but also pay a greater tax as compared to their original position. Some of those who take more leisure also obtain higher money incomes and are subject to a greater tax liability. Those who take much more leisure find their tax liability falling. There has been a change in the distribution of the tax liability in favor of those who like leisure and against those who prefer money income. This relative change favors the interpretation that some of the tax has been shifted from the indolent to the industrious.

Against this interpretation, however, there is the fact that the industrious experience an increase in their money income, and only a part of this is taken by the government. The increase in money incomes before tax appears to be evidence that they have shifted a part of their tax liability to others. The increase in money income is altogether at the expense of those who take more leisure. If some had not taken more leisure, money wage rates would not have risen in the first place, and therefore there would have been no change in relative earnings.

It seems more reasonable to conclude that the indolent have avoided a part of the original tax liability. There is the inescapable fact that their tax liability has fallen. If the government were again to redistribute the tax liability as it initially was, the indolent would be the ones who would be asked to contribute more. Furthermore, the industrious do not succeed in increasing their incomes by an amount sufficient to offset the higher prices of products. Although in the circumstances visualized, money incomes rise proportionally to the rise in product prices, the government takes a part of this increase, and therefore the industrious will have to take less output in future periods unless they wish to draw down their asset position on balance. The indolent enjoy their leisure, and the increase in product prices is, to that extent, of less concern to them. Therefore, if the industry demand for labor service has an elasticity of unity, there is some shifting of the tax liability from those who take more leisure to those who still take the same amount.

The assumption that the demand for labor service has an elasticity of unity may now be relaxed. The assumption that the overall demand for products remains constant is retained. As wage rates rise, the elasticity within the range may be greater than, less than, or equal to unity. This elasticity will depend upon the type of product, the substitution relations between labor service and real resources, and the marketing structure of various industries. The only case of interest here is one characterized by a demand elasticity for labor service of less than unity—often taken as the "normal" case.[22] Under the assumption that the demand for products is a constant, the reduction in the supply of labor is accompanied by a sufficient increase in the money wage rate to increase aggregate wage incomes in money terms. The question to be answered is whether or not this constitutes partial shifting of the tax from workers to owners of some real wealth.

For reasons similar to those already suggested for regarding a proportional net income tax as shifted partly from the indolent to the industrious, it may also be maintained that workers in general shift a part of their tax liability to owners of enterprise in this case. The latter pay higher money wages but obtain the same aggregate money return from the sale of products. Therefore their profit before tax falls. The lost income becomes part of the earnings of labor. The aggregate tax liability on owners of real assets declines, but their income also declines because of the increase in costs.

[22] If the demand for labor is elastic, there is no possibility of workers shifting some of the tax liability to owners of real resources. The aggregate income going to labor would fall in this case. Any shifting of the tax because of leisure considerations would be limited to persons within the labor group.

Although the tax liability of the industrious also increases, their added tax liability increases by only a portion of the decline in the tax liability of the indolent. In money terms, therefore, workers as a group have in this case succeeded in shifting a part of the tax to other owners of resource services.

The partial shifting of the tax to owners of real resources is not likely to be uniform. Industries which supply products which are treated as complementary to leisure may find the demands for their products increasing, whereas the reverse may occur in industries which supply products competing with leisure use of time. The latter group are apt to supply services that many people can perform for themselves. Thus no uniform increase in product prices is to be expected. In addition, when account is taken of the many varieties of labor service, it is not likely that the prices of all of them will advance as a result of the increased demand for leisure. Personal service industries may, as a result of a decline in the demand for their products, reduce their demand for labor. Wage rates may not rise because of specialization of labor services to the industry.

We need not remove the assumption of a constant demand for products in the over-all sense. Relative analysis requires some stable reference for meaningful statements about price changes. If in fact aggregate demands are expanding, the same pattern of analysis can be applied. The tax liability will automatically increase as money incomes increase. But with a proportional tax, the relation of taxes to national income will not change on this account.

The foregoing analysis can also be applied to a general and uniform sales tax which exempts leisure. As argued in chapter 6, such a tax under competitive conditions becomes a proportional income tax. Therefore the analysis of a proportional income tax in relation to choices between work and leisure may be applied also to a general system of excise taxes. Both sets of taxes favor leisure, in comparison with a system of taxation in which the tax liability does not depend upon the choice between working and not working. Sales taxes have the same effect on the work-leisure choice as do proportional income taxes.

A progressive or regressive income tax can be analyzed in a similar fashion. A progressive tax has no announcement effect on the groups whose incomes are below the first bracket rates. Announcement effects are restricted to higher income groups. To isolate the shifting possibilities of a progressive tax that exempts leisure, the background tax should be looked upon as a progressive system of taxation having zero or negligible marginal rates on money-earning pursuits. This comparison is the relevant one. It seems incorrect to hold that taxes which reduce income inequality are shiftable if they are flat-sum levies. Such taxes have no incentive aspects; they cannot alter choices between work and leisure through any change in the price of leisure, and they cannot alter the terms confronting any person in the management of resources. The only possible shifting of a system of progressive taxation occurs through its lack of neutrality with respect to choice in the management of resources including human earning power. Therefore, a progressive system of taxation is shiftable to the extent that people decide to take more leisure and in that way increase the price of their type of labor service. This means that if people are sensitive to the work-leisure choice, the supplies of some kinds of work decline and the price of that kind of labor increases. The high salaries of executives may be partly at the expense of other incomes because of progressive taxes, if it really is true, as sometimes claimed, that people shun such occupations because they do not regard the personal wear and tear incident to such tasks as worth the extra gain computed after tax. If this doubtful premise is granted, people in such jobs may therefore shift a part of their tax liability onto other groups with whom they compete for money income. In practice, this competition occurs with owners of real resources rather than with ordinary labor services, although it is extremely difficult to be specific in this area.

CONCLUSIONS

In the foregoing analysis, the effects of taxes on the work-leisure choice have been separated into those that result from distributional features and those that result from the presence of positive marginal rates. This method of analysis is basically similar to that used by Pigou. Like him, I start from the premise that a set of taxes that is distributionally neutral and that has a zero marginal rate on the gains from the management of wealth and human earning power has no effect on the work-leisure choice. According to this position, the sole function of such a set of taxes is to act as an anti-inflationary measure. The alternatives to it are direct controls designed to suppress the use of money and prices as rationing devices, debt operations designed to hold down private expenditures, or the toleration of expenditure and price inflation. The belief that an alternative to such taxes is a higher standard of private living is specifically repudiated. Taxes need have no real burden on members of the public. Under conditions of given economic efficiency, public expenditures for goods and services, rather than taxes as such, influence the amounts of commodities and services available to private groups.

Any actual system of taxes will have distributional effects. The money incomes, after deducting taxes, of some groups will be altered relatively to those of others. Those whose incomes after tax are reduced relatively will, on this account, offer more work and those who are favored by the tax system will offer less. If, however, the latter group are people at the poverty level, the redistribution may eventually permit them to supply types of labor service of greater productivity in an industrialized society by permitting more investment in training. Accordingly, a system of taxation which markedly reduces income inequality in a society may be expected to increase the supply of effective work. In poor counties, governments which can effectively and substantially reduce the inequality of incomes through tax devices may expect the opulent groups to work more and the poverty groups to supply higher quality of services. The difficulty of enacting practical measures to achieve this result continues to be a serious block to the long run progress of such peoples.

Marginal rates of tax may have the effect of inducing people to take more leisure, if the tax is of a type that reduces net earnings from work. Individual income taxes, sales and excise taxes, and import duties are of this type. Property taxes, net-worth taxes, poll taxes, corporate net income taxes, estate and inheritance taxes, and possibly spending taxes are not of this type.[23] They do not reduce the price of leisure. The effects of a system of taxation found in any country upon the work-leisure choice depends therefore upon the extent to which the tax system relies upon the first group of taxes and the marginal rates of tax accompanying that pattern. High marginal rates of taxes of the first type are likely to induce people to take some greater amount of leisure. It is this fact that

---

[23] A spendings tax has no effect on the work-leisure choice of those persons whose marginal earnings are earmarked to finance the holding of assets. Because a spendings tax exempts expenditures to acquire assets from the tax base, the marginal rate as applied to earnings is then zero. To the extent, however, people earn to finance future consumption, a spendings tax may affect the work-leisure choice.

led us to the observation that people may partly shift an individual income tax to other income recipients.

How important are high positive marginal rates of tax on earnings in inducing people to prefer leisure to work? The question cannot be settled by theoretical analysis. If the demand for leisure is highly inelastic, the effects of high marginal rates under income taxes will be small and possibly insignificant. The empirical evidence relating to this matter suggests that in fact workers in the United States at least are not sensitive to the price of leisure, and therefore the shifting possibilities of an income tax are slight and the disincentive effects are also slight. The systematic evidence available relates to some nineteen empirical studies of the shape of the supply curve of labor services. These studies have been systematically collated and evaluated by George F. Break. After reviewing the findings of these studies, he concludes: "If this information supports any hypothesis, it supports the one that the supply curve of labor is either highly inelastic or negatively sloped."[24] These findings relate to both the income effects and the price effects of wage rates and effective tax rates. They do not isolate directly the effects of the marginal rates of tax; nevertheless they are of some importance for our topic. If workers are found to work less or about the same amount at higher wage rates, one may conclude that the income effect outweighs the price effect. Theoretical analysis tells us that at higher money wage rates, people will want to work more if their income could be kept constant, because the price of leisure has risen. Actually, they appear to work less or about the same amount. This suggests that the price effect, taken by itself, is of little moment whereas the income effect is the dominating influence. Likewise, if at higher marginal rates of income tax people are found to work more rather than less, the price-of-leisure effect of the tax must be slight and the income effect is again dominating. This conclusion does not rigorously follow, but it appears to be more consistent with the evidence found in the above-mentioned empirical studies than any other, and it is also consistent with nonsystematic observation.

In social settings in which it is customary for people to mortgage themselves for a large part of their working lives, the sensitivity to the price of leisure is apt to be small. In fact the presence of these commitments leads to strong political opposition to large increases

---

[24] George F. Break, "Income Taxes, Wage Rates, and the Incentive to Supply Labor Services," *National Tax Journal*, VI (December, 1953): 352.

in income taxation because of the belief that the mortgage payments to be made on houses, household furnishings, and automobiles already allow only a small margin for ordinary living expenses, and this margin would be drastically reduced by heavier taxation. A reduction in the price of leisure is regarded by people as a small gain indeed as compared with the income effect of heavier taxation. Those who managed to escape fixed commitments by remaining single and those who are old enough to have paid off indebtedness and whose children are independent are among the few groups who may be sensitive to the price of leisure. A substantial part of the working group is not in this class.

Probably the most important consideration concerns the lack of freedom of choice to work as many hours as one pleases. If wage rates were strictly competitive prices, the supply curve of labor would have immediate relevance to the amount of work offered. Under competitive pricing conditions people could choose to work as many hours or as many days per week as they pleased; large groups of workers hired by any employer would be prepared to change employers for the slightest differential in wage rates, and there would be no financial penalty for movement. Actually, even under conditions of full employment, such a situation is only occasionally approximated. On the contrary, the actual conditions in the United States resemble more closely a system of semifeudalism. Workers are tied to particular employers in the sense that dismissal is accompanied by a severe financial penalty. These penalties have been growing. Pension programs alone are sufficient to assure a substantial financial loss to a worker even if he can secure a position otherwise as good or better. These feudal characteristics of employer-employee relations are promoted by both the workers and the employers. They are promoted by workers by placing restrictions upon the competition of outsiders for jobs, by successfully pushing wage rates above competitive levels, by rules of advancement based upon seniority, and in many other ways. They are promoted by employers in similar ways apparently on the theory that workers tied to them are more easily disciplined. Disguised unemployment is the outcome of these devices even in periods when a society succeeds in avoiding open unemployment. Patriotism alone cannot account for the ease of recruiting "retired" persons, women, subsistence farmers, and very young people into the work force in wartime. Many of these groups must be interested in remunerative employment during peacetime as well, but are kept from working in occupations for which they are suited by rules or custom and by a wage structure that is inconsistent with true full employment. To the extent that fear of loss keeps workers at particular jobs, a tax system which reduces the price of leisure may be expected to have little effect on actual choice.

In view of these considerations, it is unlikely that any significant error is made by treating income taxes as, in fact, resting wholly upon legal taxpayers and of viewing the shifting of excise taxes and import duties as completed when the owners of resources whose incomes are reduced have been identified.

I I

Effects of Taxes on Investment and Capital Values

In this chapter, taxes are studied in relation to investment decisions and tax capitalization. We shall make the assumption that people know or rather think they know the amount of gain or loss to be associated with the ownership of any particular asset. Investment theory has usually been constructed on this or some equivalent assumption. Traditionally, investment is analyzed under conditions of certainty, and the results are then modified to take account of investor risk and uncertainty. Although there are grave limitations to any theory constructed on the assumption of unique projections of asset yields, I shall follow tradition to preserve this common ground with much of the theoretical and empirical investigations in this general area. In the next chapter, taxes will be studied under conditions of investor uncertainty.

The absence of uncertainty in an investor's calculations is taken to mean that a person assumes he knows how much gain or loss he will experience over any period by owning a particular asset or asset combination. This unique projection is not a characteristic of any frequency distribution entertained by an investor. It is a definite amount.

Mere absence of uncertainty in this sense is not sufficient to assure that definite rates of return and rates of interest will emerge in a system at any date in time. All investors must also be assumed to make the same projections as to the yield of any asset. Unless this is so, a building may be expected to yield a rate of 10 per cent by some investors and 20 per cent by others at the same price. Our assumption has the convenient attribute that all assets are reducible to the common denominator of future net gain. A parcel of real estate which is believed to yield $400 annual net income is twice the "size" of a machine which is believed to yield $200 annual net income. For any prospective owner, all real assets become perfect substitutes because he attaches a unique amount of dollar gain to each. Prospective investors regard all assets as perfect substitutes if they have the same opinion about the future yield of each asset. Perfect substitution in this sense has nothing to do with the similarity of the services of the resources in question. Housing service is very unlike ditch-digging service, but houses and power shovels can be perfect substitutes for income purposes.

The net gain associated with the ownership of the asset must reflect all gains as well as all costs of management. In practice, ownership of particular assets may entail nonmonetary gains, and these are not always separable from the particular investor. Likewise, some people will not be bothered with the management of some types of assets. For a unique rate of return to emerge in a system, all gains must be expressible in monetary terms independent of the particular owner, and the differences in costs of management of different properties must be negligible.

The assumptions that people behave as if they were certain and were of the same opinion about the size of the gain associated with any asset are inconsistent with many institutional practices. For example, no rationale for the existence of a variety of securities exists under the conditions assumed. Shares of capital stock are perfect substitutes for bonds. Because different securities are not perfect substitutes in fact, sellers of securities have a motive to tailor their wares to the tastes of their customers. Uncertainty is the basic reason for variety in securities. In a world in which people are certain, the only function of private securities is to permit division of ownership of assets and their management by others.[1]

A GENERAL AND PROPORTIONAL PERSONAL INCOME TAX

The tax under consideration has a base which includes all net gains. There is no exempt income, and the rate is proportional to gain. Corporations are not taxed as such, but the proportionate shares of stockholders in corporate earnings are subject to tax. Stockholders are treated as if they were partners for tax purposes. We wish to investigate the effect of such a tax upon the incentive to invest under conditions of certainty and uniformity in yield projections.

---

[1] The impossibility of employing any particular kind of security to find "the" rate of interest is immediately evident if people do not in fact treat different securities as perfect substitutes. It is equivalent to the attempt to discover the "price" of food.

Since any future gains from investment will be taxed at the uniform rate, people assume that the net monetary reward obtainable by an asset combination is reduced proportionately. These incentive aspects of a proportional income tax may be isolated by comparison with the alternative of a system of flat-sum levies of equivalent yield on each owner of resources. This method provides a background of known characteristics for the analysis of the proportional tax. It is assumed that the yield of the set of flat-sum taxes is sufficient to prevent price inflation.

The proportional tax reduces the rate of net return after tax of each asset. If rates of return before tax are 10 per cent and the rate of tax is 20 per cent, the after-tax rate of return is now 8 per cent. Because the tax is general, it will not alter people's choices among asset holdings nor alter the rate of investment in new assets. Furthermore, the tax is not capitalized, and it is not shifted. These conclusions are close to orthodoxy in this field. But their demonstration involves investigation of some unsettled issues in investment theory.

The tax does not alter choice among asset combinations because relative gains are left unaffected by the tax. Any gain associated with the ownership of an asset is subject to tax, and therefore no one has an incentive to select certain assets in the hope of avoiding future taxes. The tax simply reduces the size of the counters used to compute gain. A proportional and general tax does not distort the pattern of investment demands.

There are complex issues involved in the conclusion that the aggregate rate of investment is not affected by the incentive features of a proportional income tax. It is true, to be sure, that any tax may reduce aggregate investment in dollar amount per period. Taxes remove money from persons' hands, and therefore they have less money to spend. Some persons will spend less for investment purposes, but not because of the incentive features of the tax. The deflationary aspect of the tax is, in any event, taken into account by comparing it with a set of already existing flat-sum levies of equivalent yield.

Investment may be financed by money which was formerly not used (hoards), money which was formerly used (gross thrifting), and money which comes into being for this purpose (money creation). Variation in hoards is not a problem under conditions of certainty. Liquidity preference is meaningful only if people are fearful of possible losses which may be experienced by holding certain assets. With certainty, earning assets are always superior to cash for investment purposes. Like the ownership of cash, real assets subject their owners to no possible loss, and unlike cash, real assets earn a return. Therefore if persons thrift more, they invest more. There is, however, the possibility that the banking system will finance some new investment—a point to be considered presently.

Thus the monetary relation between "saving" and investment under the conditions assumed is fairly simple. The troublesome term "saving" may be translated to mean "gross thrifting." This concept is defined as last period's gross gain minus present period's consumption-taking measured in money terms. Gain in this context excludes any appreciation or depreciation of identical assets held over the period. Gross thrifting equals net thrifting if depreciation of assets equals appreciation. On the basis of this definition, investment expenditures in the present period equal gross thrifting if the money supply is constant and if there is no variation in hoards.

In classical theory, saving (thrifting) and interest rates are treated as a schedule relation. The rate of saving is a direct function of the rate of interest. A proportional tax, by reducing the after-tax rate of return on assets should accordingly reduce the rate of saving. At higher rates of tax, people consume more and invest less. Thus a proportional tax would appear to reduce investment and increase consumption. These effects have nothing to do with the tax collections as such. They are results of the expectation of the future continuance of the tax.

The view that there exists a functional relation between rates of return or rates of interest and saving is based mainly, in such theories, upon the belief that people discount the future. The plausibility of the discounting doctrine depends upon how the choice between consuming and saving is visualized. In both neo-classical and Austrian approaches, a person who saves is looked upon as making a choice between satisfying his wants now or satisfying his wants at some future date. Given a dim view of human nature, one may readily conclude that people require some reward for giving up present pleasures. The term "waiting" was invented to describe this apparently hard choice which people are said to make. People who "wait" give up something definite in the present for the possibility of consuming more goods and services in the future. The implication seems to follow that they will not "wait" as much at a lower as at a higher rate of interest.[2]

The waiting theory is, I submit, a travesty on the evidence. A person who decides to thrift does by definition give up consumption in the present. But, and this is the important point, he obtains immediately what, from his point of view, is more wealth. This added wealth exists here and now. There is no waiting. The choice described by the concept of thrifting is a comparison between the utility of consuming now and the utility of holding wealth now. The insistence of Marshall, Pigou, Boehm-Bawerk, Fisher, Robertson, and many others that the choice is really between consuming now and consuming at some later date simply does not accord with the evidence. People thrift because they want to hold wealth. The reasons for thrifting are not easily catalogued, nor are they presumably the same for all people. But if people did want wealth only to consume, they should, aside from errors in estimating their own demise, end up with zero assets. The meticulous concern of many predecessors to assure that their estates are passed on intact, especially with little tax liability attached, does not fit with theories that they did not happen to get around to dissipating their assets soon enough. The reinterpretation that it is other people's future wants, not the saver's, which are relevant does not help much. In fact, there are countless arrangements made by predecessors just for the purpose of making more certain that successors will not dissipate the assets either. The trouble with the theory that people discount future wants is simple: it is an incorrect diagnosis of the choice being made.

People thrift because they wish to become wealthy. Greater wealth gives greater security; it is insurance against some types of disaster. For some, it is a source of prestige and power. It permits

---

[2] Marshall held that saving is a direct function of the level of interest rates. Although he emphasized that some people may save more instead of less at lower rates of interest, he nevertheless claimed that people on the whole will save more, the higher the rate of interest. One basis given for this conclusion was an appeal to the analogy between the level of wage rates and the amount of work people will offer. Unfortunately, this assumption is highly questionable. Basically, Marshall appears to rest the case on the theory that people discount future wants—the "waiting" conception. (See *Principles of Economics* [London: Macmillan, 1930], pp. 230–236.) Unlike Robertson, I cannot persuade myself that Marshall's analysis of the factors influencing rates of interest is fundamentally correct and only needs to be tidied up a bit to make it general and valid. (Cf. "Some Notes on the Theory of Interest," *Money, Trade, and Economic Growth* in honor of John H. Williams [New York: Macmillan, 1951], pp. 194–197.)

a person more economic freedom in many directions, including the freedom to consume more in the future if he wishes. At future dates, it enables him to save more also. The distinction between consuming and investing should not turn on the point that people like to consume but obtain no satisfaction from acquiring assets. Farmers often take more pride in the size and convenience of their barns than they do in their houses. The relevant distinction between consuming and investing is that the one does not and the other does increase productive capacity.[3]

The attempt to construct a saving schedule probably developed because of the belief that saving is somehow or other analogous to working. Given the premise that leisure is preferred to work, it is easy to believe that consuming is preferable to holding more wealth. But aside from the difficulties of such an interpretation of the work-leisure issue, thrifting and investing involve fundamentally different types of choice than do work and leisure. The resource, labor power, can be used in alternative ways, including leisure. There is no analogous resource in the case of investing. The omnibus term "capital" can be used in this sense, but if so, it should not be confused with existing nonhuman physical resources. Investing is a classification of the demands for products. We need the concept because these demands have the common characteristic that they increase the earning power of the demander in future periods if his anticipations are correct. Actually, it would be possible to give a reasonably complete account of economics without grouping demands into the consumption-investment classification. Instead, demands could be thought of in terms of demands for houses, buildings, cranes, and machines, as well as for various kinds of final services.

The actions of banking systems undermine all attempts to construct saving schedules which are treated as if they uniquely determine the money expenditures upon new real assets. Banking policies are monetary policies. They are arrived at ordinarily after considerations of many factors both within and without economics proper. These policies may take account of the thrifting behavior of people as well as their inclination, in an uncertain world, to vary their hoards. If people thrift less, banking policy may prevent any

---

[3] The above remarks lean heavily upon some ideas of Henry Simons. (See *Personal Income Taxation* [Chicago: University of Chicago Press, 1938], pp. 95–96.) The American tradition in economic thinking, so far as one may speak of a separate tradition at all, early voiced doubt of waiting conceptions. The desire of people in this country to become wealthy was too obvious to miss.

fall in the rate of investment by creating money for demanders of new real assets. The aggregate over-all demand for new assets cannot be treated as functionally related to the rate of net return after taxes when monetary policy is brought into the picture. No useful theoretical or practical purpose is served by attempting to squeeze some functional relation out of monetary policy.

The absence of any functional relation between investing and the rate of net return makes it appropriate to treat tax rates as having no effect on the rate of investing in a system characterized by certainty in projections. It follows that investors experience a lower net return after taxes on their asset holdings. Since the demand for each kind of new asset is unaffected by the future tax rate, the price of each new asset is also unaffected by the tax. The prices of old assets are determined by their substitution relation with new assets. Since this substitution is perfect under the conditions assumed, the prices of old assets are likewise unchanged by the tax. The lower income, net of tax, of each old asset is "capitalized" at the lower rate of return, net of tax. This means that the tax is not capitalized at all.

A GENERAL AND PROPORTIONAL TAX ON THE NET EARNINGS OF RESOURCES

A tax upon earnings of resources gives a type of tax fairly close to current fiscal practice. In many countries taxes are commonly levied on a base closely associated with the earnings of real assets under the control of organizations. A property tax, as administered in the United States, is a tax on the possession of real assets, mainly real estate. The federal corporate net income tax is a tax on a part of the earnings of assets controlled by corporations. The tax here investigated is levied on real assets and human earning power and is assumed to be proportional to earnings before transfer payments. No allowance is made for transfer payments except other taxes in certain cases. Thus an income which arises from ownership of securities is not directly subject to a tax.

By the use of an existing flat-sum levy on persons as a basis for comparison, we obtain the following main conclusions for a proportional tax on the net earnings of resources: (1) the tax does not affect the pattern of investment demands, (2) it does not affect the rate of investment, (3) it reduces rates of interest on securities proportionately, (4) it is partly shifted, in a special sense, to owners of securities.

As observed for a proportional personal net income tax, a tax that is proportional to earnings reduces the anticipated rate of return to be obtained from holding any real asset. In Keynesian terms, the marginal efficiency of capital schedule of each investor falls. Thus, unless "the" rate of interest falls correspondingly, the aggregate rate of investment must likewise fall. If, at the same rate of investment, each investor in real assets expects a rate of return of 10 per cent before tax, and the tax rate is 60 per cent, he can now expect a net rate of return of 4 per cent. The implication that the rate of investment must fall unless the rate of interest also adjusts is not, of course, peculiar to the Keynesian method of statement. All theories which hold that, in equilibrium, rates of net return on real assets must equal rates of interest on securities have the same implication. Thus the crucial issue becomes the effect of the tax on rates of interest.

First, consider the case where there exist only shares of capital stock and where, as a practical matter, virtually all new real investing must be done by corporations. These organizations operate under the restriction, it is assumed, that they must pay dividends in amounts equal to corporate net earnings after taxes in each period. Corporations issue only common stock. Any new investment must be financed by sale of shares to outsiders.

An old share of stock which promised to yield a return of $1.00 in future income now promises to yield a smaller return—the decrease measured by the marginal rate of the tax. If the tax rate is 60 per cent, a share which would yield $1.00 to its owner can, after the tax, yield only 40 cents. Stockholders may be expected on this account to sell shares to obtain more attractive assets in their place. But even if they attempt to turn to real assets, they are also confronted with tax liabilities of corresponding amounts. Any real asset which formerly might be expected to earn $1.00 will with the tax earn only 40 cents for its owner. Therefore, this opportunity to restore lost earning power is not available. In the absence of any nontaxed alternative method of investing, individuals have no incentive to sell common stock. Corporation managements in turn will supply securities and take cash away from investors at the same rate as in the absence of the tax on the condition that a marginal dollar of investment in real assets by the corporation will yield a return after tax sufficient to pay a 40 cent dividend on a share of stock. The supply of new shares yielding 40 cents is now identical with what the supply of $1.00 shares would be in the absence of the tax. This reduction in future dividends reflects the reduction in the earnings of real assets computed after tax. The demand for new shares yielding 40 cents is also the same as the former demand for $1.00 shares. Thus the prices of shares remain unchanged, but the rate of return on shares of stock falls in proportion to the marginal rate of the tax. Future earnings per share fall, and people are assumed to be aware of this fact in making their investment decisions.[4]

If there are some government securities outstanding, their prices rise because of the tax on corporate earnings. As already noted, the anticipated tax on future corporate earnings decreases the rate of return on corporate securities. At unchanged prices for government securities, investors will wish to hold them instead. Thus the demand for government securities rises. This higher demand is satisfied, without rationing of government securities, if their prices rise to the point where the rate of interest on them equals the rate of return on corporate securities. All securities are perfect substitutes in a world where there is no division of opinion and investors attach unique yield estimates to assets. These higher prices of government securities do not result in any reduction in the investment in corporate securities or in new real assets. In fact no exchange is necessary to bring about the new equilibrium price. Holders of government securities may simply refuse to sell at a price which yields a higher rate of return on government securities than they could obtain by holding corporate securities. The adjustment is automatic and absorbs no funds available for the financing of new real assets. Thus a proportional and uniform tax on corporate earnings in a setting in which individuals have no relevant opportunity to acquire real assets for themselves does not affect the pattern of new real investment nor the rate of investment and does reduce rates of interest on all securities, including government securities.

---

[4] If investors in corporate stocks do not correct their projections of yield, they will continuously make the "error" of overestimating income from shares and will likewise continuously overestimate the rate of return. If they behave in this fashion, the price of shares will also stay unchanged. The rate of investment in new assets will also remain unchanged regardless of whether corporate managements make the same type of error. If, however, people believe incorrectly that the income obtainable by holding some shares will be reduced by the tax on future earnings, whereas the income from others will be maintained, the prices of the former will fall and of the latter will rise. There will be greater investment by corporative managements having the favored securities for sale. If their investment outlets are restricted to assets to be used by them, *ex post* marginal rates of return computed before and after deducting tax will fall relatively to those of other corporations. Such possibilities serve to emphasize the crucial role played by anticipations in tax-investment theory.

These results have been contradicted by the analysis of E. Cary Brown.[5] Using the Keynesian theoretical structure, Brown finds that a corporate net income tax which does not permit interest deductions reduces the aggregate rate of investment by corporations and also distorts investment decisions in the direction of increasing the demand for short-lived relative to long-lived assets. Brown's remedy for the alleged adverse incentive effects on investment decisions of a corporate tax is a rapid write-off for tax purposes of the original cost of assets. His argument could be viewed as another prop for proposals for allowing accelerated depreciation for corporate tax purposes.

The chain of reasoning used to reach the conclusion that a corporate net income tax reduces the aggregate rate of new investment employs the Keynesian investment schedule concept. The tax rate shifts the investment schedule downward. At any given level of interest rates, managements are willing to spend less for new real assets. This argument follows purely from the anticipation of higher tax rates; it has nothing to do with the fact that the tax liabilities being incurred deplete corporate cash balances. The distortion conclusion follows from an analysis of the implications of discounting. The tax benefit from the allowance for the deduction of depreciation is realized over the life of an asset. The longer these tax benefits are postponed, that is, the more durable is the asset in question, the smaller is the present value of these tax benefits. In the extreme case of a perfectly durable asset, such as land, the acquisition of the asset by a corporation gives it a zero tax benefit because depreciation allowances are zero. In contrast, undepreciated gains of an asset lasting only one year are reduced less than proportionately by a proportional tax because depreciation is an allowable deduction for tax purposes.[6] The tax makes investment in short-lived assets relatively more profitable than in highly durable assets and also reduces investment in all assets.

These conclusions require the assumption that the rate of capitalization employed to discount future returns and tax liabilities is unaffected by the tax. Investment need not fall if the rate of discount falls proportionately with the after-tax net income of the asset. Thus the change in the rate of capitalization is the crucial issue. Tax capitalization is intimately associated with the effects of

---

[5] Cf. E. Cary Brown, "Business-Income Taxation and Investment Incentives," *Income, Employment and Public Policy*, Essays in Honor of Alvin H. Hansen (New York: W. W. Norton, 1948), pp. 300–316.

[6] *Ibid.*, pp. 305–309.

taxes upon interest rates—a point which has long been recognized in discussions of this topic.[7] The central issue becomes therefore what adjustment, if any, in interest rates accompanies the presence of the tax. Brown argues that interest rates need not fall because investors have the opportunity to acquire government securities, pointing out however that "in the long run," the interest rate may be changed by the corporate tax.[8] Brown's argument selects one fact for attention—the reduction in the rate of return on real assets after tax—and neglects the repercussions on rates of interest.

If corporations do the real investing and individuals hold the securities, the corporate tax must have immediate and direct effects upon "the" rate of interest. Rates of interest on corporate shares fall, and proportionately if the tax is general with respect to the future earnings of real assets. The tax reduces the earnings of corporate securities. Buyers of securities pay the same prices for shares with proportionately reduced earning power. Corporate managements are willing to supply securities in any amount necessary to absorb private thrifting only on terms which permit them to break even at the margin. If buyers, attempting to achieve a better return, turn to government securities, the prices of these rise.

For the rate of interest on government securities to remain unchanged as Brown assumes, the banking system must sell securities to mop up the money of new thrifters. The quantity of money is then reduced each period in amounts equal to the difference between what the rate of new investment is with the tax and the same rate of interest and what the rate of new investment would be without the tax. If this amount is large relative to national income, rapid deflation is initiated, and whether large or small, some deflation is inevitable. The decline in investment is directly traceable to a deflationary banking policy.[9] This, and not the tax itself, accounts for the alleged adverse incentive effects of corporate taxation. To prevent these effects, the banks need only allow the prices of gov-

---

[7] Brown's argument logically implies that all uniform taxes upon earnings are capitalized. The after-tax yields of old assets are discounted at the same rate of capitalization and therefore their prices must fall accordingly. New buyers of such assets obtain the same rate of net interest with taxes as without. It is an easy next step to conclude that corporate taxes are burdenless on those who were not around to take the capital loss when the tax was first imposed.

[8] *Ibid.*, p. 303, n. 4.

[9] Brown holds (*ibid.*, p. 314) that if interest is a permitted tax deduction, all is well; the tax neither reduces nor distorts investment. But this solution is too easy. If anticipations are unique, the rate on corporate common stock must equal the rate on debt contracts, and if anticipations are not unique, there is no meaning to equating "rates of return" to "rates of interest."

ernment securities to rise. It is wholly arbitrary to hold that a tax induces a decrease in investment when a necessary condition for this result is a deflationary banking policy.[10]

Our conclusion that a uniform and proportional tax levied on the earnings of resources reduces interest rates on securities implies that people who own long-term government debt obtain a capital gain at the time the corporate tax is imposed. This capital gain is a once-and-for-all event. Any person who holds perpetual debt (consols) at the time the tax is imposed obtains the same dollar income indefinitely. As compared to those subject to a distributionally neutral flat-sum tax, such bondholders gain absolutely. The flat-sum tax on them is abolished, but their gains before tax remain unchanged. Stockholders absorb all the tax liability. The tax passes out capital gains to bondholders, but leaves the capital-value position of stockholders unchanged. Over time, the identity of bondholders will be lost as they trade their assets with others. The government by announcing a tax on the earnings of real assets provides bondholders with the means to avoid the tax. This power lasts forever, so to speak, if the debt contracts they own last forever. If bondholders should become stockholders, the investment power of the capital gain permits them to obtain the same money income over time as they could if no tax had been imposed on corporate earnings. Stockholders obtain no capital gain and, even if some shift to bonds, they must because of the tax obtain a smaller future income.

If debt contracts are of various maturities, the capital gains vary and for some will be small or negligible. As new contracts are made, holders of debt instruments must take a cut in their incomes. Samuelson's reasoning that holders of debt contracts gain from a rise in interest rates in terms of income may be applied in reverse.[11] Over time, lower rates of interest become translated into lower incomes for owners of debt contracts. If debt contracts are obliga-

---

[10] Although Brown does not attempt to do so, his conclusions cannot be successfully rescued by an appeal to a "liquidity preference" theory of interest-rate determination. If people act as if they were certain, there is no money preference. Rather people use earning assets alone to fulfill the store-of-value desire. Money is an inferior asset under these conditions. Thus if the liquidity preference schedule is represented in the usual way, it (1) is always vertical and (2) automatically shifts to the point measuring the amount of money. The Keynesian theory of the interest rate is not relevant if people are certain. There appears to be some reluctance to accept this implication, although it has been stated in a seemingly irrefutable way by Leontief. (See "Comment," *Quarterly Journal of Economics*, LXIII [November, 1949]: 569.)

[11] Paul A. Samuelson, "The Effect of Interest Rate Increases on the Banking System," *American Economic Review*, XXXV (March, 1945): 16–27.

tions against those who manage real assets, the initial loss of earnings of the residual claimants is transferred gradually and in part to creditors. The longer the period of time during which the tax exists, the more closely a tax on the earnings of real assets approximates in its income effects a proportional net income tax levied on persons.

The fall of interest rates on government securities reduces the amount of interest payments the government must make in connection with any given amount of outstanding debt. Therefore, on this account alone, the government will need to tax less heavily; the rate of tax levied on corporations or others who manage real assets can be reduced. In this indirect way, the redistributional effects of tax and interest payments further improve the income position of those who manage real assets in comparison with that of creditors. The burden of the tax is partly removed from those whose incomes depend directly upon production and is placed on creditors.

A PROGRESSIVE PERSONAL INCOME TAX

With certainty in projections, a progressive personal income tax has no distortion effects on investment demands. Whether such a tax is viewed as altering the rate of investment depends upon the alternative with which it is compared. Any prospective investor, other than organizations, who is confronted with positive marginal rates of tax on any gains obtained from asset holdings has no incentive to change the composition of his old or new assets. As long as the marginal rate does not exceed 100 per cent, he stands to gain marginally from asset holding. Unless, therefore, a person has an incentive to consume more in the present, as the time-preference theory suggests, the announcement effects of the tax make no difference to his investment decisions. Any course of investment activity which would yield the maximum rate of return before tax will yield the maximum rate of return after tax. By assumption, all possible gains are subject to tax, and therefore he cannot hope to evade future tax liability by acquiring some assets rather than others. Actually, a progressive income tax does not catch all gains from investment. Some types of gains, notably so-called capital gains, are taxed at lower rates than are other gains. Likewise, if the tax law permits accelerated depreciation of some asset acquisitions, such as intangible drilling expenses in connection with oil explorations, taxpayers in a position to do so are given an incentive to concentrate more investment in such fields. Distortion effects of a system of progressive income taxation arise mainly from the presence of loopholes.

A progressive system of taxation reduces income inequalities as compared with a proportional system. Therefore, the relative amount of thrifting done is likely to be smaller than under a proportional system of equal yield. Unless the banking system is prepared to maintain some predetermined rate of investment, progressive taxation reduces the relative rate of investment. Wealthier groups both consume and invest less whereas poorer groups consume and possibly invest more, but on balance the aggregate amount of thrifting may be expected to fall. Productive capacity can grow at a somewhat slower pace, under a money-price system of economic organization, when a government adopts tax or subsidy measures which effectively shift income from higher- to lower-income groups. Some of the slackened growth in productive capacity in the form of new real assets is counterbalanced by the greater productive capacity of the lowest-income groups. There is no reason to assume, however, that these conflicting tendencies are necessarily or even presumably offsetting.

The incentive effect of a progressive system of income taxes on investment is a matter separate from the redistribution of income and the change in demands for products, including investment items, following therefrom. Incentive issues arise because and only because rates of tax on gains are other than zero. When people are confronted with the requirement of making definite lump-sum payments to their government, they can do nothing about the tax but pay it. The investigation of the effects of a tax measure should separate those effects following from the removal of money from people's hands and the incentive effects of the tax. Taxpayers must economize on their expenditures, including investment expenditures. But if the tax formula relates the tax payment to certain activities under the control of the legal taxpayer, taxpayers' incentives to invest can be affected. A progressive system of personal income taxation with no loopholes does not, however, change the relative marginal gains to be achieved by investment, and therefore the tax has no effects in this connection.

INCOME AND EARNINGS TAXES

The system of taxes now examined consists of a progressive personal income tax, a proportional tax on corporate earnings, and a general property tax. The progressive personal income tax corresponds to the federal individual income tax. The tax on corporate earnings corresponds to the federal corporate net income tax. The property tax corresponds to the general property tax as employed in the United States by local taxing jurisdictions. The general property tax will be viewed as proportional to the present value of assets and will be treated as approximately uniform on earnings of all real assets. It is assumed that this tax does not apply to securities of any kind or to cash holdings. Corporations as well as individuals are assumed to be subject to the property tax. These taxes are treated together because they are currently important tax devices from the point of view of yield. Furthermore, because the effects of one tax are influenced by the simultaneous presence of others, analysis of several taxes together should provide results of relevance.

An individual who wishes to acquire a real asset such as a building believes that a part of any gains he may obtain will be appropriated by a property tax and a further part by the personal income tax. The collective marginal rate of tax on the anticipated earnings of the property is not simply the sum of the rates under the two taxes if, as is the case in practice, any tax liability under the property tax is deductible from the base of the personal income tax. Thus if r_1 is the marginal rate of tax on future income under a property tax and r_2 is the marginal rate of tax on future income under a progressive personal income tax, the effective marginal rate of the two taxes taken together, r, is given by the formula: $r = r_1 + r_2 - r_1 r_2$. Thus a person whose future income would not be subject to a personal income tax because his income is below the exemption limit could expect to be subject only to the one rate, r_1. But someone subject to high marginal rates under the personal income tax would find that his rate of tax is increased only slightly by the presence of the property tax. If the property tax rate is taken to be approximately equal to 10 per cent of gains from property and the relevant rate of the progressive income tax is 80 per cent, the combined marginal rate to which future income from investment in real assets is exposed becomes 82 per cent. The higher the marginal rate of tax under the personal income tax, the less relevant is the property-tax rate.

The investment decisions of persons concerning real assets depend also upon the rate of return they can expect to realize from holding corporate securities, which for simplicity are still assumed to consist only of common stock. These decisions also depend upon the rate of interest on government securities—the assumed form of debt contracts. The effects of the combined taxes upon the pattern and volume of investment and upon capital values and rates of returns may be studied if we take as our starting point the conclusions already reached that a corporate tax lowers the rate of return on corporate securities without changing their present value and lowers the rate of interest on debt contracts by initially raising the present value of those securities. These conclusions employed the assumption that all real investing must be done by corporations. It was also assumed that corporations were subject to the rule that they must return in dividends amounts equal to net earnings after tax in each period. We drop the former and retain the latter assumption for the time being.

The property tax increases the total marginal rate of tax by less than the marginal property tax rate because property tax liabilities are deductible from the base of the corporate income tax. The effect of the property tax on corporative investment is equivalent to a somewhat higher effective rate of tax under a corporate net income tax.[12] Property taxes push up government security prices and reduce interest rates for the same reasons as does the corporate net income tax. The property tax on corporations occasions no important additional complications in this connection.

High corporate taxes create an added incentive for individuals to acquire real assets to meet their investment needs. The rates of return on corporate securities are reduced by corporate taxation. If, therefore, individuals have the opportunity, they will on this account shift to owning more real assets. It will pay to acquire real assets and rent them to corporations or others. If real assets are simple in nature, easily divisible, and if the costs of managing such assets are small, heavy taxation of corporations might prove to be impossible. Individuals would make the investment decisions, rent the equipment purchased to corporations, and the tax base of the corporate income tax would shrink accordingly.

This conclusion is modified by the presence of property taxes upon real asset holdings of individuals. The higher the rate of this tax, when stated in terms of future earnings of those assets, the greater is the preference for securities. A system of corporate tax-

---

[12] Property tax yields are, however, not sensitive to changes in earnings of the taxed assets and typically are positive even though earnings are negative. Governments therefore share in the gains from corporate activities but do not share in the losses with this type of tax—a consideration of relevance if there is uncertainty in projections of yield.

ation and of property taxation can be offsetting. This is possible if the effective rate of tax imposed by a property tax upon corporations is significantly smaller than the rate imposed on individual holdings of real assets.[13]

A progressive income tax increases the relative tax cost of obtaining income from the ownership of real assets by lower-income groups and decreases it for higher-income groups. Property tax liabilities may be large, relative to the income of poor groups. Since a property tax is a deductible item in a personal income tax, the added tax rate it imposes decreases as the marginal rate of the tax under the personal income tax increases. Nevertheless, all groups, including wealthy groups, have an incentive to avoid indirect investment through corporations as long as the effective rate of tax on corporate earnings exceeds that on the earnings of real assets imposed under a property tax. It is the difference in the effective rates of tax on real assets owned by corporations and those owned by individuals that matters. If the rates are equal, it will be a matter of indifference to all income groups whether they invest their funds directly in new real assets or acquire corporate securities. Thus a property tax acts as an offset to taxes on corporate earnings in the sense that it decreases the prospective tax gain from direct investment. The presence of a progressive income tax without loopholes does not modify this conclusion.

There remain two additional important factors to consider: (1) the effect of retained earnings on stockholder net income and (2) the exemption or low rate of taxation of capital gains. Corporate-retained earnings may or may not be reflected in the market price of securities. If they are not so reflected, because for example stockholders take the view that retained earnings will not result in a rise in future dividend payments, a policy of withholding earnings becomes equivalent to an additional proportional tax, collected at the source, on stockholders. In fact, retained earnings are additional private taxes if one adopts the legal position that managements of corporations are the representatives of the stockholders and, contrary to stockholder interest, retain earnings for the advancement of the "welfare" of the corporation. Such a policy appropriates the assets of one group for the benefit of others, and, in this respect, is similar to that of a government which taxes par-

---

[13] Dwellings, one of the most important classes of real assets held by individuals, are in some jurisdictions taxed at higher effective rates than are real assets held by business organizations. Therefore the property taxes probably do offset the corporate income tax in some degree.

ticular persons to promote the general welfare. We are not here concerned with the ethics of management practices dedicated to promoting the "corporation's interests" instead of stockholders' interests. We are interested only in the effects of such a private tax on the channels through which individuals may invest.

Earnings retention not reflected in the prices of shares has effects similar to those already discussed for a corporate net earnings tax without retained earnings. Stockholders are confronted by the private tax and the government tax which together give the "effective rate" of tax on stockholders. An additional private tax will decrease only slightly the after-tax income of stockholders in the very high brackets. If, for example, the earnings per share before the corporate income tax are $10, and the corporate tax is 60 per cent or $6.00 per share and retained earnings are $2.00 per share, a stockholder whose other income places him in an 80 per cent bracket under the personal income tax loses only 40 cents per share because of the corporate retention. By contrast, a low-income stockholder subject to a tax rate of 20 per cent under the personal income tax loses $1.60 per share as a result of the retention. But it should be emphasized that both lose. The high-income stockholder loses less because of the retained earnings for the simple reason that any action which reduces his income before tax reduces the government revenue much more than it does his after-tax income. Therefore all individual investors have an incentive to avoid investing through the corporate form and, instead, to acquire real assets or government securities. This incentive increases, the lower a person finds himself in the individual income-tax bracket structure.

The light tax treatment of capital gains is an offsetting factor provided that stockholders assume that some portion of the retained earnings will be reflected in higher future dividend payments. Since unrealized capital gains are tax-free income under the individual income tax, corporate securities can become wholly or partially tax-exempt investments so long as the gain takes the form of higher market prices of shares. If an increase in the book value of shares, because of corporate retentions of earnings, is associated with an increase in the future price of shares, stockholders are given an added incentive to acquire corporate securities. This incentive may more than offset both the corporate net income tax and the private "tax" measured by the difference between the change in book value and the change in market value in the case of a high-income stockholder, but it could scarcely do so for a low-income stockholder. As shown in the previous illustration, a stockholder subject to an 80 per cent rate under the individual income tax finds that the retention of $2.00 of earnings per share costs him only 40 cents in after-tax income. But if a share is increased in market value by $1.00, he obtains 60 cents more after-tax gain than he would if earnings had not been retained at all.[14] A low-income stockholder also obtains a tax-exempt gain of $1.00 in this illustration, but this is smaller than the after-tax gain he would have obtained if earnings had not been retained. Out of the $2.00, he would have obtained an after-tax income of $1.60. Consequently, a policy of retention of earnings as long as there is some increase in market values of shares may lead to the exploitation of the low-income stockholder.[15]

The possible distortion effects on investment of the three taxes, as well as that occasioned by retained earnings, occur because the tax system as a whole differentiates among sources of gain. If the same yield were obtained by a progressive personal income tax which included all gains, whether or not realized, in the tax base, there would be no distortion. Taxes which are levied according to sources of income, such as corporate net income and excess profits taxes, property taxes, and excise taxes, result in changing the net gains to be realized from real assets because the taxes are neither uniform nor general. The individual income tax also in practice differentiates among types of gain. Except in the accidental case when the distortion effects of all these taxes cancel one another, the direction of investment is changed in favor of lightly taxed sources of income.

Tax Capitalization

The theory of tax capitalization has been given only casual treatment in recent fiscal theory. Although discussions of interest and investment theory are frequent, few students have attempted to apply the resulting theory to taxation.[16] Under conditions of certain

[14] Clearly high-income stockholders have a strong interest in supporting high retained-earnings policies.

[15] A similar observation is stressed by W. L. Crum in an important empirical and analytical study of the effects of corporate and individual income taxes on the position of stockholders ("Taxation of Stockholders," *Quarterly Journal of Economics,* LXIV [February, 1950]: 40–42).

[16] The topic of tax capitalization has been systematically investigated by Jacob A. Stockfisch, "Tax Capitalization and Related Issues in Capital Theory" (unpublished doctoral dissertation, University of California Library, Berkeley, 1952). My own views have been strongly influenced by discussions with Dr. Stockfisch.

or unique projections of yield, full tax capitalization means that the rate of return computed after tax on an asset is identical with the rate of return if there were no tax. Tax capitalization implies, in other words, a decline in the capital value of assets relative to their net yield before tax. The reverse of this occurs when a tax increases the capital values of assets relative to income before tax. We shall call such a case *negative tax capitalization*.

The position here adopted is very close to that once proposed by Davenport. Stimulated by the discussions of the topic by Seligman and Adams, Davenport disposed of the matter in a long footnote, a part of which is quoted here to provide a starting point for our discussion. He states:

1. That no property tax, even one so general as to affect all existing properties, would in the slightest affect the interest rates of the market, if only new investment funds and other openings for new investment were left untaxed. Such a tax would amount merely to a *pro tanto* confiscation of the incomes on the burdened properties without in the slightest changing the capitalization rates.

2. That were the tax only upon new funds for investment or only upon the new properties derivative from the investment of these funds, the capitalization rate would fall approximately *pro tanto* and the previously existing properties would rise in market price without any slightest change in the incomes derivative from them, but with changes solely in the *rates* of return.

3. That were the tax imposed upon all properties, old as well as new, the net incomes would fall, and probably, though not certainly, would fall in something like the same proportion with the fall in rates of interest. No great change in present worths would result, with the exception that the less durable of income-bearing properties would suffer relatively less.[17]

In short, a tax levied only on old assets is capitalized in full, a tax on new assets is not capitalized at all, and a tax on both is not capitalized at all. These conclusions depend upon the assumption that the tax on new investment is general. Davenport took investment to mean cash, securities, real assets—in fact anything which has a present value. This is too sweeping.

Case 1. *A tax levied exclusively on the earnings of old assets*

To take a case of some importance in practice, let us concentrate again on the corporate net income tax. But let us assume, contrary

[17] H. J. Davenport, "Theoretical Issues in the Single Tax," *American Economic Review*, VII (March, 1917): 27-28.

to fact, that it is imposed with no deductions for interest on debt contracts. We again assume that all real assets outside the hands of government itself are held by corporations. Individual investors are therefore buyers of corporate securities. The first proposition to be established is that a tax on "old" assets is fully capitalized.

A tax on old assets must exempt the gain from new assets. Following Brown we may assume a tax which permits the immediate write-off of the cost of any new asset as a business expense. This means 100 per cent accelerated depreciation. If the government announces to corporations that they are liable to tax on their income from all sources, but may deduct immediately the full cost of acquiring a new asset, the government provides a part of the capital cost of the asset. If, for example, a corporate management expects that the income of an asset will be $100 per year and if its present price is $1,000, a corporate income tax of 60 per cent will reduce the future income to $40 per year after tax. But since the $1,000 may be treated as if it were a business expense in the year of acquisition, the tax liability on the corporation is reduced by $600. Therefore it costs the company $400 net to acquire an asset yielding $40 after tax per year. The result is the same as exempting the earnings of new assets from tax—in fact, it is a practicable method of tax exemption of the earnings of new investment.[18]

Accelerated depreciation carried to its ultimate extreme can be described as a decision of the taxing government to advance a part of the money to finance an investment with a proviso that it share proportionately in any gains from that investment. This is a ramification of the doctrine propounded by Mill that a tax on land means that the government owns a part of the land and that existing landowners are paying no tax.[19] The government becomes the owner of a part of the corporate assets.

---

[18] See E. Cary Brown (*op. cit.*, pp. 302–310), for a justification of the view that 100 per cent accelerated depreciation is neutral on new investment *at a given rate of capitalization*. Brown rediscovered Davenport's dictum that a tax upon old assets alone cannot affect investment, does not reduce the rate of interest, and hence is fully capitalized.

[19] J. S. Mill, *Principles of Political Economy* (London: Longman's, Green, 1909), Bk. V, Ch. II, Sect. 6 (Ashley ed.), pp. 920–921. This conception logically leads to the complete expropriation of all gains from old assets—a point the single taxers did not miss as applied to land. Once those who take the capital loss from an increase in the tax rate pass from the scene, the tax is burdenless. If one can stomach the infliction of capital losses on owners of old assets, and the single taxers had no troubles on this score, taxation becomes a business arrangement between the government and the managers of taxed assets. The government merely collects its share of the "rents"

A tax confined to the earnings of old assets, such as a corporate net income tax with accelerated depreciation, in a society in which corporations do all the real investing leaves anticipated rates of return unchanged. If such a tax is announced to replace some set of personal flat-sum taxes of equivalent yield, the prospective earnings of stockholders' existing securities fall. Consider a corporation with a million shares outstanding and corporate net earnings before distributions of $1,000,000. The tax rate is, say, 60 per cent, and thus earnings after tax are $400,000. It will be assumed that stockholders always obtain dividends equal to the after-tax corporate earnings. Investment expenditures are currently deductible in full. The corporation management has investment opportunities of various kinds, and the amount of investment it makes depends upon its ability to compete for funds with other corporations. The rate of return before the tax in question was imposed was, let us suppose, 10 per cent for all corporations including the one under examination. The rate of return on new investment is unaffected by the tax because the government contributes proportionately to corporate investment. A general tax on the earnings of all real assets, accompanied by write-offs of investment as made, is equivalent to a subsidy to new investment proportional to the tax. Thus if the corporation could have invested $100,000 to obtain marginally a rate of return of 10 per cent in the absence of any tax, it now requires $40,000 to acquire the same assets, the other $60,000 being donated by the government in the form of "forgiven taxes." The $40,000 investment will yield 10 per cent net of future tax. The future tax revenue is the government's dividend on its investment. Thus the corporation is able to sell additional shares yielding a 10 per cent rate of return. If the tax yield, which is of course reduced

of real assets without any burden to existing asset holders. Carried to its logical limit, the single-tax doctrine could be applied to all old assets existing at some date at an effective rate approaching the total undepreciated gain per period to be realized from the asset, provided that the gain of any new investment *including repairs* be tax-free. This policy amounts to wiping out property rights in old assets. The single taxers lost their bearings on this point because they failed to see that any resource, including land, has to be managed by someone, and in a money-price system 100 per cent tax rates imply either government management or no management. Logically their argument applies to any existing resources, including a human being. A person's earning power can also be nationalized by 100 per cent tax rates. This means that the government must manage him, that is, use force.

The single-tax proposal or its variant will not appeal to anyone who believes that (1) the government ought to be fair in the sense of treating people in equivalent positions in the same way, and (2) the government ought to use its taxing powers to lessen inequalities in income and wealth. The single-tax movement is fortunately dead, but its equivalent is now being resurrected under the guise of accelerated amortization.

by the allowance for accelerated depreciation, equals the needed government revenue our illustration may be allowed to stand. If the yield is insufficient, the initial rate of tax must be increased. This also increases the "subsidy" to new investment but by a smaller absolute amount.

As Davenport maintained, the capital values of old assets decline proportionately to the tax. In our illustration, old stockholders experience a capital loss of $6.00 per share. Equivalent capital losses are experienced by stockholders in all other corporations. If accounting rules permitted, corporations should immediately write down the value of their old assets proportionately to the rate of tax. For example, if a corporation owns a building which was worth $50,000, and a new one of equivalent usefulness could be constructed for $50,000, the new one would "cost" the corporation only $30,000 because the government is prepared to contribute $20,000 in reduced tax liability.

If, in addition to corporate securities, government securities also exist in the society, the effect of the government's action of taxing the earnings of old real assets only is to leave the prices of government securities unchanged. Holders of corporate securities cannot improve their position by buying government securities. The owners of old corporate securities take a severe capital loss. But at the new set of prices corporate securities again yield the same rate of interest as government securities. Prospective buyers of new securities acquire whatever securities corporations offer for sale. Rates of return, rates of interest, and rates of capitalization remain unchanged.

Tax capitalization can occur only if rates of tax are unequal, as Seligman maintained, but it does not require unequal rates of tax on the earnings of existing real assets. In fact, tax capitalization occurs no matter what differences there may be in the rates of tax on old assets, provided that no tax is levied on new assets. Taxes on old buildings but not new ones, on old machines but not new ones, and on any land (if land cannot be produced) are capitalized under conditions of certainty. The government by such a tax policy confiscates a part of the capital values of old assets and frees all subsequent holders from any tax liability which would reduce their income as compared to what it would have been if they held nontaxed assets.[20]

---

[20] It is strange to find the single taxers, many Keynesians, Fisher, and Pigou in the same doctrinal bed. All want to exempt the investment-saving process from taxation. In Pigou's case, the position is based on his theory that a general income tax involves

Case 2. *A tax levied exclusively on the earnings of new assets*

An exclusive tax on new assets requires that the government announce that some part of the prospective earnings of any asset produced or acquired by a corporation after a given date in time will be subject to tax, but that the earnings of any existing assets will be exempt. Such a tax system could be proportional to gross investment made by each corporation. Thus if the tax is 80 per cent of gross new investment—and it would have to be high to obtain yields of significance—a corporation has to pay $800 in tax for every $1,000 spent to acquire new real assets. The effect on the value of old assets of such a tax is obvious enough. Old assets rise in value since their cost of duplication is a multiple of the market price for new assets. If such a tax system does not allow the purchase of any new assets to escape taxation, rates of return on new investment decline and the capital values of old assets rise. This is negative tax capitalization. Owners of old assets are given a substantial gift by the government. Prices of debt securities rise, and their owners obtain windfall gains. As they must make new contracts, however, their incomes fall, and the treasury's problem of financing the national debt without incurring heavy interest charges is partly solved.

The next logical step would be to consider a general and proportional tax on the earnings of all assets. However, we have already done this in the sections headed "A general and proportional personal income tax" and "A general and proportional tax on the net earnings of resources." That analysis provided the conclusion that rates of return and rates of capitalization computed after tax are proportionally reduced by the tax. If this is correct, there is no tax capitalization in such a case and Davenport's dictum is again reinforced.

Case 3. *Partial taxes levied on the earnings of some new and some old assets*

In practice there are ways one may invest without being subject to full rates of tax or to any tax at all. Exemption of some income, such as interest on state and local securities, from the income tax

---

double taxation of "saving." (See *A Study in Public Finance* [London: Macmillan, 1947], pp. 132–133.) The alleged double-tax interpretation arises from the view of saving as implying "waiting." Consistently applied, the tax exemption of future income from investment is a social policy of partially wiping out previously existing property rights.

makes it a partial levy. It is convenient to use a system of partial *excise* taxes as an illustration of partial taxes upon the incomes of owners of resources. In chapter 6 we argued that under competitive conditions a partial excise tax may be but need not be diffused. The theory there developed was not applied to the effects of the tax on the pattern of investment. We may now attempt to repair this deficiency and at the same time suggest a theory of possible relevance for any *ad rem* system of taxation which is unequal.[21]

A set of partial excise taxes reduces the money incomes obtained from (1) resources located in the taxed fields, and (2) resources that compete for income with those in the taxed field. The latter group of resources includes those which have their earnings lowered because the demands for their products fall as the prices of the taxed commodities rise.[22] In any event, except in special cases, a partial system of excise taxes may initially leave the incomes of large groups unaffected.

Partial excise taxes reduce the incomes obtained from certain resources which can be and normally would be produced under economic conditions. Corporations in the taxed fields, for example, may own physical resources which are specialized to the taxed products. Their earnings are smaller because of the tax. Therefore, if such corporations must compete for investment funds, they cannot expect to sell securities on the same terms as they could if corporate earnings were not effectively taxed. Their securities become less attractive and fall in price. By the same token, other securities become more attractive and rise in price. There is therefore positive and negative tax capitalization. To earn a higher rate of return, taxed corporations must restrict their investment to the more promising lines whereas corporations in exempt fields push investment further. Rates of return fall in both exempt and taxed industries. They fall in taxed industries because of the tax-induced decline in rates of return. They fall in exempt industries because the rate of investment is stepped up, and the rate of return declines as investment increases. If this rate of return does not decline, investment falls even further in the taxed field. This change in the pattern of investment relieves the financial pressure on taxed firms in two ways. The reduction in the rate of increase in new assets supports the earnings of old assets. In a society in which

[21] Progressive rates under the personal income tax occasion no inequality relevant to investment decisions since the levy relates to gains of one person from any source.

[22] This means that the demand for the taxed product is inelastic, and people lower their demands for other products.

monetary policy attempts to stabilize the money value of a growing output, service prices need not fall over time. New resources compete for income with old resources in a setting of growing total income. In the taxed fields, fewer new resources come into being to compete for income with old resources and, therefore, the earnings of old resources rise in money terms. In other fields, the reverse movement occurs. If therefore corporations are in effective competition with one another for the dollars of investors, the tax is partly shifted away from the resources in the taxed fields to those in other industries. Given time—that is, if the tax is very "old"— this shifting process will eventually result in spreading the tax burden from physical resources in taxed industries to all physical resources.[23]

These results require that the corporations whose incomes fall compete for investment cash with others. If each corporation retains earnings for investment purposes and does not appeal to outsiders for funds, there need be no shifting of excise or other taxes through the investment process. This point is especially important in applications of the theory. Large corporations in this period of economic development are to an important degree financially independent of outsiders for investment finance. Investment decisions inside corporations need not be subject to the discipline involved in marketing new securities. The poor financial prospects of some corporations do not necessarily decrease the rate of investment in real assets. Tax shifting through changes in the pattern of investment is at best a clumsy and halting process in a social system in which investment decisions and their financing are made by corporate managements.

---

[23] This type of shifting can occur only through time. If the tax is repealed, owners of resources in the taxed field will experience some capital gains and owners of resources in nontaxed fields will experience capital losses.

12

Uncertainty, Taxes, and Investment

"Thus we reach the important and somewhat unexpected conclusion that the imposition of the tax will increase the total risk taken."[1] This theory, formulated by Domar and Musgrave in one of the most significant theoretical studies of the relation between taxation and risk-taking in the recent literature in economics, means that a proportional income tax which permits full loss offsets increases the inducement of investors to hold "risky" assets. Among other implications, their analysis also leads to the conclusion that people will hold less cash and more of other assets at higher rates of tax. Taxes induce people to take bigger chances. No finding could be more at odds with prevailing sentiment concerning the relation between risk-taking and investment than this.

High taxes are criticized frequently and with feeling because of the belief that taxes reduce the willingness of people to take risks. If Domar and Musgrave are correct in their findings, objections to high rates of tax on investment income must be made in spite of, not because of, the effect of taxes on the inducement to assume risk. Any such judgment involves the value premise that it is better for a society if investors select more "risky" assets, and this might be challenged. The proposition that high rates of tax with full loss offsets induce people to become less conservative in their investment decisions, if correct, has important implications for the relation of taxes to capital values and to the pattern and rate of investment. It is thus desirable to examine carefully the basis of the Domar-Musgrave thesis.

THE DOMAR-MUSGRAVE ANALYSIS

The tax under discussion is a proportional income tax, levied on the total net gain of any person, which subsidizes losses at the same

---

[1] E. D. Domar and R. A. Musgrave, "Proportional Income Taxation and Risk-Taking," *Quarterly Journal of Economics*, LVIII (May, 1944): 411.

rate it taxes gains. Any loss is compensated and at once by the government.

Of the various methods currently used for constructing a rationale for investor uncertainty, Domar and Musgrave choose the subjective frequency approach. A particular wealth owner is visualized as attaching various probabilities of gain and loss to any class of asset he might hold. The gain g is the actuarial value of the gains expressed as a percentage of the value of the assets in question, and the loss r is the actuarial value of the losses similarly expressed. The yield, y, $(g-r)$, is the difference between the expected gain and loss thus expressed.[2]

Investors examine the possible noncash assets they might hold. Of those to which they attach the same estimated loss, they choose the ones with the highest yields. The result is their "optimum asset curve," shown for a particular investor as OBA (fig. 25). It means the maximum amount of yield for any given amount of loss a person estimates he could obtain by holding various assets including cash.[3] Thus if an investor considers holding common stock, those shares of stock which promise in his opinion to give the higher yields without increasing his expected risk or loss are preferred. He can take more risk and expect greater yields by holding the unproved shares, and he can always reduce his risk by increasing the proportion of his assets held in the form of cash. Thus the line OBA shows the maximum estimated yield of various assets, measured along the horizontal axis, for each given amount of risk, measured along the vertical axis. At the origin, a person holds only cash and takes no risk and gets no yield, it being assumed that the market does not pay interest on cash holdings. At higher points, the amount of cash held decreases, and instead, short-term government securities and similar conservative assets are held. At yet higher points, even less cash, fewer short-term securities, and more long-term bonds are held. At point A a person holds almost no cash

---

[2] The use of the yield y in the analysis to mean the positive element on which the investor focuses might be challenged on the ground that it assumes a person would never acquire an asset for which his estimate of y is zero. It seems improper to assume this because it is a behavior rather than an estimate assumption. Some people might acquire an asset whose expected yields add to zero or are negative because they like to gamble. Therefore, it might have been better to use the expected gain g and the expected loss r to summarize the two crucial aspects of the assumed subjective frequency distribution. See, however, *ibid.*, pp. 394–395.

[3] The construction implies that people dislike risk in the sense that if two asset combinations entail the same risk, an investor would always prefer the combination with the greater yield.

and is perhaps betting all his wealth on a favorable outcome from holding shares of stock of new corporations.

The optimum-asset curve summarizes an investor's estimates of gain and loss for various asset combinations. A theory of investor tastes must be introduced to explain the actual assets he will in fact hold. Investor attitudes may be represented by an indifference map reflecting the hope of gain and the fear of loss, of which the curves NK, PC_tL, and MBH are shown in figure 25. The behavior

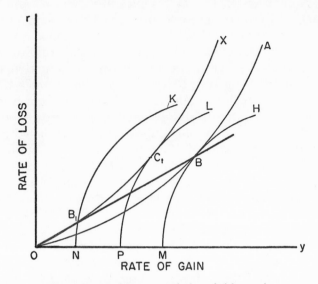

Fig. 25. Domar-Musgrave relation of risk to gain.

assumptions behind these representations are of course crucial. It is postulated that investors dislike risk, or loss, and that the marginal disutility of expected risk increases with increasing risk. These assumptions provide the basis of the indifference curves showing the relation between expected yield and loss rates in figure 25. In the absence of any tax, an investor would select the asset combination represented by point B, that is, the point at which the indifference relation between yield and loss is just tangent to the estimated rates of gain and loss as represented by OBA.

A proportional tax with full-loss offsets reduces both his prospective gains and his prospective losses. Any gain he may realize will be subject to tax, and therefore his gain after tax is reduced proportionally.⁴ But, if the government subsidizes losses, or what amounts to almost the same thing, allows full deductibility of losses, his possible loss *after* tax is also reduced proportionally. Thus if a person contemplates a possible loss of $100 on an invest-ment of $500, the presence of a proportional tax with full-loss offsets levied at a rate of 60 per cent reduces his possible after-tax loss to $40. If the gain he expects is $300 on the investment, the tax reduces the possible after-tax gain to $120. Thus the ratio of his possible after-tax loss to his possible after-tax gain remains unchanged by the tax. The government offers to share in his losses in the same proportion that it will share in his gains.

Graphically, the after-tax gain and loss with full-loss offsets is represented by the line OB_1B for the asset combination shown at point B on OBA (fig. 25). It is a straight line through the origin because the tax reduces both estimated loss and gain proportion-ally. Thus an investor, having reached his preferred asset position in the absence of the tax, now finds that his estimated gains and losses after tax are reduced. The line OC_tX is the optimum asset curve after tax for a given rate of tax. This altered position is represented by the point B_1 for the assumed rate of tax. But at B_1 he now finds that he is taking less risk after tax than he prefers, and therefore he moves to point C_t on the indifference curve PC_tL. This indifference curve is higher than NK where he initially found himself after the tax was imposed. To reach C_t an investor reshuffles his assets, selecting those with greater possible before-tax loss than the combination represented by point B. Thus the con-clusion stated at the outset of this chapter follows. The higher the rate of tax, the less conservative are investors in choosing asset holdings. They become less conservative in two ways: (1) among earning assets, they hold "riskier" assets, and (2) they hold smaller idle balances.

It is sufficient for this conclusion that the marginal disutility of risk increases with increasing risk, granted the subjective frequency approach to uncertainty. If the marginal utility of income is con-stant, it nevertheless follows that people will take more risk at higher as compared with lower rates of tax, provided that full-loss offsets are allowed.⁵ Economically, this means that if a government confronts investors with a tax on gains and an equivalent subsidy

⁴ This result is consistent with the observation that, with unique projections, a proportional tax reduces prospective gains proportionally.

⁵ Domar and Musgrave stress this implication. See *ibid.*, p. 403, n. 9 and references therein.

of losses, the private risk to which persons believe they expose themselves is thereby reduced. Since they dislike risk, they are induced to take more risk.

Domar and Musgrave restrict their analysis to an investor whose possible assets consist of securities and cash. The argument is not explicitly generalized to real investment decisions. Yet, if the same assumptions are made, the some logic may be applied to wealth formation. A corporation management, for example, is confronted with a variety of real assets it may acquire. If the subjective frequency approach to uncertainty is adopted, the management selects assets, at any set of prices, to maximize expected yields for each amount of expected loss. In the absence of any tax, the management would select those earning assets and that amount of cash which maximize its position, which means in this context the combination consistent with the highest indifference curve between the actuarial values of possible losses and yields. In the presence of a tax with full-loss offsets, the amount of risk associated with any investment is reduced proportionally. Since the corporation is exposed to less risk with a tax than in its absence, the management would presumably take more risk. Again, it is sufficient that the marginal disutility of risk increases with increasing risk. If the management's desire for corporate income diminishes with increasing income, it will take still more risk, in the hope of increasing earnings after tax and will thereby attempt to offset for its stockholders some of the decrease in corporate earnings occasioned by corporate taxation.

Thus the tax on the earnings of real assets increases the demand for them in the sense that investors hold less cash and hence more earning assets than they would hold in the absence of the tax. This development is distinct from the money-removal or deflationary effects of current taxation of corporations. Only the "incentive" aspects are considered in the argument. A corporate income tax must, to be sure, reduce the amount of dollar investment which corporations can finance out of internal funds, just as a personal income tax reduces the amount of consumption and investment expenditures that a person can finance who is subject to the tax.

RISK AND THE PATTERN OF INVESTMENT

The foregoing analysis suggests that a person will take more total risk, that is, possible loss before tax, the higher the rate of tax to which he is subject if he is also promised full-loss offsets. Since cash is, in the relevant sense, a riskless asset—it has a conventional invariant price—people hold less cash and more of other assets. Thus apart from effects of the tax upon the composition of their noncash assets, the tax induces people to bid up the prices of earning assets in general. By contrast, we found that a proportional income tax under conditions of certainty would leave the demands for assets unaffected. (See p. 282.)

The increase in the money demand for assets by investors as a result of a tax is a transitional development. Once a tax has been in effect for some time and the demands for earning assets have presumably already adjusted, investors continue to hold less cash or more of other assets than they would if the tax had not been imposed. Whether this matters in any important degree cannot be readily determined. Any general shift away from cash may be compensated by a decrease in the quantity of cash. The banking system may, in other words, supply additional securities for investors to hold, and destroy the cash that would have been used to bid up the price of securities. Whether or not the compensation is made, any likely change in the rate of tax is not apt to matter significantly. The economy may be expected to adjust to such changes in choices between holding cash and other assets. Since tastes are changing for many other reasons more or less continuously, there is little reason to place much emphasis upon the mere fact that taxes with full-loss offsets may induce investors to hold less cash and more earning assets.

The more significant implication, perhaps, is that investors will seek, because of heavy taxes, those securities and real assets which are regarded as entailing greater risk. The choices which people make in their asset holdings are of great significance to the development of an economy. The investment decisions of one generation determine in large measure the kinds of productive capacity available to the next generation. Although there is a general disposition to regard so-called "risky" investment as better than conservative investment from the point of view of the development of an economy, it is by no means self-evident that this is true. An economy may advance faster if people invest in ways which result in more productive capacity rather than in risky ventures which merely result in losses. Any conclusions based on criteria established to rate investments on grounds of social desirability would not be likely to show that investments entailing greater risk are per se superior to those which entail less. High tax rates with full-loss offsets are not necessarily an economic blessing merely because they are believed to induce people to take more risk.

If people choose more risky assets at higher rates of tax, prices of risky assets rise and prices of safe assets fall. But the precise meaning of such a development is not clear unless people rate securities on the basis of the degree of risk in some definite pattern. It must be kept in mind that risk in the sense here used refers to a state of mind. It is altogether consistent with the foregoing analysis for some investors to regard the holding of government bonds as very risky and gold prospecting on Manhattan as very safe. Unless, therefore, the tastes of investors follow more or less the same pattern, there is no way of knowing how the demands for particular securities and particular real assets are altered by a general increase in people's willingness to take chances.

Financial conventions may be sufficiently definite to permit some guesses concerning the likely effects of a reduction in possible private losses upon the demands for various types of securities. Short-term government securities are commonly viewed by investors as entailing less risk than long-term securities, all United States government securities are viewed as entailing less risk than the debt contracts of business organizations, and these in turn are viewed as entailing less risk than some shares of stocks. People and organizations may be expected to shift their investment preferences from government securities to corporate securities if they decide to take greater chances of loss.

Real assets cannot readily be classified as to the degree of possible loss even by an appeal to convention. Although assets having short life expectancies may be considered by many investors as more conservative investments than long-lived assets, we need only recall that many fingers have been burned in inventory speculations to doubt that life expectancy is particularly relevant in a classification of assets by degree of possible loss. Perhaps assets used to produce more resources entail more risk than assets used to produce consumption items. But after such a generalization is qualified for the many exceptions, it is questionable whether much of significance would remain. For sheer possibility of large gains and losses, large-scale vegetable growing can rarely be equaled.

The possible loss accompanying the ownership of any asset depends very closely on who does the owning. The equipment to produce steel would be a hazardous investment for a company attempting to break into the steel business, but the same assets could be relatively safe for established companies. Uncertainty, referring as it does to a mental process, is difficult to project to external things. Probably no distinguishable change in the pattern of the demand schedules for particular real assets resulting from a change in risk is ascertainable by theoretical analysis. Perhaps the most that should be said is that a government measure which reduces the private risk of owning assets alters the demands for particular real assets, increasing some and decreasing others.

The Domar-Musgrave analysis leads to the implication that a proportional tax which is completely general, that is, which subsidizes losses at the same rate at which it taxes gains, is not neutral with respect to investor choice. In security markets, the tax induces people to prefer more risky assets and to hold less cash. In the real asset markets, the tax likewise induces investors to increase their demands for what they regard as riskier assets and to hold less cash.[6]

---

[6] The use of the subjective frequency technique of rationalizing investor choice has been attacked on the grounds that an investment decision made today is in a measure unique and therefore the frequency probability technique is not applicable to it. Shackle in particular has emphasized this criticism. (See G. L. S. Shackle, *Expectation in Economics* [Cambridge: University Press, 1949], pp. 109–127.) His own important contribution to this subject is an attempt to provide an alternative method of rationalizing investor choices which is closer to a theory emphasizing subjective attitudes toward the unknown than to a frequency distribution. There are, it seems to me, two very different issues at stake in the rationalization of investor choice. Investors' choices might possibly be arrived at on the basis of an assumed known frequency distribution of gains and losses from past similar investments, but in fact investors may simply not engage in such calculations. Or it may be claimed that the use of a frequency technique by any investor is inherently unreal in the sense that he could not validly use such a method even if he tried. Each venture is "unique." Shackle appears to base his criticism mainly on the latter objection. To answer Shackle's objection, it is sufficient to point to instances in which investors do in fact employ a frequency approach to their investment decisions. There are innumerable such illustrations. Oil companies keep records of past experiences of themselves and others in drilling and do use such information in deciding where to drill new wells. Furthermore, they appear to assume that out of each number of wildcat wells attempted, only some will yield oil in quantity. The use of past experience appears to be the basis for the better record of regular oil operators than of syndicate groups motivated by the strong hunches of some enthusiast. Depreciation calculations, which are closely related to investment decisions, appear to be based on assumed average experience. No one really knows how long a particular machine will function, but there is evidence about that class of machines *and people who use such evidence will be right more often than those who do not.*

The telling criticism of the subjective frequency approach is that some investors in demanding some assets do not appear to rely on any better evidence than their own inexplicable hunches. Animal spirits, as Keynes has stressed, rather than sober calculations are highly important features of both real investment and security purchase decisions. This characteristic of investors makes all attempts at rationalization, including Shackle's, irrelevant. Economists must, then, fall back on the bare fact that people simply like to own certain assets. This emphasis gives a taste theory of invest-

A Proportional Tax on the Earnings of Real Resources

A corporate income tax is used here, as in the last chapter, to illustrate a tax levied on the earnings of real resources. Such a tax affects two types of investment decisions, those of corporate managements in making real investments and those of individuals in choosing between corporate and other assets.

If corporate managements are calculating, in the sense that they base their investment decisions on past evidence of the gains and losses associated with the ownership of particular classes of assets, and if they have an aversion to the possibility of losses, a proportional tax accompanied by full-loss offsets on the future earnings of assets will operate in the direction of inducing them to demand more risky new assets. The government takes a part of the possible loss, and therefore the acquisition of the same assets makes the investments more conservative than in the absence of the tax. Granted the assumption of the increasing marginal disutility of risk, the conclusion follows that as a result of the tax with loss offsets, corporations will hold less cash and more earning assets and will select earning assets of greater possible loss before tax. Further, the higher the rate of tax, the more risk managements will presumably take. If, in addition, diminishing marginal utility of income describes their behavior, they will take still more risk because of corporate taxation.

Corporation investment decisions depend upon the ability of the management to finance its needs. If a corporation must apply to outsiders for investment finance over and above the amount of investment necessary to compensate for the depreciation of existing assets, the rate of investment and possibly the pattern of investment of any one corporation depends upon the willingness of outsiders to acquire corporate securities. Let us assume that corporations pay out dividends in amounts equal to net earnings.

---

ment choice. Tastes of some investors for particular real assets and securities cannot be explained any more than can the tastes of particular people for ice cream or for beer. The theory of investment demands becomes indistinguishable from the theory of consumption demands in this case, and discussion in terms of possible gains and losses and of attitudes toward risk becomes irrelevant. I see no objection to the use of the frequency method of analysis for the explanation of some investors' demands for some assets and a taste theory for others. In fact, this has been done in economic analysis for some time. The demand for assets in the form of household appliances is usually assumed to be based on the tastes of the buyer. The demand for debt contracts such as personal loans is usually assumed to be based on average experience with securities of that type.

When a proportional tax is imposed on corporate earnings, owners of new corporate securities will find that the dividends per share are smaller because of the tax. If individuals have only the choice of holding corporate assets or real assets which they can manage for themselves, the amounts of various corporate securities they are willing to hold and to acquire at any set of prices depend upon the substitution pattern between these securities and real assets. Different people will presumably react differently to the prospect of lower average future dividends as a result of heavy corporate taxation. Those who are wealthy can avail themselves of the opportunity of investing in nontaxed real assets and, on this account, may sell some of their existing holdings of corporate securities or refrain from buying as many new corporate securities. Because real assets held for income purposes are typically available only in large chunks, small investors cannot always afford to shift from securities to such assets. In addition, wealthy investors frequently act on the advice of experienced persons and they have more experience themselves; therefore they are apt to pay close attention to the tax-induced reduction in the dividends from corporate securities. Yet another consideration is the costs of management. Economies of scale are available to the wealthy investor because he can hire others to look after his properties and can design his holdings to reduce costs of management.

Many persons in the middle- and lower-income groups have tastes for assets of the kind associated with household activities, such as houses themselves and appliances of one kind or another. They hold much of their wealth in this form. If such assets can be owned free of future taxes, there is some incentive even for these investors to shun corporate securities in favor of household assets because of corporate taxation. But people in this group differ widely in their attitudes toward the securities of impersonal organizations. Optimists bent on becoming rich present an opportunity for corporate managements to obtain more cash. Some have investment tastes which are limited to real assets directly used by them, savings deposits, and cash. Because they are not interested in corporate securities, corporate taxation does not directly affect them. In the absence of other taxes, wealthier investors are likely to shift away from corporate securities to other assets. Corporate investment financed by sales of securities declines because of corporate taxation. The decline occurs, not because of "risk" considerations in any direct sense, but because some people can be expected to pay attention to prospective reduced income from corporate securities as compared with income from other assets in choosing the form in which to hold their wealth.

If the proportional tax is levied on the earnings of all real assets including those owned within corporations, there is no incentive to shun corporate securities because of tax considerations. Such a tax must, of course, apply to assets owned and used by a person, to prevent an increase in the demand for them at the expense of other asset holdings. If all people were calculating in the sense of projecting the tax against future gains, there should be no change in the tastes for assets of various kinds other than a preference for riskier assets. But people in the mass do not appear to be highly calculating in this respect. Real assets which they like will be held or acquired without reference to the future tax liabilities which such ownership will entail. A taste attitude toward investment suggests a lack of attention to future tax liabilities as well as to future gains and losses. The motivation is the immediate enjoyment of possession of the asset, including the enjoyment of thinking how durable it is. Securities may not give enjoyment in this way. People who are calculating about corporate securities, but not about the ownership of houses, automobiles, and deep-freeze boxes, may be expected to discriminate against corporate securities even if all real assets are uniformly taxed. However, persons who treat real property as closely competitive with securities are not apt to be influenced to any marked degree by a uniform tax on the earnings of all real assets. Calculated judgment should, in any case, lead them to select much the same assets as they would in the absence of taxation.

There is a possibly significant exception to this conclusion. A proportional tax on the earnings of real assets accompanied by full-loss offsets directly affects the persons making the real investment decisions. Where, as in the large corporation, one group owns the securities and another group does the managing, persons who have a choice between holding income property and corporate securities will directly obtain loss offsets by a proportional tax on earnings from real assets but no such loss offsets on income from their security holdings. But it is the managements of corporations who mainly obtain loss offsets. Whether this influences the demand for corporate securities will depend upon the attitudes of security holders to the lesser apparent risk in corporative operations. If existing and prospective security holders have pretty much the same views about possible losses and gains as do managements, corporate securities should, in the opinion of security holders, subject them to smaller possible losses. But investors are also concerned with the possible losses from changes in market prices of corporate securities.[7] This risk of loss is not reduced by full-loss offsets on corporate earnings, and therefore a general and proportional tax on the earnings of real assets accompanied by a subsidy at the same rate on the losses may decrease the prices of corporate securities relative to the prices of old real assets.

A tax on the earnings of all real assets operates to increase the demand for old debt contracts, and, over time, to lower the pattern of interest rates. For reasons already noted, people who treat corporate securities as substitutes for debt contracts will, because of corporate taxation, prefer debt holdings at the same prices. The prospective yield of any given claim to corporate assets is reduced by the tax. Provided that no tax is levied on the yield of debt contracts, people shift their demands partly from corporate to government securities thus bidding up their prices. The precise amount of the reduction in yield rates on government securities depends upon the substitution pattern existing between government debt contracts and other assets. In the extreme case of an isolated government bond market, isolated because the securities held by certain organizations are limited by rules or custom to government debt, taxation of the earnings of real assets need not affect yield rates on government securities. Otherwise, taxation levied on the earnings of all real assets becomes an instrument of the government to hold down the interest expense of a given outstanding debt.

The demand for new private debt contracts will rise because of taxes on the earnings of real resources and for the same reasons. In addition, the quality of these contracts at any given terms improves as a result of taxation of earnings with full-loss offsets. It

---

[7] Keynes stresses this point (see *The General Theory of Employment Interest and Money* [New York: Harcourt, Brace, 1936], pp. 149–163). But for some reason he chooses to regard variation in the prices of shares as having nothing to do with the financing of real investment decisions (*ibid.*, p. 151, n. 1). Such a modification would undermine the theory that real investment decisions are determined by investment schedules and "the" interest rate. This insistence upon debt contracts as being in some sense or other crucial in real investment decisions is an orthodox but a highly limited view of the facts. Debt contracts constitute at most only one of the many possible ways of financing investment. The loanable-funds approach is also objectionable on this score. Exclusive of government debt, debt contracts are a relatively small part of existing securities measured in capital values. Yet economic thinking has persisted in treating debt contracts and rates of interest as if they were the whole story.

improves because the government reduces the private risk of the issuers of these securities by offering to share in any losses. A banker contemplating whether or not to acquire the promissory note of a local business organization will find that a tax with full-loss offsets levied on the business reduces the possible loss the bank might experience by holding the note. If the assets which the business acquires eventuates in a loss, the government pays a part of the loss and thereby improves the ability of the debtor to meet his obligation to the bank.[8]

A tax on the earnings of assets reduces the potential private after-tax gains. Thus through its tax policy, the government becomes a kind of income-bond holder. Since the gains from any new investment must be shared with the government, the amount of this income which the business could contract away to creditors is reduced, provided that interest is not a permissible deductible expense as a strict earnings tax implies. As the tax rate approaches 100 per cent, the amount of earnings which could be assigned in the form of interest approaches zero. Corporate managements would, in this event, be unable to supply a debt instrument with a positive yield. Thus the higher the rate of tax on the earnings of real assets, the lower are interest rates. The interest rates on new debt contracts fall on this account, despite the improvement of the quality of the contract because of the decrease in the possible loss associated with any given investment program.

---

[8] The seller of the debt contract has some choice in the method of financing any projected investment expenditure. If the business is a corporation and a market exists for its securities, it may choose to sell shares instead of debt. Which method is employed depends fundamentally upon attitudes toward possible loss. From the point of view of business management, an increase in debt contracts outstanding increases its possible losses in a number of ways. When the contract comes due, there may not be a favorable setting in which to market other securities to obtain cash to pay off existing contracts. This type of adverse development can be cumulative, as Hart has emphasized. (Albert G. Hart, *Money, Debt, and Economic Activity* [New York: Prentice-Hall, 1953], pp. 199–205.) Once a business begins to have trouble with some creditors, it is likely to have trouble with others. There is a loss of face in the business community if debt contracts are not met on schedule. Such considerations favor financing in a fashion which does not occasion embarrassment if a period of losses is experienced. There is the further and perhaps even more fundamental consideration that the sale of debt endangers the sovereignty of the management in investment decisions. Perhaps no common generalization is much more wrong than the one that creditors have less power over real investment decisions than do the "owners." In corporations of size, the management has much more to fear from creditors than it has from potential new stockholders. Aside from tax considerations, the possible adverse effects of indebtedness are sufficient to explain why business organizations are reluctant to rely on debt methods of financing.

PROGRESSIVE INCOME TAXES

A progressive income tax with full-loss offsets may not be altogether feasible. If gains are realized, they are taxed at the rates appropriate to that income bracket, whereas if losses are realized, taxable income is smaller and is therefore taxed at lower marginal rates. There are of course many other technical difficulties in framing a tax law designed to compensate taxpayers for losses at rates equal to those on gains on their investments. If an investment decision would, in the judgment of the investor, make only the difference of shifting his income within a small tax-bracket range, allowance for deducting losses in computing taxable income would reduce the risk almost proportionally. At high levels of income, a progressive income tax approximates proportionality in its rate structure. Since investment decisions of a tax-conscious sort are apt to be more relevant to high-income than to middle-income investors, a tax law which permits full deductibility of losses from other income is almost equivalent to subsidizing losses at the rate applicable to gains. If, in addition, averaging is employed, any bias of the tax legislation against risky assets is further reduced.

If the only tax is a progressive income tax with full-loss offsets, the tastes of investors for assets of various kinds will, on the basis of the Domar-Musgrave analysis, induce them to take more risk and to hold less cash. The government reduces the after-tax loss to the investor. Granted the usual premise that investors prefer to avoid losses, the government, by offering to share in these losses, operates in the direction of favoring riskier investments. In practice, favorable tax treatment of some types of gains from investment would appear to be a much more significant factor in investment choice.[9]

---

[9] Exemption of the interest on the debt contracts of state and local governments in the United States income tax laws does not necessarily reduce the demand for other securities. If governments are intent on offering these securities for sale in any case, and this question involves political issues primarily, some groups will hold these securities. Groups who stand to gain taxwise from the exemption are induced to demand more of these securities and thus bid them away from other investors. There is no presumption that the demand for corporate securities declines on this account unless those excluded by the high price of municipal securities are biased against corporate securities.

The fundamental objections to exemption of interest from tax are the resulting sabotage of equity principles in the income tax and the encouragement which low yields give to state and local governments to adopt the politically easy method of increasing debt instead of taxes to finance expenditures and transfer payments.

IMPLICATIONS FOR TAX CAPITALIZATION

According to the Domar-Musgrave analysis, a proportional tax on income increases, if anything, the prices of assets. Therefore, if one may speak of tax capitalization at all under conditions of uncertainty, there is a tendency toward negative tax capitalization. For reasons already mentioned, these effects probably have little significance when banking policy is taken into account.

If taxes are levied only on old assets, their prices may be expected to fall even if people are uncertain. People must be not only uncertain but also rather muddleheaded to be willing to pay the same prices for old assets which are subject to tax in a setting in which the government announces that all new assets may be owned free of tax. It is of course conceivable that people might always gamble that the tax will be repealed and always find themselves in error. But if the general pattern of taxation in a country has persisted for some time, eventually people will awake to the fact that they can acquire a new asset without acquiring a tax liability and will therefore prefer such assets. Thus the same general pattern of asset prices found for conditions of certainty will presumably emerge under conditions of uncertainty. Exemption of new assets from tax accompanied by heavy taxation of old assets will force down the prices of old assets. Old houses subject to property or other taxes can be expected to sell at lower prices if people can acquire new houses free of tax.

If taxes are restricted to new assets, the reverse pattern of asset pricing will emerge. People will prefer tax-free assets, hence prices of old assets will rise. Prices of new assets subject to tax will nevertheless have to be in line with the costs of producing them. The relation between the prices of new real resources and the prices of services is not apt to be subject to significant variations in actual economic systems. Resources can be and are produced during each moment in the history of a society. New resources are produced by the organization of the services of previously existing resources, and the costs of producing new resources are closely tied to the prices of these services. In an aggregate sense, the prices of new resources are a sample of the prices of existing services, and therefore the relation between them over time must be close to constant. Under conditions of uncertainty, it is true that the relation between the present value of an asset and its future net earnings is a vague notion because people are guessing about the amount of the future net earnings. The earnings may be losses instead of gains. But the relation between capital values of new resources and current prices of services can be computed from observable data rather than from assumptions concerning investor attitudes. Tax capitalization may, and perhaps must, be thought of in terms of these objective market facts. If taxes are levied only on new assets, there is little room for a change in the relation of the prices of current services and the prices of new assets. It would be surprising if the prices of old assets should fail to rise relative to the prices of new assets in these circumstances. Whatever we wish to mean by tax capitalization if investors are uncertain, an observable rise in the prices of old assets relative to new in a setting in which old assets are exempt from tax would suggest that people are influenced by tax considerations in the valuations they place on assets.

Significant changes in capital values because of taxes are unlikely if taxes are levied on a basis of a general means test applied to persons, such as a personal progressive income tax without loopholes. Theoretical analysis does not suggest reason for alarm about the possible adverse investment incentive effects of such a tax, provided that losses are treated consistently as negative gains and provided that averaging devices are employed to eliminate discrimination against persons with highly fluctuating incomes. Since, in addition, the corporate device separates the managers who buy real assets from the persons who own claims to the assets, a tax system that obtains the bulk of the revenue through personal means-test taxation does not affect directly a major part of real investment decisions. Any adverse incentive effects in such a system of taxation would take the form of individuals refusing to acquire corporate securities. Heavy taxation of corporate earnings by government, the retention of earnings, and the light taxation of other assets are sufficient causes for investors especially among the less wealthy to prefer assets other than corporate securities.

Uncertainty in investor projections gives the same general pattern of results in terms of asset pricing as that found for unique projections. An asset that carries some special future tax liability with it will be valued at a lower price on that account. People may, to be sure, simply ignore these future liabilities. If investment decisions are made altogether on the basis of animal spirits rather than of sober calculations, tax considerations become irrelevant. But animal spirits are not apt to overcome altogether the known advantages of tax gains possible by investing in oil property or in state and local securities.

Special taxation or special exemptions of some types of investment are of less importance to investors whose tastes in assets are
confined to those assets which the government treats alike for tax
purposes. The opportunity of a corporation to invest in tax-free
assets of a kind which have no relevance to its operations may not,
in any direct way, affect its investment choices. The institutional
limitations on investment choice arising from the specialized nature of business and financial organizations has the effect of reducing the importance of unequal taxation of various types of assets.
If investors could actually acquire any type of asset, whether a
security or a real resource, the pattern of investment would, in all
likelihood, be affected by special taxation in a much more marked
degree than appears to be true in practice. Special tax concessions
present opportunities for limited groups of investors. Severe taxation of some types of assets or some methods of owning assets
becomes a permanent hardship on other groups. There is no presumption, in a world of limited investment choice, that heavy
taxation of assets such as houses is equally diffused among investors
in general by reduction of the realized after-tax rate of return on
all assets.

These "maybe" theoretical results of taxation on investment
decisions under conditions of investor uncertainty should not ob-
scure fundamentals. A general system of taxation based on a personal means test or a general system of taxation levied at equal
rates on the future earnings of assets reduces the after-tax gains of
investors. Even if people do not consider future taxes at all in their
investment decisions, they will find themselves paying taxes. Realized after-tax rates of return must fall as compared with a no-tax
setting. Owners of real assets and of claims to real assets both suffer
a reduction in their after-tax gains. Partial taxation of the earnings
from both old and new real resources other than human resources
is also virtually certain to reduce the rates of return computed after
tax for the owners of those assets.

Low interest rates are a direct consequence of a tax policy which
relies heavily on taxes levied on the earnings of real resources in
comparison with a tax policy levied on personal income after all
transfer payments. A shift away from corporate, property, excise,
and import levies toward taxes levied on income of persons computed net of transfer payments made by them would result in
higher market rates of interest on securities. Even under conditions
of uncertainty, a tax policy which makes the ownership of real

assets expensive lowers the income from security holdings. It directly lowers incomes of types of securities that are residual claims to earnings, and through the process of substitution it lowers the prices of debt contracts. Debt holders, as well as stockholders, pay a part of the tax cost resulting from *ad rem* levies.[10] Thus organizations and persons holding debt contracts who would be exempt under a progressive individual income tax which allows personal exemptions are effectively taxed indirectly through the reduction in the amount of interest income they obtain. Taxes levied on personal gains regardless of source do not seem to be shiftable in any significant sense. (See p. 258.)

Partial taxes which reduce the earnings of some classes of resources may or may not be shifted to others through the investment process. They are definitely shiftable from persons who own residual claims to persons who own contractual claims. This type of shifting can occur only in an institutional setting in which assets are jointly owned. If each real asset were owned in fee simple by a particular person, no issue could arise because debt contracts would not exist.

Partial taxes are also shiftable in principle if the pattern of capital formation reflects differences in future tax liabilities. A tax on the ownership of houses is shiftable to owners of other assets if in fact people reduce their demands for new houses relative to other assets. But, under conditions of uncertainty, demands need not shift in such a fashion. When people's tastes for assets are not rigorously correlated with future after-tax yields, it may not be taken for granted that extra taxation of some assets reduces the future supply of their services.

---

[10] At the time these taxes are introduced, owners of fixed-income securities obtain some capital gains, depending upon the life of the contracts. If contracts last forever, they can indefinitely escape any tax which reduces earnings of real resources. In practice, debt contracts are typically of such length as to permit an eventual reduction in the income of such persons.

Index

Accelerated depreciation for tax purposes, 279 ff.
Acreage restrictions, 29
Adler, J. Hans, 218 n. 10
After-tax rule, 76
Aggregation in social accounting, 73–80
Alimony payments: as similar to tax payments, 17; treatment in social accounting, 75
Allocation of resources: and monopolistic pricing, 160; and private gain, 99; between government and private ends, 20 ff.; ideal, 99
Announcement effects, 129, 141; and distributional effects, 241 ff.; defined, 14–16, 125; of positive marginal rates of tax, 236 ff.; of subsidies, 164
Anti-inflationary effect, 121; of excise taxes, 129–133, 140; of net worth taxes, 235; of poll taxes, 141
Assets, 87–92; as determinants of consumption, 91; as determinants of investment, 93–98
Automobiles and excise taxes, 137–138

Bain, Joe S., 45 n. 6, 152
Bale concept, 191–192, 197, 199
Bankers and credit analysis, 94
Banking policy: and quantity of money, 96; and tax capitalization, 269; in relation to saving schedules, 264–265; neutral, 118
Banking theory in social accounting, 75 n. 23
Bankruptcy, 63, 66
Banks, 64, 86
Bastable, C. F., 172 n. 2
Benefits: and costs, 49 n. 9; of government functions, 21, 38
"Better off": defined, 120; related to wealth, 229
Black, Duncan, 8–10, 227 n. 1, 243–244, 246 n. 20
Blough, Roy, 70 n. 20
Boehm-Bawerk, Eugene von, 263

Boulding, Kenneth E., 104 n. 17
Bowley, A. L., 58–59 n. 4
Break, George F., 6 n. 4; quoted, 256
British White Papers, quoted, 67–68
Brown, E. Cary, 123 n. 1, 268–270, 279 n. 18
Brown, Harry Gunderson, 2, 7 n. 5; on shifting of sales taxes, 124, 128–129
Budgets: balanced, 2, 130; underbalanced, 131
Budget studies, 103–104
Burden of taxes, 53; concept of, 120; ethical judgments about, 120; excise taxes, 165; import duties, 174, 176, 182, 189, 196, 210; on consumers, 3; personal taxes, 228, 244, 249, 254
Business organization, defined, 43

Canons of taxation, 2
Capital gains, effects of light taxation of, 271 ff.
Capital values as determinants of expenditures, 83–84
Capitalization of human earning power, 86, 93. See also Tax capitalization
Carroll, J. J., 128 n. 6
Cash value, 85–86
Causation: and announcement effect, 15; and overpricing, 170; and speculative history, 17; and taxation, 162, 170; and the consumption function, 108; in national income computations, 71, 80
Central banks and international trade, 203, 206, 208–209
Certainty in projections, 259–260
Cigarette taxes, 48, 72, 118
Clarification as a method of analysis, 3 ff.
Clark, Colin, 58 n. 4
Classical tradition, attack on, 6
Classical indictment of excise taxes, 171
Classification of government ends, 21 ff.
Cohn, Gerhard, 58 n. 1
Commodity taxes, shifting of, 127, 138. See also Excise taxes
Communism, 79 n. 28

[303]

Index

309

Simultaneity: of consumption and investment, 108; of production and output, 4, 5
Simultaneous variation of different taxes, 8–9, 141–142
Single tax doctrine, 279–282
Social accounting, 55 ff.
Socialism: and estate taxes, 115; and incentives to work, 245; and price controls, 170; applicability of theory to, 19; money-price systems under, 39 n. 2
Spendings tax, 255
Stevens, R. W., 178 n. 16
Stigler, George F., 104 n. 17, 139 n. 15
Stine, O. C., 60 n. 9
Stockfisch, Jacob A., 277 n. 16
Stockholders as affected by corporate income taxes, 266
Stocks as determinants of flows, 96
Stone, Richard, 58–59
Subsidies: and price control, 168–170; and social accounting, 59–60, 66–67; announcement effects of, 164; consumer, 28, 31, 169; distinguished from public functions, 36–37; flat-sum, 230; general excise, 143–145; in kind, 2, 23, 30 ff.; partial excise, 145 ff.
Supply schedules: of saving, 262; of work, 255
Swedish economics, 100 n. 2
Symmetry: Edgeworth's doubts about, 197; of import and export taxes, 174, 181, 197

"T" accounts for national banking systems, 206, 208
Takers, concept of, 39
Tariff schedules, U. S., 225
Tariff theory, 3. See also Import duties
Tastes: and import duties, 196; and price and reallocation effects of taxes, 126; and social accounting, 69; and supply of work, 231; for assets, 294
Taussig, Frank W., 185 n. 25
Tax capitalization, 265, 277 ff.; and pattern of investment, 268; and uncertainty, 299 ff.; main discussion of, 267 ff., 299 ff.
Tax discrimination as procurement device, 47
Tax-exempt securities, 282–283, 298 n. 9
Tax-exemption: of earnings of new assets, 280–281; of earnings of old assets, 282; of leisure, 237–238

Tax-forgiveness, 46–49; and social accounting, 57
Tax-induced collusion, 157–159
Tax-induced price discrimination, 48
Taxes. See Excise, Import, etc.
Tax neutrality: in announcement effects, 16, in distribution effects, 141
Tax theories: as an influence on price policies, 161–162; and simplifying assumptions, 6–7
Taxing the foreigner: by import duties, 19; Mill's views on, 172; Pigou's views on, 173
Terms of trade: as affected by import duties, 181; spectacular change in, 187; summarized, 223–224; with fixed exchanges, 216–217, 220
Thin, Tun, 234 n. 6
Thrift, objectives of, 263–264
Thrifting: defined, 116; gross, defined, 261; related to consumption, 117
Time: and analysis of excise taxes, 142; and the Keynesian consumption function, 106–107; concept of the present, 13, 17; in relation to money, 85–86; Whitehead's views on, 107
Timeless production, 43
Transfer income: and accounting theory, 66; and ethics, 64; defined, 58; and international trade, 75
Transfer payments: and income equation, 84; as one class of government financial activities, 1, 24, 52; taxes as a form of, 53
Truth in economics, 7

Uncertainty. See Risk
Undercharging by government, 28
Underemployment: and government costs, 49; and monopoly, 154–155; and subsidies, 164–165. See also Full employment
Underpricing: and suppressed inflation, 166; defined, 165; shifting of excise taxes under conditions of, 165 ff.
Unemployment: and imperfections in pricing, 41–42; disguised, 155 ff., 257
United States, Department of Commerce, 59, 218 n. 10
Used-up tax, 228 ff. See also Pigou
Utilitarian doctrines, applied to taxation, 81

Value judgments, 2. See also Ethics

Value of marginal product, two meanings distinguished, 145
Vickrey, William, 238 n. 10
Viner, Jacob, 191 n. 30, 202 n. 2
Von Mering, Otto, 152 n. 2

Wage income and excise taxes, 157
Wage rates: condition of stability of, 229–230; effects of income taxes on, 246 ff.
Waiting: and costs of government, 50–52; and rates of interest, 262–263
Wald, Haskell P., 243 n. 17
Warburton, Clark, 70 n. 20
Waste: and rationing devices, 35–36; and taxes, 122; from subsidies in kind, 30, 33
Wealth: as determinant of consumption, 91; object of thrifting, 263
Wealth effect, 231
Wealthy groups and leisure, 235
Welfare: of corporations, 275–276; general, and government enterprise, 25

Welfare economics, 120; and international trade, 198
Welfare tests: and social accounting, 76 n. 25; applied to pricing of highway service, 35
Whitehead, Alfred North: on contemporaneous independence, 107–108; on questions of scale, 6 n. 2
Wicksell, Knut, 100 n. 2
Wine industry and excise taxes, 160
Work: and labor unions, 232; and leisure, 227 ff.; and rationing of government services, 33; by-products of, 238; effect of taxes on supply of, 16; supply of, during wartime, 234
"Worse off": and government use of resources, 233; and import duties, 210–211, 216–217; and the work-leisure choice, 242 ff.; defined, 120

Yntema, Dwight, 75 n. 23
Young, Allyn, 34

Zero rates of tax, 234